Economic Policy i

Contemporary Political Studies Series

Series Editor: John Benyon, *University of Leicester*

Economic Policy in Britain

Wyn Grant

palgrave

First published 2002 by
PALGRAVE
Houndmills, Basingstoke, Hampshire RG21 6XS and
175 Fifth Avenue, New York, N. Y. 10010
Companies and representatives throughout the world

PALGRAVE is the new global academic imprint of
St. Martin's Press LLC Scholarly and Reference Division and
Palgrave Publishers Ltd (formerly Macmillan Press Ltd).

ISBN 0–333–92889–X hardback
ISBN 0–333–92890–3 paperback

This book is printed on paper suitable for recycling and
made from fully managed and sustained forest sources.

A catalogue record for this book is available
from the British Library.

Library of Congress Cataloging-in-Publication Data

Grant, Wyn.
    Economic policy in Britain / Wyn Grant.
        p. cm—(Contemporary political studies)
    Includes bibliographical references and index.
    ISBN 0–333–92889–X
        1. Great Britain—Economic policy—1997– 2. Great Britain—
Economic policy—1979–1997. 3. Great Britain—Economic policy—
1964–1979. 4. Great Britain—Economic policy—1945–1964. I. Title.
II. Series.
HC256.7 G73 2002
338.941—dc21   2002017000

10   9   8   7   6   5   4   3   2   1
11   10 09 08 07 06 05 04 03 02

Printed in China

Contents

List of Tables

Preface

This book arises from many years' experience of teaching the third year Making of Economic Policy module at the University of Warwick as well as a postgraduate module on Problems of Economic Management. The Making of Economic Policy module has been taught with a succession of economists all of whom have increased my respect for their discipline. In the late 1970s and 1980s I taught the module with the late Shiv Nath with whom I wrote a book on economic policy. The module was then taught for several years by Jim Bulpitt, an original thinker on a wide range of issues. After Jim's premature death, I started to teach on the module again, at first with Professor Lord Skidelsky. It was a real privilege to teach with someone with such a powerful intellect, a profound range of knowledge stretching across several disciplines and direct experience of the world of politics and policy. His successor, Geoff Renshaw, brought to the module a sophisticated understanding of economics and a relentless questioning of my assumptions and beliefs that I found refreshing and challenging. He also helped me with the collection of statistical tables for the book.

The Making of Economic Policy course at Warwick was established by Professor Malcom Anderson. He is now an emeritus professor of the University of Edinburgh, a citizen of France and actively involved in both academic writing and policy work in Brussels. When I first came to Warwick he was effectively my mentor, although we did not use that term in the 1970s. He offered me invaluable advice on the development of my research and teaching. I owe him a lasting debt and this book is dedicated to him.

Steven Kennedy, my publisher at Palgrave, guided the development of this book with his usual care and thoroughness, making a number of invaluable suggestions for its improvement. I would also like to thank an anonymous reader for the comments provided. In the department at Warwick, Peter Burnham has many shared interests, not least in the historical development of economic policy in Britain in the second half of the twentieth century. Despite our different theoretical perspectives, we have had many fruitful discussions, not least on trips to the Public Record Office. Nicholas Crafts of LSE provided me with his latest unpublished work on relative economic decline which was of great assistance in the final stages of writing. In the different world of football, Alan Curbishley offered a role model of the virtues of calm deliberation under much greater pressure than I ever have to face. As always, I owe a great debt to my wife, Maggie. Hopefully, the twenty-first century will offer a more successful and fairer economic setting in which my granddaughters, Clarissa, Lauren and Victoria, can grow to adulthood.

WYN GRANT

Introduction

Economic policy since the Second World War has been concerned with influencing the behaviour of the economy as a whole with the objective of securing key objectives such as low inflation, low levels of unemployment and high rates of economic growth. These objectives were pursued by government manipulation of policy instruments including interest rates, taxes and control of the money supply. The emphasis after 1945 was thus on macroeconomic policy, the attempt to control economic aggregates through the manipulation of economic demand. A number of other policies were seen as having an effect on the failure or success of economic policy – for example education policy and skill formation – but these were seen as distinct arenas of policy. Policies that focused on the meso or micro levels of the economy were categorized separately, for example industrial policy and regional policy.

This traditional approach changed with the election of the Thatcher government in 1979. Not only was the traditional ordering of priority objectives reversed, with greater emphasis given to the control of inflation rather than unemployment, but also the methods used to achieve them changed. There was a new emphasis on the supply side of the economy in contrast to the previous emphasis on the demand side. The new orthodoxy was summarized by Nigel Lawson in his 1984 Mais lecture:

> the proper role of [macroeconomic and microeconomic policy] is precisely the opposite of that assigned to [them] by the conventional postwar wisdom. It is the conquest of inflation, and not the pursuit of growth and employment, which is or should be the objective of macroeconomic policy. And it is the creation of conditions conducive to growth and employment, and not the suppression of price rises, which is or should be the objective of microeconomic policy. (Lawson, 1992, pp. 414–15)

The Blair government has built on the economic foundations established by Thatcher and Major, retaining an attachment to sound

1

money, but giving a greater emphasis to sustained growth and to an element of redistribution. The major change in the conduct of economic policy under Blair was the immediate surrender to the Bank of England of one of the key instruments utilized by governments, the control of interest rates. This forms part of a larger trend towards the depoliticization of economic policy (Burnham, 1999, 2001).

Even if it is becoming more depoliticized, economic policy has not lost its central role in the political process. One of the indicators of this continuing centrality is the enhanced role of the Treasury in the Blair government. The perceived competence of governments in managing the economy is an important factor in the voting decisions made by electors and has been one of the explanations of the electoral success enjoyed by New Labour. The success or otherwise with which the government manages the economy influences all other areas of public policy. If the economy enters a recession, tax receipts fall and spending on social security rises. Increasing taxes could lengthen the recession, so government either has to cut public spending or borrow more money (or probably some combination of both). This funding shortfall then affects the extent to which public services can be maintained or improved, a key concern of the electorate.

Key issues and disputes in British economic policy

These have centred on the key objectives of economic policy and how they might be achieved. The precise mix of objectives has differed over the postwar period, but the level of employment and the rate of inflation have always been at the heart of debates about economic policy. Added together, as they have been by many commentators, they form the 'misery index' (Brittan, 1995, p. 130) (Table 1). The term 'was invented by the late Arthur Okun' (Dornbusch and Fischer, 1990, p. 547). Until 1970 this was in single figures (apart from one year which was influenced by high inflation because of the Korean War). It peaked at 30.5 in 1975, but was also high in the early 1980s, finally falling to single figures again in 1997. Up until 1979 higher priority was given in practice to the employment objective, but since 1979 the emphasis has been on inflation. Since around 1960 a high and sustainable rate of economic growth has been an objective. Until the early 1970s a principal objective of

Table 1   Inflation, unemployment and the misery index

Decade	Inflation mean (%)	Unemployment mean (%)	Misery index
1950–59	4.1	1.5	5.6
1960–69	4.6	1.9	6.5
1970–79	12.9	3.7	16.6
1980–89	7.6	9.6	17.2
1990–99	3.9	7.2	11.1

Notes: lowest unemployment figure, 1.1% (1955); highest unemployment figure, 11.5% (1986); lowest inflation figure, 1.5% (1954); highest inflation figure, 26.7% (1975); lowest misery index, 2.8 (1954); highest misery index, 30.5 (1975). The measure of inflation used is YBGB = GDP (expenditure) at market prices deflator (seasonally adjusted). This is the broadest of three available measures of inflation. It includes prices of all goods and services that are included in GDP. The longest unemployment series is BJCA (a technical term for the claimant count). This goes back to 1950 and is labelled 'claimant count' in modern terminology, but used to be called 'registered unemployment'. The misery index used here is the sum of the mean annual unemployment rate and the mean annual inflation rate for each decade. Thanks to Geoff Renshaw for collecting data and calculations and to Mark Stewart for advice.

policy was sustaining a fixed exchange rate, and associated with this was a need to manage balance of payments difficulties. A fixed exchange rate is one where the pound is maintained at a predetermined level (or fluctuates within a very narrow range) against some other currency, the dollar in the earlier postwar period. If the exchange rate can vary against that of other currencies, it can be devalued to boost exports (which become cheaper in foreign currencies) and restrain imports (which become more expensive in pounds). If the exchange rate is fixed and overvalued, as it often was in Britain, the economy will suffer a series of balance of payments crises in which imports of goods and services outweigh exports.

The major political parties tried to differentiate themselves in terms of the degree of state intervention in the economy. This debate centred particularly on an adversarial argument about the merits or otherwise of public ownership of key sectors of the economy. In practice, apart from the denationalization and renationalization of the steel industry, this debate produced few practical effects as the distance between the parties was far less than they pretended was the case. Up until 1979, both Conservatives and Labour accepted the idea of a 'mixed economy' in which there was substantial government intervention, both through direct ownership and other means. Both parties provided substantial subsidies to firms in difficulty and to encourage economic development in the less successful regions.

After 1960 both parties agreed on the need to improve Britain's economic performance, compared with its competitors, usually measured in terms of a higher rate of economic growth. The parties had different explanations of the causes of poor performance with the Conservatives emphasizing trade union power and Labour paying more attention to underinvestment. There was, however, general agreement that government intervention in some form had to be part of any solution. It often seemed, however, that the objective of both main parties was the more effective management of decline. The Thatcher government made the reversal of decline one of its key objectives, seeing the accommodation with labour as one of the main obstacles that had to be overcome (Gamble, 1988). In taking such a stance the Thatcher government was obliged to breach an important part of the postwar economic settlement which had coopted organized labour into economic policy-making, leading eventually to a weak form of corporatism known as tripartism. In its continental European form, corporatism involved the cooption of key interests, particularly organized labour, into the economic policy decision-making process on the assumption that they would help to implement the agreed policies. The decentralized and fragmented trade union movement made it difficult to use such an approach to policy-making in Britain.

Similarly, although there was disagreement among the parties about the extent to which redistribution should be an objective of policy, both of them accepted the idea of the redistribution of income and some limited redistribution of wealth. This was achieved through a progressive tax system, centred on direct taxation, the funds raised being in part used to provide a variety of welfare services that were of particular benefit to the less well-off members of the community. The Thatcher government substantially changed taxation policy, significantly reducing the higher rates of income tax, and shifting the tax burden from direct to indirect forms of taxation. The unpopular community charge or 'poll tax' was one of the causes of her ultimate downfall. She would have also liked to make inroads into the welfare state, but, apart from a significant reduction in spending on public housing, it remained largely intact.

Until 1979 there was broad agreement between the two main political parties on the importance of maintaining full employment. The Thatcher government gave greater importance to the control of inflation, although arguing that sustainable employment would not be possible without sound finances and low inflation. This provoked disagreement between the parties about the ranking of objectives and also about the efficacy of different policy instruments in achieving them. Between the early 1960s and 1979, both Conservative and Labour governments relied considerably on incomes (and to a lesser extent prices) policies as a means of controlling inflation under conditions of employment. After 1979 the Conservatives placed a new emphasis on the control of the money supply and public-sector borrowing.

These policy instruments were controversial and brought very mixed results. The debates about the control of inflation in the 1980s led to a new emphasis on rules in the conduct of economic policy that would establish credibility for government actions in the judgement of other economic actors, not least the financial markets. New Labour

> deepened [a] commitment to the 'rules-based' economic strategies begun by the Major administration. 'Rules-based' approaches attempt to build counterinflationary mechanisms into the economy by reordering part of the government's responsibility for economic policy onto non-governmental bodies. (Burnham, 2001, p.136)

How different is New Labour?

The Labour view of recent economic history, as set out by Tony Blair, is that Thatcherism brought about important and necessary changes in the British economy, but it is now necessary to move beyond Thatcherism. Nevertheless, Labour's economic policies have been built on an unmistakably Thatcherite platform, tightened by the introduction of new rules governing the conduct of fiscal policy. The control of public expenditure under the first Blair government was almost certainly tighter than it would have been under a re-elected Conservative government. Heffernan observes (2000, pp. 65–6) that the Blair government has taken up four economic policy objectives of the Thatcher and Major governments:

(1) Ensuring financial stability by promoting sound money and placing the reduction of inflation at the heart of both fiscal and monetary policy; (2) placing the market at the centre of economic life through deregulation and the rejection of direct state intervention; (3) Privatisation of state-owned industries and utilities so withdrawing the state from direct control over economic activity; (4) Controlling trade union activity by legislation and (together with other measures) so disciplining the labour market.

In political terms, New Labour was anxious to differentiate itself from both Old Labour and from the Conservatives. The 'philosophy' of the Third Way offered a means of doing this, even if it was largely constructed after the Labour victory in 1997 in two books written by Giddens (1998a, 2000). Much of the thinking behind the third way was imported from the United States (Deacon, 2000; Giddens, 2000, p. 3). The Clinton Democrats did not accept the Reagan and Thatcher view that government was the problem, not the solution; they did not want to revert to big government, but they thought that government was a tool that could be reinvented and used more selectively in the twenty-first century. Government needed to be more limited in its use of resources and to target them on real needs.

The third way accepted the reality of government failure: 'Government and the state are the origins of social problems as well as markets'. (Giddens, 2000, p. 28). However, it was accepted that 'Markets can't even function without a social and ethical framework – which they themselves cannot provide' (Giddens, 2000, p. 33). The vision of economic policy was predicated on a normative and empirical acceptance of the realities of globalization. Third-way politics was characterized as a 'globalizing political philosophy' (Giddens, 2000, p. 122), and it was accepted that 'Economic globalization, by and large, has been a success' (Giddens, 2000, p. 124). The question, for whom, is not one that fits very well into the third way.

The third way sought to develop a new mixed economy involving 'a wide-ranging supply-side policy which seeks to reconcile economic growth mechanisms with structural reform of the welfare state' (Giddens, 2000, p. 52). There is quite an emphasis on regulation as a tool of an active government; it is argued that 'greater regulation of economic life, in some respects, and some contexts, is necessary' (Giddens, 2000, p. 84). If one looks at the justifiable grounds for regulation given in Giddens (1998b) they are quite extensive. The third way therefore provides an intellectual under-pinning for the development of a regulatory state. More generally, its critics saw it, at best, as an attempt to find some compromise between neo-liberalism and old-style social democracy, but tilted towards the former.

Even if the third way offers a less distinctive and clear philosophy than is sometimes claimed, the economic policies followed by New Labour are not the same as those of the Conservatives. The Conservatives would not have introduced a minimum wage, signed the social chapter of the Maastricht Treaty so as to open up new rights for workers, or used the tax and benefits system to introduce an element of redistribution in favour of working families. However, the similarities and continuities outweigh the differences. As Heffernan observes (2000, p. 173), 'in terms of objectives as well as methods, "New" Labour offer a distinctive political strategy dramatically at odds with the Thatcherite project.' New Labour is working within the terms of a new political settlement initiated in 1979. Policy will continue to develop in new directions, but such initiatives as using private provision in the public services are entirely consistent with a market-based approach to economic policy.

Do all these developments mean that the ideology and the politics have been taken out of economic policy and it has become increasingly a matter of the application of predetermined rules within a broad market-based consensus? In many respects, yes. The state has lost many of its old roles in economic policy: owner; manager of the macro economy; and provider of subsidies. It has gained one new important role, as a regulator, so that many writers have come to use the term 'regulatory state'. Economic management has become increasingly a managerial task, as illustrated by the fact that Gordon Brown's big project in the second Labour government appeared to be improving productivity: worthy, but hardly exciting. There is, of course, one major exception to this trend towards depoliticization – the debate about whether Britain should join the euro. Many of the fierce ideological disputes of the past have, however, transferred to the international level and the fight against globalization. For young political activists, the appropriate targets are not national governments but the European Union (EU), international summits and the World Trade Organization (WTO).

Globalization and the autonomy of the nation state

In the middle of the twentieth century the place of the state in the making of economic policy in Britain and other western countries seemed secure. Keynesian economics provided a politically accept-able toolkit for achieving full employment. It involved the use of counter-cyclical demand management to avoid recession. Even if it was necessary to enter into negotiations with the Americans about the management of the international system of economic manage-ment, the nation state was seen as the principal decision-maker in matters of economic policy. It might be constrained, but it was sovereign.

By the beginning of the twenty-first century, the empirically and normatively contested concept of globalization cast a shadow over debates about the continued viability of domestic economic policy. Those writers who doubted whether there was a new phenomenon called 'globalization' emphasized 'that, in proportional terms, levels of cross-border trade, migration and investment were as high (if not higher) in the late nineteenth century as they were in the run up to 2000' (Scholte, 2000, p. 19; see Hirst and Thompson, 1996). Those analysts who thought that something rather more significant than accelerated internationalization was occurring emphasized the mag-nitude and speed with which sums were traded across international financial markets and the consequent rapidity with which a minor national crisis could become a major global one. Analysts in the former camp argued that the events of 11 September 2001 signalled the end of globalization, while those in the latter group argued that it might be slowed down, but would not be reversed.

Certainly one view that was often heard was that, at least in economic policy, the system of nation states established by the Treaty of Westphalia in 1649 was coming to an end. According to this account, responsibility for the shaping of economic policy was likely to flow both upwards and downwards. At the international level, the International Monetary Fund (IMF), the World Bank and the WTO came to be perceived as major sources of economic power, even though the WTO is in many respects a very weak organization. For many observers, they were simply the institutional face of market power. At a seminar of major international economic deci-sion-makers attended by the author, someone posed the question 'Who calls the shots? Not us, say the international financial insti-tutions, it's the G7 finance ministers [the grouping of leading economic powers]. Not us, say the finance ministers, it's really the markets.'

There was also the prospect of a downwards shift of authority from the level of the nation state. An understandable reaction to the development of a global economy is to demand that political power be devolved to a local level so that people can have some influence on their own immediate circumstances. As globalization proceeds, the value of more immediate identities increased. In Britain this was reflected in the creation of a Scottish Parliament and a Welsh Assembly, the Scottish Parliament having the power to levy additional taxes. Within Scotland in particular, the terms of political debate were increasingly constructed in Scottish terms.

One response to these dilemmas was to argue that political control of globalization was only possible at a Europe-wide level. The EU could be seen as an attempt to build a dynamic European economy that was distinctive from that of the United States in so far as it tried to offer a higher level of social protection. Its neo-liberal critics argued that the result would be a more regulated, less flexible and more rigid economy unable to compete in a globalizing world economy. In any case, there was a paradox at the heart of the enterprise. The EU represented both an attempt to facilitate globalization through the construction of an internal market and an attempt to constrain it through policies designed to achieve a 'social Europe'.

Structure of the book

Whatever the importance of globalization, the EU and subnational governments, significant economic policy decisions are still taken at the level of the nation state. In order to understand where we are, we need some knowledge of how we got there, particularly for students for whom the first government they can remember is that of John Major. Chapter 1 therefore reviews the historical development of economic policy in Britain since the Second World War, identifying the distinctive features of the British economy and economic policy together with the major periods in the development of economic policy and the key issues that were faced in them.

Chapter 2 considers in greater depth the arguments about the impact of globalization on the making of economic policy advanced in this chapter. It reviews the roles of the leading global governance agencies that attempt to provide some form of policy coordination in the global economy. It also considers the extent to which economic policy-making has shifted to the EU level. Chapter 3 reviews the general theoretical perspectives available on the making of economic policy. It covers issues about market failure and government failure, the increasing influence of Polanyi's work, and a range of theoretical perspectives from Keynesianism to Thatcherism.

Chapter 4 is the first of three chapters concerned with specific aspects of policy. It examines the development of monetary policy in Britain and the implications of economic and monetary union for economic policy. Chapter 5 is concerned with one of the areas of policy in which the main decisions are still taken at the nation-state level – taxation and public expenditure. Chapter 6 extends to the discussion to policies concerned with the supply side and competitiveness, including skill formation, competition policy and transport policy.

The final three chapters before the conclusion are concerned with aspects of the decision-making process. Chapter 7 reviews the evidence on the extent to which election outcomes are influenced the way in which governments manage the economy. Chapter 8 is concerned with the core executive institutions involved in the making of economic policy in Britain, particularly the Treasury. Chapter 9 looks at the influences outside the core executive in terms of the influence of Parliament, the role of the media and of organized interests. Chapter 10 attempts to bring together the various issues examined in the book in a review of the future of economic policy.

This book is meant to be an analytical, rather than a prescriptive, work. Nevertheless, some indication of the author's own value position is appropriate. Crouch (2000, pp. 3–4) has drawn on the work of van Apeldoorn to distinguish between pure and embedded forms of neo-liberalism (not dissimilar from the distinction made between pure and social market approaches in Grant, 1982, pp. 13–17). What Crouch also calls 'European neo-liberalism' identifies 'a need for markets to be embedded in certain wider institutions if they are to receive infrastructural support and social consent, though the aim remains as little actual interference with markets as possible' (*ibid.*, p. 4). Although the author is sceptical of the benevolence and efficiency of government, he would see a case for intervention, for example, to improve the general living conditions of the least well-off sections of society or to protect the environment. He is, however, relatively agnostic about the mechanisms by which objectives are achieved (market, state, non-governmental or, most likely, some combination of all three). The overall position taken is a social market one, but with a considerable emphasis on social provision if only to ameliorate the harsh inequalities which a pure market system can generate and from which all citizens are losers in the long run.

1

From the Postwar Settlement to Thatcherism

Introduction

The British economy in the postwar period can only be fully under-stood in terms of Britain's unique industrial history. The three key terms that need to be understood here are: early industrialization; empire, and individualism. The term 'industrial revolution' has become a contentious one for economic historians, not least because more recent work has shown that the acceleration of economic growth was slower than had earlier been supposed (Crafts, 1985). There had been manufacturing industries in Britain before the late eighteenth century and 'already in the 1700–60 period Britain had a relatively high proportion of the labour force in industry' (Crafts, 1985, p. 64). However, traditional industrial production was trans-formed by the application of steam power, the development of the factory and a series of technical innovations, initially in the textile industry. By 1840 'Britain had a far higher proportion of exports in manufacturing than any country achieved, by far the highest urban-ization level, by far the lowest proportion of the labour force in agriculture' (Crafts, 1985, p. 60).

Why should Britain be the first country to industrialize? A whole book could be written on this subject, but some key factors can be selected (Owen, 2000, pp. 10–11):

- A relatively commercially oriented (since mediaeval times) and increasingly efficient agricultural sector which generated capital and released labour for industry.
- Based on the political settlement of 1688 (the so-called 'Glorious Revolution'), a stable and orderly polity – essentially an aristo-cratic oligarchy under an often incompetent but generally harm-

less monarchy with an ability to accommodate commercial interests, for example through Parliament.
● An endowment of mechanical and craft skills built up through
long-established trades (often luxury goods industries stimulated
by high consumer demand). The inventors and innovators of the
industrial revolution came from this background.
● An efficient transport system (canals, later railways), facilitating
regional specialization and 'industrial districts' which assisted
skills formation and technical development.
● An abundant energy source (coal).

The imperial experience

Because it is a distant memory for current generations, it is easy to
forget the extent to which the British economy was configured by
the experience of Britain as an imperial power. Indeed, it produced a
mindset that persisted into the middle of the twentieth century and
influenced Britain's attitude towards the emerging European
common market in the 1950s. From the time of the Commonwealth
under Cromwell, Britain sought, if not always systematically or
consistently, to build a global empire based on its naval strength.
Once industrialization occurred, the empire offered an assured
source of agricultural goods and raw materials and a protected
market for British manufacturing exports. However, it meant that
Britain was overreliant on the export of goods to less advanced or
semi-industrial countries (Crafts, 1985, p. 161).

The emergence of this pattern of exchange involved the defeat of
agricultural protection through the repeal of the Corn Laws and the
endorsement of a system of free trade that suited an economically
dominant Britain. As Britain's economic strength weakened from
the late nineteenth century onwards, the political strength of protectionism increased, leading to the introduction of imperial preference (favourable treatment for imports from the empire and the
'dominions', countries such as Australia and Canada). First introduced in 1919, it formed part of a general system of tariff protection
introduced in 1932. The general consequence was to shield the
British economy from competition and thus remove an important
stimulus for its reorganization.

The ethos of individiualism

Because the British economy was the first to industrialize, largely through the efforts of individual entrepreneurs, there were important consequences for the role of government. It produced a very individualistic ethos that confined the state to a spectator role in contrast to the 'developmental state' that emerged in Germany (Marquand, 1988). Systematic approaches to training and research and development received relatively little support. An important consequence was that Britain performed badly in the second or 'scientific' industrial revolution at the end of the nineteenth century. This was particularly noticeable in the key new chemical industry where Germany outperformed Britain in terms of technical innovation. Britain was also relatively slow to apply electricity to industrial production and to adopt new 'Fordist' systems of automation and plant organization, although they may have been more applicable to a country like the United States with a workforce of unskilled immigrants (Crafts, 2001, p. 22; Lewchuk, 1989). Britain 'was unable to take advantage of a higher growth path based on the opening-up of higher returns to investment in education and science' (Crafts, 1985, p. 160).

The experience of decline

In 1910, Britain still had the highest per capita income and the highest percentage of exports by value in manufactures of any European country (Crafts, 1985, p. 54, 60). However, the United States was increasingly challenging Britain's position: 'One of the consequences of the First World War was to consolidate the position of the US as the world's leading industrial power' (Owen, 2000, p. 23). Britain's share in the value of world exports of manufactures declined from 33.2 per cent in 1899 to 21.3 per cent in 1937 (Gamble, 1994, p. 17), and by 1973 it was to shrink to 9.1 per cent (Crafts, 2001, table 9). The strains of fighting the Second World War meant that by 1945 the economy was effectively bankrupt and dependent on American aid to survive. Awareness of problems of relative economic performance grew and much of the debate about postwar economic policy, particularly after 1960, became dominated by discussion of the phenomenon of relative economic decline. This debate, and the extent to

Table 1.1   The UK's ranking in terms of real GDP/person, benchmark
              years 1870–1999

1870	2nd (after Australia)
1913	4th (after Australia, New Zealand, USA)
1950	7th
1973	12th
1999	17th

Source: based on Crafts (2001), table 1; measurement basis is $1990.

which it was a particular ideological construction or reflected an
objective economic reality is considered more fully in Chapter 3.

This debate did reflect an economic reality in the sense that the UK
continued to slip down tables measuring levels of real GDP/person,
an approximate measure of prosperity (see Table 1.1). The single
most important explanation of relative economic decline appears to
be poor productivity performance that in turn reflects a number of
other factors such as powerful but decentralized trade unionism
that affected investment and innovation and deficiencies in vocational training. Before the Second World War, British performance
was principally deficient when compared with the United States,
but in the postwar period it was the continental European economies
that started to overtake Britain. A consensus view on the causes of,
and remedies for, relative economic decline is not possible because,
ultimately, judgements become highly political and value laden.

The Second World War and modern macroeconomic policy

The Second World War was a watershed in the development of British
economic policy, representing the beginning of modern macroeconomic policy. It marked the beginning of modern macroeconomic
policy manifested in what is often called the postwar settlement by
which its proponents mean a broad and implicit accommodation
between political parties and/or employers and labour involving
greater state involvement in the economy, industry and welfare provision. The extent to which there was a new postwar settlement has
been challenged, and one should not forget that there were quite
substantial interventions in industry in the interwar period. Nevertheless, the experience of fighting the war through a command economy
had a lasting effect on the conduct of economic policy.

The postwar settlement

The broad outlines of the postwar settlement may be sketched out as follows. First, there was a commitment made in the 1944 White Paper on Employment issued by the wartime coalition government to 'high and stable' levels of employment. What this meant was not defined quantitatively, and Beveridge planned a postwar social insurance system that assumed unemployment at 8.5 per cent. However, the commitment to 'full' employment became the leading objective of postwar economic policy and influenced the conduct of politicians up until the 1970s. Second, in order to maintain full employment, the government resorted to Keynesian techniques of aggregate demand management, particularly using fiscal policy instruments, so that taxes were cut when the economy turned downwards and raised when it appeared to be overheating. Third, running the economy at or near full employment inevitably created inflationary pressures. The answer the Treasury favoured to this dilemma was incomes policy (sometimes accompanied by price restraint and dividend control policies). The first of these policies was introduced in 1948. In the 1960s and 1970s, these policies became a semi-permanent feature of the conduct of British economic policy.

Fourth, the resort to incomes policies further increased the political displacement of the trade union movement which had already been granted a new status by the postwar settlement. As a corollary, the organized employers also became more important. The unions and the not particularly well-organized employers proved unable to act as 'governing institutions' engaged in a positive partnership relationship with government:

> It may be more realistic to regard the employers and unions...as veto groups, with the power to prevent governments from acting when their vested interests were threatened, rather than as architects of policy. If so, the effect of the war must still be reckoned as far-reaching. The veto groups were now entrenched at the centre of power. (Addison, 1987, p. 18)

Fifth, the immediate postwar period saw a massive increase in social expenditure, particularly arising from the establishment of the National Health Service. It has been estimated that 'between 1936 and 1950 there was, in real terms, an increase of 80 to 90 per cent in social expenditures without counting food and housing subsidies. The largest single element in this increase was the NHS' (Dell, 2000,

p. 138). It has been argued that, at a time when the economy was in a dire condition and the country was in debt to the United States, Britain spent beyond its means. Attention was distracted from the urgent task of improving industrial performance by the delivery of a social dividend that had not been earned (Barnett, 1986; Dell, 2000). In political terms, however, the Labour government elected with a large majority (although only by 48 per cent of those voting) had little choice but to deal with the desperate postwar housing shortage and deliver the promised National Health Service. The argument that Britain spent beyond its means is, in any case, sometimes exaggerated.

Periods of economic policy

Postwar economic policy can be divided, arbitrarily but conveniently, into a number of distinct periods:

- 1945–51: wartime recovery and nationalization under Labour.
- 1951–60: Keynesian macroeconomic management, but no extension of state intervention in the economy and some retreat.
- 1960–67: the 'Brighton Revolution' and the hope of modernizing the economy through government intervention in partnership with the employers and the unions, ended by the shock of devaluation in 1967.
- 1967–79: a period of uncertainty and transition. Traditional macroeconomic instruments lose their efficacy; the economy is battered internally and externally, producing 'stagflation' – low growth, high unemployment and high inflation. The economy is starting to restructure away from its traditional reliance on manufacturing, but the experience is a painful one.
- 1979–90: the postwar settlement is replaced by a new Thatcherite settlement. There is a shift in policy priorities and changes in policy instruments; success is mixed, but the course of British economic policy is changed.
- 1990–97: Thatcher is a hard act to follow and Major's record is blighted by Britain's humiliating withdrawal from the exchange rate mechanism, although the economy is in good shape by the time he leaves office.
- 1997– Blair and Brown accept the Thatcherite settlement, but gradually shift policy in a new direction. They are helped by a

benign global environment, but hopes that the business cycle has been abolished are undermined by the threat of recession in 2001.

The years of austerity

The grim years of austerity that followed the Second World War now seem a long way away. Rationing, utility furniture, bomb sites, fuel shortages, the struggle to earn dollars seem to belong to another world. The Labour government of 1945–50 is, however, generally viewed with a measure of nostalgic affection. The conventional wisdom has been that 'Britain had never – and still hasn't – experienced a progressive phase to match 1945–51' (Hennessy, 1993, p. 454). The Labour Prime Minister, Clement Attlee, has come to be regarded as one of the great prime ministers of the twentieth century.

The postwar Labour government was seen as constructing what is often referred to as the *Keynesian welfare state*, and this remained the dominant paradigm within which economic policy was framed until the 1970s. What that offered was full employment plus 'cradle to the grave' welfare provision by the state. Much of the welfare state had been constructed before the Second World War, but Labour added the essential ingredient of the National Health Service which purported to offer healthcare free at the point of the delivery on the basis of need. By the beginning of the twenty-first century, it was all too apparent that it was a patchwork quilt of a service with the quality provided often determined by the postal code of the recipient. The Organization for Economic Cooperation and Development (OECD) condemned health outcomes in the UK as 'mediocre in some respects' with the 'quality of health care delivery ... not up to par' (OECD, 2000, pp. 143–4).

Nevertheless, establishing the Health Service at all against the initial opposition of the doctors and against a difficult economic background was a considerable achievement. The Labour government also had to construct a macroeconomic policy for the first time: 'Macro-economic policy was born in the years after the war and survived more or less unchanged for at least two more decades... The very concept of managing the economy was new and little understood' (Cairncross, 1985, p. 19).

It should therefore be no great surprise that for much of the time the postwar Labour government did not really know what they were doing. One might have expected an emphasis on economic planning but, 'Labour still had no clear and coherent policy on planning' (Leruez, 1975, p. 37). It was not until 1947 that Cripps was to produce a well-regarded document on the subject against the background of the fuel crisis which simply served to forcibly underline the limitations of any attempt at planning (Cairncross, 1985, p. 304). The government had persisted with various physical or direct controls of the economy longer than in other countries, but these elements of a command economy gradually had to be withdrawn as it sought to build a better working relationship with business.

Nationalization

If the government had any notion of what it wanted to do in terms of economic management, it was nationalization, particularly of the so-called 'commanding heights' of the economy. Electricity was already to quite a large degree publicly owned or supervised; gas had a considerable measure of municipal ownership; and the railways had been merged into four companies and were on the verge of bankruptcy. It seemed unlikely that the necessary capital for developing these essential elements of infrastructure could be raised privately. Similarly, there was little sympathy for the coal-owners who were widely regarded as poor employers. It was only when the government nationalized steel that they encountered significant political resistance, opposition that was mobilized even more effectively when they contemplated nationalizing sugar.

A major problem with the nationalization exercise was that 'Very little thought had been given to the organisation of the nationalised industries either in the Labour movement or in Whitehall (Chester, 1975, p. 1025). In part this was because what mattered was eliminating the supposed evil of capitalist control in a nationalized industry, and the actual way in which this was done was seen as being of secondary importance. In any case, an appropriate model offering a mixture of accountability and autonomy was on hand in the form of the so-called 'Morrisonian' public corporation. Morrison as Lord President of the Council was in charge of the nationalization programme and followed the model he had set out for the London Passenger Transport Board when he was Transport Minister in the 1929–31 Labour government. The postwar nationalizations were, however, seeking to pursue a variety of incompatible objectives. While they could be subsumed within the idea of the public corporation this was 'only at the expense of avoiding discussion as to the degree of independence which the Boards should be allowed and the extent to which they should be required to pay their way' (Chester, 1975, p. 1035). Ministers had to wrestle, without great success, with some of these confusions in successive postwar governments. Despite devaluation in 1949, and a relatively successful experiment with incomes policy, more fundamental problems of economic performance also remained unresolved.

Greater prosperity: Keynesianism, Butskellism and Robot

Britain entered the 1950s with Keynesian orthodoxies of economic management well-established. The term 'Butskellism' (a combination of the names of the last Labour chancellor, Gaitskell, and the first Conservative chancellor, Butler) was coined to reflect what was seen as a new economic consensus, although it may be more of a coincidence than is sometimes realized. There was quite a big difference between Gaitskell and Butler on both economic policies and economic philosophy. What is clear is that the Conservative government elected in 1951 had no wish to engage in confrontation with the trade unions, and indeed did everything it could to conciliate them. Within the Economic Section of the Treasury, 'All of us were Keynesians and very much aware of being so' (Henderson, 1986, p. 4).

Maintaining full employment was the principal objective of policy. 'The political pressures on the Government in the 1950's to give high priority to the maintenance of full employment were very strong' (PRO: T267/12, p. 13). Quite what full employment meant was still undefined, but when unemployment began to rise above 2 per cent in 1958, reflationary measures were taken. The restraint of inflation was of less importance than later in the postwar period. It was not until Peter Thorneycroft became Chancellor in 1957 'that it became a primary aim of policy' (PRO: T267/12, p. 13). The term 'economic growth' was not used until the end of the decade; economic expansion was sometimes referred to, although usually implicitly in relation to the full-employment objective. 'The rate of economic growth achieved was not prominent in debates on the Government's conduct of economic affairs in the way that it became in the early 1960's however' (PRO: T267/12, p. 13).

Maintaining sterling as a reserve currency within an international fixed exchange rate regime produced recurrent balance of payments crises. There was a tension here with full employment objectives. As the Treasury put it with its usual caution, 'the aim of maintaining sterling as a reserve currency is quite separate from maintaining full employment' (PRO: T267/12, p. 13).

The Robot episode

However, in 1952 an attempt was made within government to challenge the orthodoxy of a fixed exchange rate and move to a managed or 'dirty' float. The slogan used by its advocates was that of 'take the strain off the reserves and put it on the rate of exchange'. The attempt failed, but the fact that it was made at all was significant. It was conducted in great secrecy at the time, but has been the subject of considerable debate 40 years later because it was one point when the orthodoxies of postwar economic policy were seriously challenged. It was called 'Robot' after the initial letters of the names of the three principal actors involved – Leslie Rowan, George Bolton and Otto Clarke.

The plan had three main elements: the floating of the pound; full convertibility of what was known as 'overseas sterling'; and the blocking of 90 per cent of non-sterling balances held in London. The broader significance of these proposals was that they represented an attack on the domestic and international postwar settlement. In particular, it was claimed that it implied an end to the full-employment commitment, although the long postwar boom might have secured full employment in any case. Unsurprisingly, this triggered off what one observer has termed 'perhaps the most bitter arguments of the postwar years in Whitehall' (Cairncross, 1985, p. 245). The passions aroused did not prevent it from also being 'the fullest . . . and most sophisticated' debate over the issue of exchange-rate parity (Cairncross, 1985, p. 270).

The strongest support for the plan came from the Bank of England (who emphasized convertibility) and the majority of Treasury officials who emphasized floating but also saw it as a way of controlling the propensity of politicians to increase public expenditure. It fell to the Chancellor, Butler, to put the case to Cabinet which he did with characteristic, but in this case unfortunate, diffidence. Meanwhile, the opposition mobilized effectively. Lord Cherwell, who had the ear of Churchill, was a key opponent.

The debate was very much settled in domestic terms with ministers expressing a fear of high unemployment and of antagonizing the unions. It was evident that the postwar settlement was already cemented as orthodoxy and that ministers were very risk-averse. What was striking was the absence of attention to external factors, illustrating the largely domestic construction of economic policy during that period. Not much attention seems to have been given to the likely reaction of the United States which, although it would have welcomed convertibility, would not have endorsed the dismantling of the Bretton Woods system of fixed exchange rates. There was 'a confidence, even over-confidence in Britain's ability to restructure the world in its own interests and confront successfully its domestic problems' (Bulpitt and Burnham, 1999, p. 19).

Robot may be seen as more than a policy shift that would have allowed a more effective pursuit of existing objectives. In Bulpitt and Burnham's view (1999, pp. 22–3), 'Robot was a strategy to employ market forces to bring about the necessary supply-side revolution in Britain.' What was attempted was a financial *coup d'état* that would have broken the power conferred on the employers and unions by the postwar settlement. This objective was not achieved until the election of the Thatcher government in 1979. In the meantime, the failure of Robot meant that the postwar settlement had to be deepened by constructing more elaborate tripartite arrangements to contain inflation and to pursue the newly-emphasized objective of economic growth.

These elite discussions did not enter public debate. As far as the majority of the people were concerned, the dominant narrative of the 1950s was increasing prosperity. After emerging from the period of austerity after the war, which effectively lasted until the early 1950s, the population of Britain had entered a new era of conspicuous consumption leading to greatly increased levels of car ownership and the acquisition of a wide range of consumer durables. This was encapsulated by Harold Macmillan's much misquoted comment from his speech at Bedford football ground in June 1957 'most of our people have never had it so good' What is not usually quoted is his subsequent warning:

> What is beginning to worry some of us is 'Is it too good to be true?' or perhaps I should say 'Is it too good to last?' ... Our constant concern today is – can prices be steadied while at the same time we maintain full employment in an expanding economy? Can we control inflation? This is the problem of our time. (Horne, 1989, p. 64)

The reason 'you have never had it so good' was often misquoted was that it captured the spirit of the times, as did the slogan under which the Conservatives won a large majority in the 1959 general election under the slogan 'Life's better under the Conservatives'.

The Brighton Revolution and the shift in economic policy

Few people have heard of the Brighton Revolution, but it was one of the most important events in the postwar conduct of British economic policy. As Brittan comments, 'The year which saw the greater part of the new thinking was 1960, although it is about the least remembered of all the years of that decade' (Brittan, 1964, p. 228). With the exception of 1979, most of the great shifts in economic policy have taken place not after elections, but midway through the life of a government. Thus:

> Many of the new policies which Labour was later to proclaim as distinctively its own had already emerged in the far-reaching appraisal which went on inside the Treasury and other government departments around 1960–61. (Brittan, 1964, p. 227)

Although the Brighton Revolution was essentially a *coup d'état* within what we would now call the 'political class', it is necessary to sketch in the broader context within which it occurred. Despite the public optimism generated by increased prosperity, the economic establishment was seriously worried at the end of the 1950s. The morale of the political class had already been badly shaken by the Suez episode in 1956 which showed that Britain was not the great world power it thought it was, but at a time of crisis was dependent on the Americans. One consequence was a renewed interest in the common market and European developments generally. It soon became evident that the continental European economies were growing much more rapidly than Britain. Between 1950 and 1973, GDP per person in international dollars grew by 5.0 per cent in West Germany; 4.9 per cent in Italy; 4.0 per cent in France; and by only 2.4 per cent in the UK (figures from Crafts and Toniolo, 1996, p. 6). Having said that, it should be noted that the economy performed strongly in the 1950s and 1960s relative to its historical record in terms of such key indicators as inflation, employment and growth (see Table 1.2).

It was the employers who took a leading role in stimulating new thinking. A key figure was Sir Hugh Weeks, the chairman of the

Table 1.2   Rates of growth of real GDP/person, selected
periods, UK 1870–1999

	Growth rate (% per year)	UK ranking (against other countries)
1870–1913	1.0	2
1913–50	0.9	4
1950–73	2.4	7
1973–99	1.8	12

Source: derived from Crafts (2001), table 2.

Economic Policy Committee of the Federation of British Industries
(FBI) and a typical 'industrial politician' with experience as a civil
servant, on a quasi-governmental body and in business:

> It began, as so often in Britain, with a dining club, which began meeting
> early in 1960, bringing together industrialists and economists to discuss a
> wide range of economic problems relating to growth (Leruez, 1975, p. 85)

It was this private dining club convened by Weeks that was to pave
the way for the events in Brighton in November.

An important role was also played by what we would now call
think-tanks, notably Political and Economic Planning. Externally,
the OECD's predecessor, the Organization for European Economic
Cooperation (OEEC), also played a role in an attempt to get Britain
out of its stop–go cycle and on to a steadier and higher rate of
growth. However, France played the key external role. It was anticipated there that Britain would eventually join the common
market, and it was hoped that it would do so as an advocate of
planning rather than *laissez-faire*:

> Around this time there was a steady stream of visits by businessmen and
> civil servants between the rue de Rivoli and the rue de Martignac (the
> respective Paris homes of the Ministry of Finance and the Plan) on the
> one hand, and the Treasury and the FBI headquarters in Tothill Street on
> the other. (Leruez, 1975, p. 87)

The FBI decided to convene a conference of the economic establishment in Brighton in November 1960. Leading businessmen were
there, but also the Treasury, the Bank of England and the nationalized industries. One of the important consequences of Brighton was
the new emphasis attached to economic growth as an objective. In

presenting the conference's report, Sir Hugh Beaver 'stressed that the achievement of a faster rate of growth might be the best way of achieving stable prices and a sound balance of payments, not the other way round' (Brittan, 1964, p. 240).

How was economic growth to be achieved? The answer provided was through indicative planning, but what did this mean? In essence, agreeing on a range of economic indicators and incorporating them into the planning of public expenditure, but also investment decisions by private companies. One of the conclusions of Brighton was 'that government and industry [should] "agree on an assessment of expectations and intentions to be placed before the country as a framework for economic effort during the next five years"' (Blank, 1973, p. 152).

The British thought that they were adopting a version of the model of planning pursued so successfully in France. In fact, the French model was far more *dirigiste* than they believed it to be, or would have been acceptable in Britain which did not have a 'strong state' tradition. In order not to alarm the British, the French soft-pedalled the elements of compulsion in their Plan and emphasized the 'indicative' elements. As an unfortunate consequence of this French attention to British sensitivities, the British 'drew up two sound plans but gave little thought as how to implement them' (Leruez, 1975, p. 89).

The new mood induced by Brighton had a number of significant consequences for economic policy. Britain applied for membership of the common market as it was then known, and although the application was eventually vetoed by de Gaulle, what was significant was that it was made at all. It was not until the 1967 application made by Wilson, however, that the political class (although not the country) was united around the idea of European membership.

The National Economic Development Council (NEDC) was set up, bringing together the employers, the unions and government. Brittan saw the NEDC as introducing 'indicative planning to Britain' (Brittan, 1964, p. 234). With its own staff it provided an alternative source of advice to that offered by the Treasury, with a greater emphasis on the importance of economic growth as a policy goal. Its period of greatest influence was possibly from 1962 to 1964, after which it lost some of its staff and its influence within the Department of Economic Affairs (DEA). Although economic development committees were formed to review the problems of particular industries, these were seen as having an educational rather than a policy-making role, while the staff of the NEDC was viewed with some suspicion because they were not formally civil servants (PRO: BT258/2498).

The planning of public expenditure was reformed in line with the recommendations of the Plowden Report to introduce a systematic element of longer-term planning. The government edged towards an incomes policy, at first through the largely ineffective National Incomes Commission and its 'wise men'. A 'pay pause' in the public sector had been attempted in 1961, but was widely unpopular and soon breached. In 1962 a 'guiding light' for pay increases was announced which turned out neither to guide nor illuminate. Rather more effective was a new set of policies towards the nationalized industries which were required to earn a return on their capital assets rather than breaking even in the medium run, a policy which led to hidden cross-subsidization and the maintenance of services which were neither economically nor socially justified.

The Wilson government and devaluation

The Wilson Labour government came into office in October 1964 with high hopes that it would achieve significant improvements in the management of the British economy. The atmosphere was a more subdued version of the sense of entering a new era of modernization of the British economy and governing institutions that accompanied the election of Tony Blair in 1997. In particular, business had considerable confidence in the new government. After Blair became leader of the Labour Party there was some attempt to revitalize the reputation of the Wilson government. Nevertheless, when one revisits these events, it is difficult to escape the conclusion that this was a government which quickly abandoned its economic strategy and whose conduct was thereafter dominated by short-term political considerations. From the perspective of the Treasury, the period from 1964 to 1970 was 'a period of frustration and disappointment' (PRO: T267/22). It represented 'the final flourish of the attempt to manage the economy and manipulate domestic demand by levers in a context of fixed exchange rates and vulnerability to balance of payments crises' (Deakin and Parry, 2000, p. 181).

Wilson's own explanation is that for all but a year of the government's life, its work was 'dominated by an inherited balance of payments problem' (Wilson, 1971, p. 17). Those who were not alive at the time may not appreciate just how much the discussion of economic policy was dominated by the balance of payments; Labour's chances of re-election in 1970 were damaged by a single month's blip in the balance of payments. In part, this emphasis on the balance of payments reflected a popular misperception that they were the equivalent of a set of company or household accounts. However, the existence of a fixed exchange rate enhanced the importance of the balance of payments. Unfavourable figures produced pressure on the pound that then had to be defended by domestic policy measures. Even when devaluation did occur, it was a move from one fixed exchange rate to another.

When Labour came into office, the pound was overvalued. International experts took the view that 'sterling was in fundamental disequilibrium and ought to be devalued by 10–15 per cent' (Brittan, 1971, p. 291). This reflected the fact that

> the competitive position of the United Kingdom was weakening under the combined influence of rising money wages and slower growth in productivity than in other industrial countries... the relief afforded to the balance of payments throughout the 1950s by a steady improvement in the terms of trade could not be expected to continue for another decade. (Cairncross and Eichengreen, 1983, pp. 156–7)

What the Government could not face up to was the choice between devaluation and deflation:

> The result was an eventual devaluation, which in all time but the technical sense was forced, at the worst possible time internationally, when resources not only of foreign exchange, but of confidence, patience and credibility had all been nearly exhausted. Trying to get the best of both worlds, the government succeeded in achieving the worst. (Brittan, 1971, p. 293)

Devaluation was discussed in 1964 at a meeting of the three leading ministers concerned with economic policy (Wilson, Brown and Callaghan) and senior civil servants and economic advisers two days after the election. It was decided not to devalue, and discussion of the subject was thereafter largely suppressed, a practice assisted by the dominance of economic policy-making by the 'Big Three' of Wilson, Brown and Callaghan.

The decision not to devalue was essentially a political one. 'In October 1964 a decision to devalue the pound would, to say the least, have been a highly unorthodox step for a new (and very inexperienced) Labour Government to take' (Bruce-Gardyne and Lawson, 1976, p. 122). There is an interesting contrast with the immediate decision of the 1997 Labour government to transfer the fixing of interest rates to the Bank of England. However, the 1964 Labour government had a majority of only four. Of more importance was Wilson's anxiety not to have Labour labelled as the party of devaluation. He was also concerned about offending the Americans which was apparently a matter of great importance to both Wilson and Callaghan.

In any case, Wilson argued that 'the basic problems of the British economy were physical and structural' (Brittan, 1971, p. 292). Labour placed great faith in the National Plan and the institutional separation of the Treasury and the Department of Economic Affairs (DEA) as means of realizing its objective of promoting economic growth. The problem with the Plan was that it posited a growth rate of 25 per cent over a six-year period and then asked industries what the implications of such a growth rate might be for them (Leruez, 1975, p. 171). The results were not surprisingly somewhat optimistic. The DEA was supposed to provide a growth-oriented challenge to Treasury orthodoxy, but it was effectively outmanoeuvred by the Treasury when it came to the distribution of functions.

Labour did not want to go down the deflation path because of the consequences for the level of unemployment, but in 1965 pressure on the pound forced it to take its first package of deflationary measures. This package convinced some observers that 'the government had abandoned its growth and employment objectives, and would be prepared to deflate to the extent necessary to maintain the exchange rate' (Brittan, 1971, p. 309). In July 1966, the government was forced to adopt another broadly-based package of restrictive measures, in effect signalling the beginning of the end of full employment.

By July 1966 the government had a large majority in the House of Commons. Why, then, did it not devalue? Wilson subsequently regretted that he did not devalue then (Bruce-Gardyne and Lawson, 1976, p. 138). This time there was a discussion in Cabinet, but the proponents of devaluation were an ill-assorted group of the right and the left and Wilson had little difficulty in outmanoeuvring them. At one time it appeared that Callaghan might join forces with Brown in supporting devaluation, but he was persuaded to change his mind in a private meeting with Wilson, the master tactician.

Devaluation was thus 'delayed well beyond the point of maximum advantage... until after heavy forward sales of sterling had been made... ministers were unwilling to contemplate action that would have the advantage of surprise' (Cairncross and Eichengreen, 1983, p. 141). One of the factors that had changed during 1967 was that it was become increasingly evident that Britain would not be allowed to enter the common market unless it devalued sterling. Gloomy balance of payments forecasts and a continuing drain on the reserves led the government with no palatable alternative to take the decision it had sought to avoid in November 1967. As one would expect from the so-called 'J-curve' effect, (Tew, 1978, p. 356n) the benefits took some time to arrive and there were doubts whether the new parity could be maintained. By 'the first quarter of 1969 the current balance moved into surplus and in the second quarter this surplus... was substantial' (Blackaby, 1978, p. 49).

The government should have devalued earlier and much of the responsibility for the failure to do so must rest with Wilson himself. The best outcome would have been a floating rate, but that could not be countenanced at the time by the international monetary authorities. As it was, the Americans were concerned by the devaluation of the pound which they saw as the first line of defence against the dollar. The inflation produced by the Vietnam war eventually led the Americans to abandon the Bretton Woods system, the first step being taken by the Smithsonian agreement of December 1971 which widened the bands of permissible fluctuation. Healey notes (1990, p. 412), 'It would have been impossible for Britain to adjust to all the changes in the world economy during my period as Chancellor without the new international currency regime of floating exchange rates.'

The failure of modernization and a period of transition

Both the Labour government from 1964 to 1970 and Edward Heath's Conservative government from 1970 to 1974 advanced a rhetoric of modernization which is echoed by the present Blair government, although Heath was preoccupied with a problem of trade union power which did not trouble Blair. Both governments failed in their efforts to modernize the economy. Too much faith was placed in what could be achieved by setting up new institutions, whether government agencies or mergers of large firms.

Both governments attempted to tackle the problems presented by a fragmented, decentralized, increasingly militant and powerful trade union movement. Both attempts failed. These were also the last governments to take regard of full employment as the over-riding objective of economic policy. The pursuit of this objective produced discontinuities in policy, most evident in the Heath gov-ernment's 'U-turn' of 1972 when it abandoned its experiment with more market-oriented policies and reverted to intervention.

In retrospect the 1970s can be seen as the most troubled decade for postwar British economic policy. The 'misery index' of the combined unemployment and inflation total increased rapidly, and the trade unions dominated the landscape of economic management. The first oil shock and other commodity price rises triggered much higher rates of inflation. Nothing much could be done about com-modity prices, but governments could try to control domestic sources of inflation. 'The crucial issue in 1974 and for several years thereafter was seen as pay, and hence economic policy was seen quite largely as a process of negotiation with the leaders of the TUC' (Britton, 1991, p. 19). With inflation reaching an annual rate of 26.9 per cent in August 1975, an emergency and quite effective £6 a week limit to pay increases was introduced in the summer of 1975.

Seen in retrospect, the 1970s were a decade of transition in British economic policy.The country faced three crises, although they were imperfectly understood at the time. First, a structural transform-ation was beginning to take place in the economy with a shift from a manufacturing-based to a services-based economy. However, there was still a strong (and partly gender-biased) preference in favour of manufacturing as a more worthwhile way of making a living. The 'assumption that only an industrial future is possible for Britain' (Gamble, 1981, p. 31) was widely shared. Hence, attempts were made to shore up the crumbling industrial economy with policies that often enabled marginal businesses to stay afloat and generally slowed down the process of transformation.

Second, there was a crisis of economic orthodoxy. Keynesianism still ruled supreme in the Treasury, but it was clearly not working any longer. What emerged as the policy rule was, ' "frustrated Keynesianism". Policymakers saw a need for counter-cyclical fiscal policy, but were inhibited from taking decisive action by fears of yet-faster-inflation and yet-wider-deficits on the balance of pay-ments' (Britton, 1991, p. 20). The monetarists were gaining ground in the media and the City, but monetarism had not yet displaced

Keynesianism as the dominant policy orthodoxy; there was simply too much intellectual and personal capital invested in neo-Keynesian perspectives.

Third, there was a debate about whether the country was governable any longer. Heath had posed the question 'Who governs Britain?' and the response of the electorate in February 1974 had been, 'If you can't, we will choose someone else.' The result was close, however, with the Conservatives winning more votes than any other party, although fewer seats than Labour. With Labour back in government, a more general debate started which brought together neo-liberal critics on the right and Marxists on the left, academics as well as partisan polemicists.

Certainly the extent and depth of the pessimism was noticeable:

> Although no one has produced a plausible scenario for the collapse of the present British system of government, the fact that people are talking about the possibility at all is in itself significant, and certainly we seem...to face the sort of 'crisis of the regime' that Britain has not known since 1832, possibly not since the seventeenth century.' (King, 1975, pp. 294–5)

However, as Rose (1979, p. 369) pointed out, 'In a very general sense, any problem of political authority contains the seeds of its own resolution. If effectiveness and consent decline drastically, then a regime is repudiated'. The ungovernability debate was part of the death pangs of neo-Keynesian social democracy. After 1979 it was replaced by a new order based on a neo-liberal paradigm. In other words, the political system had enough elasticity and resilience to generate a new set of solutions, even if the transition period was painful.

In retrospect it is easy to interpret the course of events as inevitable, and the path to a new paradigm was a rocky one. The left of the Labour Party had not found it hard to interpret the failure of the 1964–70 Labour government to achieve significant change as a betrayal of socialist principles. A frequently quoted slogan was offered by Tony Benn that called for 'A fundamental and irreversible shift in the balance of power and wealth in favour of working people and their families' (Benn, 1979, p. 11). Wilson was at his most adroit in heading off this challenge from the left, first in securing the exclusion from the manifesto of a proposal to nationalize the 25 largest companies, and then in isolating the left within the Cabinet. The 1975 referendum result decisively confirming Britain's membership of the European Community was a setback for the left and enabled Wilson to remove Tony Benn from the industry ministry and move him to the less significant energy department.

The 1976 IMF crisis

The 1976 crisis was provoked by a fall in the value of sterling, which fell below two dollars in March and on 28 September as the Chancellor and the Governor of the Bank of England arrived at Heathrow on their way to the annual IMF conference, by a further 4.5 cents to $1.64. This was in line with its broad level at the end of the century, but at the time the downward fall seemed out of control. Healey broke off his journey and, 'On 29 September a formal application was made to the IMF for support amounting to $3.9 billion, the largest sum ever requested of them' (Dell, 1991, p. 237).

There was an alternative policy scenario available in the form of the 'New Cambridge' school which, in effect, advocated pulling Britain out of the international financial system and imposing substantial import controls to create a siege economy. The substantial public expenditure cuts required by the IMF were not acceptable to large sections of the Labour Party. As in 1966, however, opposition within the Cabinet was divided into groups on the left and the right. The Benn group on the left did not want to have too much to do with the group led by the intellectually formidable Crosland. Crosland in essence argued that the government should call the bluff of the IMF (and, by implication, the Americans). The threat of isolating the British economy and reducing defence commitments would result in far more favourable terms. In the end, however, Crosland backed down, claiming that he had not been convinced by the counter-arguments but did not want to bring down the government.

Healey notes (1990, p. 435) that 'An agreement with the IMF is like the Seal of Good Housekeeping Approval: it is regarded by the markets as a guarantee of responsible economic management.' Its effect was to 'limit the freedom of action of the government' (Britton, 1991, p. 32) and more specifically to require them to make cuts in public spending and to agree a target path for Domestic Credit Expansion.

What was the significance of the events of 1976? Considerable importance has been attached to a speech made by Callaghan at the Labour Party conference that was seen as a repudiation of Keynesianism and the postwar settlement. Callaghan argued that the option of spending one's way out of a recession no longer existed and that full employment could not be guaranteed by a stroke of the Chancellor's plan. Healey also started to publish the monetary forecasts that had been used in private to guide policy. There was, however, no general policy shift from Keynesianism to monetarism. There was something of a vacuum in the conduct of economic policy, which became increasingly apparent as the influence of the IMF settlement waned:

> The 'cautious' Keynesians, both ministers and officials, remained in power for a few years yet, and the approach to economic policy which they supported was not altogether abandoned. But their intellectual position was much weakened by the events of 1976 and quite different ideas about the aims and instruments of policy were becoming influential even in the Treasury and Bank. (Britton, 1991, p. 33)

A new political settlement?

It is very easy to fall into the trap of exaggerating the coherence of Thatcherism or the extent to which Mrs Thatcher was able to achieve her objectives. There was no grand scheme: policies (such as privatization) were adopted when it seemed politically expedient and others were effectively dropped (such as monetarism) when they no longer served a useful purpose. Tactical retreats were made when it did not seem opportune to progress further on a particular front. In other words, Thatcherism was highly political in the sense that one of its priorities was to win elections and secure the continuation of the Conservative Party in office. Thus, one interpretation of the Thatcher period is that 'The principle [sic] aim of those who took office in May 1979 was to achieve a governing competence through a reconstruction of that traditional centre autonomy enjoyed by British governments prior to the 1960s' (Bulpitt, 1986, p. 34). What this meant was that the Conservative Party would have enough freedom in office to pursue its own political agenda unconstrained by outside interests such as business and the unions.

Mrs Thatcher made it clear that she was running a 'conviction' government that had little time for the equivocations produced by the consensus politics of the previous 30 years. 'I'm not a *consensus* politician or a *pragmatic* politician. I'm a *conviction* politician' (*Observer*, 25 February 1979). As soon as she was able, she got rid of almost all the moderate 'One-Nation' Tories in her Cabinet. The Conservative Party was remade in a new populist image. 'The ultimate objective of Thatcherism in government was to use the state to promote neo-liberal reforms in economic strategy' (Heffernan, 2000, p. 57). There was no doubt in the minds of ministers that they had embarked on a 'complete change of direction' (Lawson, 1992, p. 69). This involved a shift from the postwar emphasis on the management of demand to a supply-side strategy (particularly in the late 1980s) and a replacement of full employment by the control of inflation as the single most important objective of economic policy. Nigel Lawson saw 'the commitment to full employment, come what may' (Lawson, 1992, p. 70) as an error made by previous governments.

The economic and political landscape was transformed in two areas in pursuit of these policies. Almost all of the nationalized industries were privatized; government was no longer responsible for a core section of the national economy, a burden that had sometimes threatened to overwhelm it. The trade unions were substantially weakened through a combination of measures: legislation which constrained their activities; the suppression of major strikes (particularly by the miners); the erosion of the manufacturing and public sectors from which they had obtained their greatest strength.

Policy instruments changed as well. The comprehensive incomes policies which dominated the 1960s and 1970s were out of favour. Consequently, there was no need to engage in intensive consultations with the employers and the unions. Tripartite discussions between the government, CBI and TUC were no longer at the heart of economic policy-making; the government's approach was to set out clear objectives that it said it would adhere to in order to influence expectations. A framework for macroeconomic policy was provided by the Medium-Term Financial Strategy (MTFS) which set out a four-year path for the money supply defined as M3. 'The MTFS was intended to be a self-imposed constraint on economic policy-making' (Lawson, 1992, p. 67), an equivalent of the gold standard and the Bretton Woods system in the past. Unfortunately, this proved somewhat difficult to control and by 1982 narrow (M1) and wider (Private Sector liquidity, PSL2) aggregates began to appear in government statements, as well as money GDP. Nevertheless, Lawson argued that the MTFS met its broader objectives, for 'although the monetary targets were missed, the spirit of the strategy was observed, as a result of which inflation was reduced far more than our supporters... would have believed possible' (Lawson, 1992, p. 413).

Nevertheless, Lawson was very sensitive to the deficiencies of money supply targets and the volatile relationship between the quantity of money and the price level or nominal GDP (Lawson, 1992, p. 417). In order to pursue his overall objective of real growth against a background of price stability, he needed another policy instrument and it seemed to him that the clearest, operationally, was the exchange rate target. 'An exchange rate target requires an anchor country with reasonably stable prices to which the domestic currency can be tied' (Lawson, 1992, p. 419); which led him into a policy of shadowing the deutschmark and advocating British membership of the Exchange Rate Mechanism (ERM).

This policy led to increasing tensions between Lawson and Mrs Thatcher. Mrs Thatcher claims that she did not know about this policy until she was interviewed by journalists from the *Financial Times* in November 1987 (Thatcher, 1993, p. 701). Thatcher thought of dismissing Lawson but, in effect, admits that his political strength prevented her from doing so (Thatcher, 1993, p. 702). Eventually, Lawson resigned in 1989 opening his resignation letter with the cardinal truth, 'The successful conduct of economic policy is possible only if there is, *and is seen to be*, full agreement between the Prime Minister and the Chancellor of the Exchequer' (Lawson, 1992, p. 964). By 1989, interest rates were very high, peaking at 15 per cent in October, and inflation was rising. Lawson's actions after the 1987 stock exchange crash had triggered an unsustainable boom. Nevertheless, Lawson was a Chancellor who made a difference and the Treasury was at the centre of policy-making in a way that was not going to happen again until Gordon Brown became New Labour's Chancellor in 1997.

The Thatcher government's objectives

One of the central objectives of the Conservative government was to reduce the share of taxation and public expenditure in the national economy. When the Conservatives came into office in 1979, total managed expenditure was 44.4 per cent of GDP. It then rose to a peak of 48.3 per cent in 1983 against a background of recession. It reached a low of 39.4 per cent in 1989 and then rose again under the Major government, finally falling back to 41.6 per cent in their last full year in office. The subsequent Labour government in fact achieved a sharper fall in the ratio. What this reflects is that much of public expenditure is politically difficult to reduce because it is largely made up of popular public services (health and education) or transfer payments (pensions, child benefits and so forth) (figures from Lipsey, 2000, p. 11).

In terms of taxation there was little shift in the overall take from 35.5 per cent in 1979–80 to 37.25 per cent in 1990–91 (figures from Lawson, 1992, p. 1081). Taxation as a proportion of national income 'remained higher than it had been under Labour' (Lawson, 1992, p. 986), which Lawson attributes to the need to reduce substantially an inherited Budget deficit. Nevertheless, the structure of taxation did change; there was a substantial shift from direct to indirect taxation, and income tax rates were significantly reduced. When the Conservatives came into office, the top rate of tax on earned income was 83 per cent and that on savings income was 98 per cent: both were reduced to 40 per cent.

Inflation initially rose to over 20 per cent, fell back sharply in the early 1980s and then peaked again at 10.9 per cent in September 1990, before falling back again. Lawson admits that although inflation during his time as Chancellor was under 5 per cent it was 'not good enough' (Lawson, 1992, p. 989). The Conservatives could, however, claim to have undermined the assumption that inflation was a given and to have paved the way for the low and stable rates of the late 1990s. Nevertheless, the 'misery index' of inflation and unemployment rates for 1980–95 was 16.0 for the UK, compared with 9.3 for Germany. In both 1955–79 and 1980–95 the UK was above the median for advanced industrial countries and 'the ranking of the UK is very similar in both periods' (Crafts, 1997, p. 55).

Summarizing the government's broader performance, Crafts notes the short-term productivity gains from shaking-out inefficiency. Factors such as better industrial relations and an improved quality of investment 'suggest that there may have been a relative improvement sufficient to prevent further economic decline relative to Europe' (Crafts, 1997, p. 62). From a growth perspective, the government's performance might seem positive but

> for those whose main concern is the distribution of income, the overall outcome might be regarded as negative. Inequality, measured purely in terms of income, has increased more rapidly in the UK than elsewhere. (Crafts, 1997, p. 62)

The Major government

The story of the economic policy is dominated by the events of 'Black' or 'Golden' Wednesday that was one of the most extraordinary events in postwar British economic policy (there is a more detailed discussion in Chapter 4). The Major government was forced to leave the exchange rate mechanism that Britain had joined in 1990 in humiliating circumstances; membership of the ERM had supposedly been at the centre of government economic policy. Although the consequent devaluation was beneficial for the British economy, the Conservatives lost and failed to regain one of their most precious electoral assets, their lead in perceptions of economic competence over Labour.

The Major government continued the Thatcher tradition of making 'the single target of macro-economic policy...the minimization – or elimination – of inflation'. One important innovation that was continued under Blair was the setting of an inflation target, expressed as a range. The three other traditional goals of high growth, low employment and a trade balance were 'regarded as residuals whose achievement is contingent on a favourable inflation outcome, although Major gave more emphasis to growth from 1993' (Wilks, 1997, pp. 689–90). This had been signalled in comments made by Major on television in October 1992 when he had declared, 'A strategy for growth is what we need, a strategy for growth is what we are going to have' (quoted in Lamont, 1999, p. 296).

This is not a remark that would have been made in the Thatcher period, nor would monetary indicators have been treated so casually as a monitoring range formed one of a number of indicators that included house prices (Lamont, 1999, p. 276). The public-sector borrowing requirement rose, partly as a consequence of the recession, partly as a result of additional spending requirements made before the 1992 general election. Mrs Thatcher let it be known that Major 'had permitted public expenditure to rise too far' (Dorey, 1999, p. 223). The tax burden rose as well, but Major remained true to the Thatcherite canon of cutting direct taxes, placing the burden on indirect taxation including some new taxes that came to be known as 'stealth taxes' because their impact was not intended to be immediately apparent. Unfortunately, Major's second Chancellor, Ken Clarke, incautiously let it be known that the cost of budget measures over three years 'was equal to an extra 7p on the standard rate of income tax' (Major, 1999, p. 683). The loss of the claim to be a tax-cutting party further damaged the standing of the Conservatives with their natural supporters, helping to pave the way for a New Labour government which assured voters that it had lost the 'tax and spend' habits of the past.

New Labour

One of the ways in which New Labour signalled its separation from Old Labour was to transfer responsibility for the setting of interest rates to the Monetary Policy Committee of the Bank of England. It was a step that John Major had not been prepared to contemplate. No government likes giving up control of a key policy instrument, but New Labour took this decision within a few days of taking office, an interesting contrast with Old Labour's reluctance to contemplate devaluation in October 1964.

In the area of fiscal policy, government actions became more constrained and rules-based with the passage into law of a Code of Fiscal Stability. At the centre of the Code were two rules governing fiscal management. The first is the so-called 'golden rule' which requires that government will borrow only to invest and not fund current spending. The second rule is a debt rule that requires that the ratio of GDP to public-sector debt be held at a stable and prudent level.

Conservative spending plans were accepted for the first two years in office at both the departmental and aggregate level. In the 2000 Comprehensive Spending Review, however, the government announced substantial increases in public expenditure. This was against a background in which total managed expenditure in 1999–2000 was just 37.7 per cent of GDP, lower than any year since 1963–64. On the projections at that time, even by 2003–04, government spending as a share of GDP would be lower than when New Labour came into office.

Labour broadly accepted the post-1979 settlement constructed by Thatcher; its broad objectives were similar to those of the preceding Conservative governments. But this does not mean that Labour's policies were identical to those of the Conservatives. For example, the tax and benefits system was used to help the less well off: 'One considerable achievement of the Brown Chancellorship so far . . . is to put a halt to the redistribution that for almost two decades was widening economic inequality in the United Kingdom' (Moran and Alexander, 2000, p. 115).

Nevertheless, an underlying premise of New Labour's economic policies, at least for Tony Blair, has been that globalization is a real phenomenon that seriously constrains the domestic economic policy freedom of any national government. Whether the 'enigmatic and even secretive' (Deakin and Parry, 2000, p. 182) Gordon Brown shares this perspective is less clear. As was emphasized in the introduction, globalization is a highly contested concept; anyone studying contemporary economic policy has to make a judgement about its extent and its impact on the freedom for manoeuvre in domestic economic policy. It is this issue which is considered in the following chapter.

2

Globalization and Europeanization

Introduction

Globalization is probably the most contested concept in contemporary social science. Globalization gurus like Tony Giddens assert that the 'old globalization' debate about whether globalization is taking place is over; the reality of globalization has to be accepted and we should be moving on to a 'new globalization' debate about appropriate responses to it. However, whether there has really been a shift from a long-running process of internationalization, interrupted by a long phase of protection from the First World War to the 1970s, to something genuinely different that we can label globalization remains contested. Indeed, some commentators saw that the events of 11 September 2001 might bring about the demise of globalization (Roach, 2001). In any event, this is not simply an academic debate about appropriate labels; globalization constrains the range of economic policy options available to nation states, and the most extreme versions would deny any autonomy to the nation state in economic policy matters at all.

The globalization debate is often of low quality. It can reduce to listing a number of global brands, without reflecting how many brands are not global, or to seeing airport duty-free shops as a metaphor for the global consumer, or treating the Teletubbies as some kind of global icon. Nevertheless, the debate attempts to address a central question of vital importance to the type of society in which we live: are states the masters of markets or are markets now the masters over the governments of states (Strange, 1996, p. 4)? If the answer is broadly in the affirmative, then we need to be thinking about the construction of new and more effective forms of economic governance at the regional and global levels.

What is globalization?

There is very little agreement about what globalization is. Scholte (2000, pp. 15–16) sets out five alternative definitions in terms of internationalization, liberalization, universalization, westernization and deterritorialization. He prefers this last definition which sees globalization as the spread of supraterritoriality:

> Following this interpretation, globalization entails a reconfiguration of geography, so that social space is no longer wholly mapped in terms of territorial places, territorial distances and territorial borders. (Scholte, 2000, p. 16)

It is open to question, however, whether social geography was ever entirely territorial.

The understanding of globalization preferred here is of a continuing (although not irreversible) process which reduces the significance of national boundaries as an impediment to the free movement of capital, goods and services and (to a far lesser extent) of labour. To use a metaphor employed by Giddens, a softening of borders means that they become more like frontiers once again (Giddens, 1998, p. 20). This process has its limits, however. 'There has been no comparable relaxation of immigration controls to accompany the liberalization of trade and capital flows' (Crafts, 2000, p. 29), which might imply that this is a process driven more by the interests of capital than by the needs of people. Despite such important exceptions, globalization is seen as 'a significant trend, but one that coexists with other developments and is far from complete' (Scholte, 2000, p. 17).

Scholte defines the approach adopted here that emphasizes economic integration and the removal of government-imposed restrictions to transactions between countries as liberalization, a global world being one 'without regulatory barriers to transfers of resources between countries' (Scholte, 2000, p. 45). From his perspective, 'The long-established liberal discourse of "free trade" is quite adequate to convey these ideas' (Scholte, 2000, p. 45).

In fact, however, globalization extends far beyond free trade. The regulatory barriers that would need to be removed to establish a global world go beyond the economic to encompass the social. As those barriers start to be removed, a Polanyian 'double movement' is likely to come into play and forms of resistance are likely to increase. Globalization is a 'tendency to which there are countertendencies' (Hay and Marsh, 2000, p. 6); a backlash against global-ization is possible. Roach's (2001) core argument is that globalization rests on enhanced cross-border connectivity. The terrorist attacks of September 2001 may impose what amounts to a new tax on cross-border linkages because cross-border flows will cost more and take longer. In addition, there may be psychological effects which lead companies to look inwards. It could be argued, however, that when border flows are of information rather than goods, modern technol-ogy reduces the impact of interruptions to the movement of persons or products.

Nevertheless, globalization is neither stable nor irreversible. The world economy at the beginning of the twenty-first century is signifi-cantly driven by the American economy. The events of September 2001 deepened an already evident slowdown in the US economy. Although analysts differed about the likely length and intensity of any global slowdown, the result of a major world showdown could be 'antipathy to international capital mobility and free trade leading to widespread adoption of policies aimed at reimposing controls' (Crafts, 2000, p. 31). Even with the continuation of good economic times, political mobilization around the impact of globalization on the north–south divide or on the environment may intensify. There may also be tensions between demands for increasing social protec-tion for workers and pressures for greater mobility of capital, less regulation and lower levels of taxation.

In broad terms, globalization can be seen as a process in which international trade grows faster than national output; foreign direct investment grows faster than trade; and international financial markets undergo a complete transformation. Figures for 1979–96 show that

> The average annual increase in world trade was 5.2 per cent, nearly 2 per cent higher than world output growth (3.3 per cent)...In contrast, international financial market activity has grown by more than 14.9 per cent! (Annaert, 1999, p. 37)

Even though the World Trade Organization (WTO) has greater authority than the General Agreement on Tariffs and Trade (GATT) it replaced, that greater authority has to be exercised carefully and is conditional (see p. 51). The acceleration of inter-national trade could be seen as a return to the considerable eco-nomic interdependence that existed before the First World War. Taking such a view too far, however, would be misleading: 'The nature of international trade is in several respects quite different now compared with one hundred years ago and it plays a much larger part in world economic activity' (Crafts, 2000, p. 25). Trade before the First World War was centred on goods and raw materials, whereas services have now grown in importance. Foreign direct investment in that period often took the form of portfolio investment unlike the complex web of direct investment undertaken by multinational companies later in the twentieth century. In the 1990s, transfers between foreign affiliates of multinationals increased by nearly twice as much as global trade.

Foreign direct investment has been an important phenomenon since the nineteenth century. The evidence suggests that 'the book value of foreign direct investment relative to world GDP is probably only a couple of percentage points higher now than in 1914' (Crafts, 2000, p. 27). Much of the increase in trade and foreign direct investment has occurred between the United States, the European Union and Japan. Indeed, there is a sense in which if globalization means anything, it is the increasing integration of the economies of the USA and the EU. 'In 1996 about 50 per cent of the US foreign direct investment position was in the EU, and almost 60 per cent of EU foreign direct investment was in the USA' (Blank and Taillander, 1998, p. 12). The developments in trade and in foreign direct investment could be comfortably accommodated within a model of accelerated internationalization.

It is when we turn to the financial markets that we see something qualitatively different to what has existed before, a highly integrated market system in which small disturbances in one location can have far-reaching and uncontrollable consequences. In such a system of 'casino capitalism' (Strange, 1986) it is difficult for governments or even for international bodies to control events:

> Since the 1970s the variety of financial instruments, the number of financial markets in the world, the magnitude of investments in financial instruments, and the volumes of trading have all skyrocketed well beyond any previous levels. (Scholte, 2000, p. 116)

Transactions on foreign exchange markets expanded fifteenfold in the two decades to 1998 (Scholte, 2000, p. 79), there has been a massive expansion of global deposits, and a tremendous growth in financial derivatives markets. The globalization literature is susceptible to 'gee whiz' superlatives, but international financial markets are perhaps one area where they are justified.

A number of forces are driving these developments. There has been a remarkable growth in foreign portfolio investment; foreign assets/world GDP grew from 17.7 per cent in 1980 (about the level at the beginning of the First World War) to 56.8 per cent in 1995 (Crafts, 2000, p. 27). The enhanced activity of multinationals in such areas creates an expanding market for cross-national financial transactions and new financial instruments. Electronic communications have been a necessary but not a sufficient condition of these developments. Once global markets emerge, they acquire a momentum of their own. Markets come to be seen as 'more powerful than the states to whom ultimate political authority over society and economy is supposed to belong' (Strange, 1996, p. 4).

Three perspectives on globalization

In this book we are particularly concerned with the implications of globalization for the conduct of economic policy at the level of the nation state, and in particular Britain. Baker and Seawright (2000) provide an analytical framework that distinguishes between three different variants of the globalization literature: hyperglobalism, national political economy and open regionalism. Each of these has different implications for national policy-making.

'The proponents of hyperglobalism argue that the changes introduced by globalization are so profound that they have altered irrevocably the political economy context of national policy-making' (Baker and Seawright, 2000, p. 8). This is the kind of literature which Hay and Marsh (2000, p. 4) portray as 'business globalization' which predicts the 'withering away of the state at the hands of footloose multinational corporations and capital'. Ohmae (1990, p. 172) argues that 'national borders have effectively disappeared and, along with them, the economic logic that made them useful lines of demarcation in the first place'. In fact, the globalization of consumer tastes that he asserts has already occured has its limits. Airport duty-free shops may be the precursors of a borderless environment, but it has not arrived yet as anyone who has attempted to cross the border between Canada and the United States can testify.

If the hyperglobalists are correct, the policy implications 'are considerable, since there is little if any room left for discretionary policies aimed at protecting, subsidising or fine-tuning the national economy' (Baker and Seawright, 2000, p. 8). Any government that attempts to pursue its own distinctive policy is liable to be punished by the financial markets. With the option of protection no longer available, 'governments have learnt that they must implement policies which command confidence in the financial markets' (*ibid.*). It is in relation to the power of the financial markets that the hyperglobalism argument has its greatest strength.

The national political economy approach sees the world as still conforming to an international rather than a global model:

> This view recognises that there have been significant changes in the way in which the international economy has been organised in the last thirty years, but it insists that it has not mutated into a global economy and that nation-states, on the whole, have not declined in power. (Baker and Seawright, 2000, p. 10)

It follows that 'opportunities for states to exercise autonomy in economic policy making remain considerable, and are shown to be so by the diversity of response and experience which is evident around the world' (*ibid.*). It should not surprise us that such a complex phenomenon as globalization should not necessarily produce policy convergence (Wincott, 2000); it is undoubtedly the case that globalizing forces are still significantly mediated by national economic and cultural structures. Much of the evidence collected in areas such as welfare policy suggest that national differences influenced by key decisions that created 'path dependencies' persist. Nevertheless, distinctive national economic structures and styles such as 'Rhineland capitalism' are under increasing pressure to conform to international orthodoxies. Moreover, governments that attempt to pursue policies out of line with prevalent thinking may find that they cannot sustain such independent courses of action as happened in Britain in 1976 and France in 1981/82. The autonomy of governments has always been constrained to some extent by international economic forces, but it seems plausible to suggest that those constraints are becoming more limiting.

The open-regionalist approach is closest to the one that is taken in this book. It starts from the assumption that globalization is a contestable historical process rather than an outcome. There is an acceptance that, particularly in relation to global financial markets, 'the economic trends which make up the new world economy of the last thirty years are qualitatively new, but it does not accept the more extreme formulations of the hyperglobalism thesis' (Baker and Seawright, 2000, p. 12). Nation states remain an important set of political actors, but there has been some erosion of their decision-making capacity. An important part of this perspective is the argument that regional formations such as the EU are not protectionist fortresses, but rather 'they facilitate the creation of a new political space ... and the elaboration of new forms of governance' (*ibid.*).

Europeanization of economic policy

The conclusion drawn from the open-regionalist approach is that 'traditional goals of national economic management are now best pursued at the collective level of the European Union, rather than left to the nation-state alone' (Baker and Seawright, 2000, p. 12). From this perspective, 'perhaps the existence of the EU has produced a different form of globalization in western Europe from that in other parts of the world' (Wallace, 2000, p. 49). Wallace goes on to argue that the various collective policy regimes of the EU, which will be examined in more detail in later chapters, may have

> enabled West European countries to function as a more self-sufficient economic entity than might otherwise have been the case. Thereby west European vulnerability to the broader phenomenon of globalization may have been reduced. (Wallace, 2000, p. 49).

At the heart of the Europeanization of economic policy is economic and monetary union, and this is discussed fully in Chapter 4. There are, however, other areas of economic policy in which the EU is active. One of the most notorious is agricultural policy with the CAP producing a type of European agriculture that is internationally uncompetitive, subsidy-dependent and environmentally damaging. The experience of competition policy has been more positive and is discussed more fully in Chapter 6. The EU has also pursued a policy designed to promote high technology, although at one time this seemed to be based on a forlorn effort to replace 'national' with 'European' champions by propping up firms in difficulty or at least in need of additional investment funds. The pursuit of ambitious policies in the area of high technology continues to be a difficult area of operation for the EU (Lembke, 2001).

Trade policy

Trade policy is an area in which the EU has operated since the formation of the common market. Trade or 'commercial' policy was made an exclusive European Community competence under the Treaty of Rome. The common commercial policy was based on the three principles of a common external tariff, common trade agreements with third countries and the uniform application of trade instruments across member states. As the significance of international trade negotiations has increased, so has the importance of the EU's role in this area. Although there is no trade council of ministers as such, there are well-established mechanisms for making trade policy. The General Affairs Council makes a decision that negotiations are to be started and issues a negotiating mandate: 'The actual conduct of trade negotiations is the responsibility of the Commission, acting on behalf of all EU member states' (Nugent, 2001, p. 307).

Two broad critiques have been advanced of the EU's conduct of trade policy. One, from the Eurosceptics, is that trade policy has become unduly politicized, producing strains in relations with the USA and other countries. Redwood claims (2001, p. 4) that 'The EU, as a deliberate act of policy, escalates trade disputes with the US, seeking to establish its own position as an important player in trade negotiations and in the day-to-day management of trade relations.' The number of trade disputes between the EU and the USA might be regarded as curious given their generally friendly relations and the fact that their trade is broadly in balance. Most of the disputes, however, arise in agriculture which is the most politicized sector of the economy in both Europe and the United States. Farmers on both sides of the Atlantic receive high levels of subsidy and protection and the attempts to maintain these subsidy regimes inevitably produce international trade disputes. The various efforts to establish joint conflict management mechanisms between the EU and the USA do not generally extend to agriculture. The USA seems to have backed away from the determination to reduce assistance to farmers embodied in the Freedom to Farm Act. Radical reform of the CAP is often predicted, but is yet to occur. There is no general EU effort to provoke trade conflicts with the USA, but there has been a policy failure in terms of reform of the CAP.

A second critique, from a more integrationist perspective, is that the EU's negotiating position is still too much influenced by the particular interests of powerful member states. Once again it is agriculture where the most serious problems have arisen. In the Uruguay Round, the Blair House agreement was supposed to have resolved the outstanding issues on agriculture between the USA and the EU, but France was in effect able to insist on the negotiations being reopened (officially 'clarified'). The final outcome embodied in the 'Blair House 2' or 'Breydel' was even more favourable to France's position. Britain's consistent position has been to favour a more liberal approach by the EU to international trade questions; however, particularly on agricultural issues, it has lacked sufficient support to bring about change.

The position taken here would somewhat modify the emphasis placed by the open-regionalist perspective on the role of the EU to point to the desirability of the construction of a multilevel governance system of economic policy-making. Some tasks, such as economic development, might be undertaken at the subnational level; others would remain at the national level, some would be transferred to the regional (EU) level and yet others would require reinvigorated agencies of global economic governance.

The Blair government and globalization

Before they start to construct an economic policy, governments have to make an assessment of the globalization phenomenon. In summary, they have to decide whether it is happening and, if so, whether they approve of it and, if not, whether and how they intend to resist it. The Blair government's general approach to this set of questions was to see globalization as a challenge and an opportunity rather than a threat. Its underlying assumption was that 'an increasingly liberalised global economy is broadly beneficial' (Wilkinson, 2000, p. 183).

It could be argued that the arrival of globalization as a widely discussed phenomenon was politically convenient. It could be deployed as part of the process of converting 'old' into 'new' Labour. It made it possible to argue that any government's room for manoeuvre was limited and that powerful international financial markets demand a market-based philosophy. As Hay and Watson argue (1999, p. 155):

> It is the discursive construction of globalization, rather than globalization *per se* which is driving political change in contemporary Britain... globalization acts as a convenient *post hoc* rationalization for a logic of tax cutting which the Labour Party has already internalized.

Blair's analysis of globalization started from the belief that 'The determining context of economic policy is the new global market. That imposes huge limitations of a practical nature... on macro-economic policies' (*Financial Times*, 22 May 1995). Given that Blair apparently views globalization as both a normative and an empirical imperative, what is there left for government to do in the sphere of economic policy? The Prime Minister elaborated his own views of what he saw as the three key tasks for 'centre-left' governments in his meeting with President Clinton in February 1998:

> One was that, as a result of globalization, it was essential that domestic governments held to fiscal and monetary prudence. Second, that there was a role for government, but that was not in extensive economic regulation but in empowerment with the equipment of the individual to make the markets operate better. Thirdly, that we have to construct a tax and benefit system which was sound and helped to make work pay. (Senior British Official, 1998, p. 1)

Critics argue that globalization produces winners and losers and the third way 'adopts the world-view of the winners' (Giddens, 2000, p. 24). Alongside the celebration of globalization by writers like Giddens, there is a concern about its more negative effects. The suggestions about how to deal with these negative consequences are not very precise, but there is a much greater emphasis on government regulation than neo-liberals would feel comfortable with. Giddens acknowledges the problem of government failure, but argues that 'Government needs to play a regulative role across the board' (Giddens, 2000, p. 45). This is clearly at variance with conceptions of globalization as deregulation:

> Though New Labour has committed itself to follow what it perceives to be the logic of globalisation and operate within the parameters it deemed to dictate, it has always committed itself to pursuing this agenda in conjunction with the promotion of certain environmental, social and developmental issues. It has committed itself... to a kind of *socialised* neo-liberalism. (Wilkinson, 2000, p. 138)

Global economic governance

Globalization has seen an intensification and extensification of the reach of market-driven economic forces. One response is the construction of institutions at the regional level, such as the EU, that can mediate globalization. Another, and not mutually exclusive, response is to enhance the capacity for policy coordination possessed by global governance agencies. Political institutionalization at a global level has not kept pace with economic change. In part, this reflects the fact that we still live in a world in which nation states are important; many new ones have been formed as breakaways from existing states, suggesting that the status of distinct nationhood is still attractive. Both new and old nation states are reluctant to sacrifice too much authority to international bodies. Global governance agencies operate in an environment almost as constrained as that faced by nation states, and, above all, this is because of an underlying continuity – 'globalization leaves capitalism as entrenched as ever, if not more so' (Scholte, 2000, p. 21).

The World Trade Organization (WTO)

The WTO has become a particular target of opponents of globalization. Portrayed by some as the 'World Terror Organization', its attempts to secure freer trade are seen as a threat to environmental standards and the rights of workers in developing countries. The supporters of free trade have, however, sometimes seen it as the 'Water Treading Organization', making insufficient progress towards the world of free trade. Although traditional protectionist barriers such as tariffs have been significantly reduced, world trade is still managed rather than free. The WTO is a more effective organization than the General Agreement on Tariffs and Trade (GATT) that it replaced in 1995, but it has a number of substantial weaknesses. As Vines observes (1998, p. 74), 'It is essentially a fragile body' which has 'rather limited leadership, research and interpretive capacity'. It has by far the smallest secretariat of all the international organizations despite having to service a complex network of committees and an increasing range of responsibilities (see Table 2.1).

Table 2.1 Size of secretariats of global governance agencies

World Bank	11303
International Monetary Fund	2700
Organization for Economic Cooperation and Development	1850
World Trade Organization	500

Sources: web sites of organizations.

> In 1996, the WTO budget was equivalent to about 9.5 minutes of the value of world merchandise trade in 1995 . . . and to a little more than 7.5 minutes of 1995 world trade in goods and services combined. (Blackhurst, 1998, p. 39n)

The gap between what serious analysts of the organizations observe and journalistic portrayals is immense. A not untypical portrayal appeared in the *Independent on Sunday* headed 'The hidden tentacles of the world's most secret body'. Its account of the WTO continued:

> It can stop us choosing what we eat. It can strike down laws passed by even the strongest, democratic governments. It can start or sanction trade wars. And it can set at naught the provisions of international treaties which have been solemnly ratified by the world's nations. (*Independent on Sunday*, 18 July 1999)

Most of the statements contained in this quotation are either wrong or gross distortions of the actual position. Nevertheless, they feed popular perceptions at a time when 'new age' politics are gaining ground. The advocates of free trade thought that they had won the intellectual battle by demonstrating that protectionist barriers benefited neither producers nor consumers. All that was needed was to find a more effective mechanism to overcome the particularistic interests of national governments or regional trading blocs like the EU. It was thought that the WTO and its disputes-settlement mechanism had provided that. The WTO now faces a struggle on new and uncharted territory that cannot simply be resolved by coopting non-governmental organizations or making additional concessions to developing countries. In addition, any future world recession could lead to a reversion to more traditional protectionist politics.

The GATT was set up as part of a trinity of organizations that emerged from the postwar world economic settlement sponsored by the United States, the other two being the International Monetary Fund (IMF) and the World Bank. The original intention had been to set up a more powerful International Trade Organization, but this objective was frustrated by opposition in the United States. Nevertheless, the GATT was able to make progress in reducing tariff barriers through a series of negotiating 'rounds', the most significant of the early ones being the Kennedy Round (1964–67) and Tokyo Round (1973–79). In part this was possible because the United States as the hegemonic power was prepared to bear some of the costs of freeing up trade as part of its cold-war effort to bolster western economies against those of the Communist countries. Freer trade also suited American multinationals. However, as the world economy ran into increasing difficulties in the 1970s, the predominant free-trade coalition in the United States began to erode. Countries began to resort to a number of non-tariff barriers to trade such as bilateral arrangements that imposed 'voluntary export restraints' or 'orderly marketing agreements' on newly-industrializing countries.

The long drawn out Uruguay Round which began in 1986 and was concluded with the Marrakesh Agreement in 1994 revitalized global governance arrangements in relation to world trade. Agriculture had been effectively excluded from earlier trading rounds, but the Uruguay Round brought it back within the supervision of the world trading system through an Agreement on Agriculture. What was important about the Agreement on Agriculture was not so much the substantive outcome, which allowed the EU in particular to retain high levels of agricultural protection, but the fact that agriculture was firmly established as part of the world trading agenda.

Another important aspect of the Uruguay Round was the establishment of a General Agreement on Trade in Services that reflected the increasing share of services rather than primary products or manufactures in world trade. As in agriculture, what was important was not so much what was contained within the agreement itself, but the basis that it provided for future negotiations. Since the conclusion of the Uruguay Round, important agreements have been concluded on financial services and telecommunications, as well as on information technology products.

Above all, the Uruguay Round led to the creation of a new trade dispute-settlement system 'that is sometimes seen as the crowning glory of the WTO' (Wolfe, R., 1999, p. 217). The GATT did have a dispute-settlement mechanism, but its operation could be blocked by a single country and there were no deadlines for coming to a decision. It is therefore not surprising that it never resolved a trade dispute valued at more than 10 million dollars. Between its introduction in January 1995 and November 2000, the new mechanism dealt with 213 requests (162 distinct matters) leading to 41 issued reports.

Once a decision against a complainant has been made, the scope for authorized trade retaliation through sanctions is greater than under the old GATT arrangements. Supporters of the new arrangements see it as a move towards a more rule-based system for settling international trade disputes, with a body of trade jurisprudence being established. One concern about this more effective arrangement is that it means a loss of sovereignty for WTO members.

The system of liberalizing international trade embodied in the WTO faces three main challenges. First, the WTO is clearly under-resourced in terms of the range of tasks it attempts to undertake; it is still operating very much in terms of a GATT secretariat model. It is, of course, a member-driven organization in which the Geneva delegations play an important part, and the larger member countries in particular do not want a 'proactive, assertive secretariat' (Blackhurst, 1998, p. 41). Nevertheless, the present secretariat is not large enough to function properly in terms of servicing meetings and providing advice. This suggests that what the larger and wealthier countries really want is a forum in which they can cut deals between themselves.

Second, the benefits of freer international trade and the greater prosperity it brings may be increasingly taken for granted. Political coalitions in favour of free trade, particularly in the United States, have been significantly weakened. However, the events of September 2001 may have strengthened the case for free trade and encouraged the United States to resume more of a leadership role as part of its efforts to reconstruct the international order. The anti-globalization movement may have lost some of its intellectual authority, with some of its energy and capacity being diverted into the anti-war movement.

Third, environmentalists point out that greater trade may bring prosperity, but it also leads to greater movement of goods which contributes to global warming and pollution problems. Efforts to protect biodiversity may be endangered if domestic rules are seen as incompatible with free trade. Developing countries are concerned that most of the benefits of free trade go to those countries that are already wealthy, reinforcing existing global distributive imbalances.

Although the WTO is a 'one country, one vote' organization, power has hitherto largely been exercised by the 'quad' of G7 members (the USA, the EU, Japan and Canada). However, their combined power was of little value in the failed talks at Seattle. The combined effect of a lack of preparation by leading members of the WTO and opposition by developing countries and demonstrations on the streets meant that the hope of launching a new 'Millennium Round' of trade negotiations could not be realized. The old WTO model of mutual adjustments between rich countries, often at the expense of other participants, does not really work properly any more, but no one has come up with a new model to replace it.

Organization for Economic Cooperation and Development (OECD)

The OECD originated with the Organization for European Economic Cooperation (OEEC) set up to manage the Marshall Plan which helped to rebuild Europe's economies after the Second World War. It became the OECD in 1961 with an initial membership of 20 countries in Europe and North America. The membership has now expanded to 29 to include countries such as the Czech Republic, Hungary, Mexico and South Korea. This number is a much smaller membership than the (continually increasing) 138 members of the WTO, or the 182 countries that belong to the International Monetary Fund (IMF) and the World Bank. It reflects the fact that the OECD is still primarily a club of rich, like-minded countries that produce two-thirds of the world's goods and services.

The OECD has also been described as a think tank or an unacademic university. It would be easy to dismiss it as a 'talking shop', but this would be to overlook the importance of the agenda-setting function in politics. The way in which ideas emerge and become accepted can be as important in the political process as the exercise of power by established interests. Indeed, one way to overcome their veto power is to develop new concepts and arguments. An interesting example is the way in which the OECD was involved in the development of new methodologies to measure the overall level of subsidy (including tax reliefs) made to agriculture. This led to the now widely accepted Producer Subsidy Equivalent (PSE) and Consumer Subsidy Equivalent (CSE). This certainly drew attention to how extensive agricultural subsidies had become, although admittedly it did not bring about a significant reduction in their size.

The OECD does see itself as a setting where members can exchange ideas on practice leading to better-informed domestic policy formation. 'The OECD is the only international agency in which officials from ministries of finance and economics are able, if they so wish, to review systematically questions of microeconomic policy' (Henderson, 1998, p. 126). Its annual reports on the economies of its member states receive serious attention from decision-makers and the economic and financial media. The OECD sees its role of seeking to coordinate domestic and international policies as par-

ticularly important under conditions of globalization, and in under-
taking such a task it can be argued to have certain advantages:

> The OECD combines (1) a diverse portfolio of interests, concerns and
> expertise, and (2) a dense and continuing network of contacts within
> member governments and other international agencies. These make it
> possible for the secretariat to handle subjects and issues that cut across
> professional dividing lines . . . Among international agencies the OECD's
> distinctive contribution is to be found, not so much in particular areas of
> policy, but rather in the way it handles topics, its mode of operation.
> (Henderson, 1998, p. 126)

The very scope of the OECD's activities is both a source of
strength and a limitation. Its range of interest enables it to look at
issues, such as ageing in society, across traditional departmental
boundaries. In this way, it can move the debate beyond the assumptions of entrenched policy communities. However, this breadth of
perspective also means 'that no one department feels closely identified with, and fully informed about, its activities as a whole, which
are likewise not well known to a wider public' (Henderson, 1998,
p. 7). One consequence of its lower profile is that it has not been the
target of angry demonstrations against globalization in the way that
the World Bank and the WTO have. The OECD is really an organization for the political class in wealthy countries, a role that has
both strengths and limitations. Its reliance on consensual decision-
making sometimes slows down the speed with which it acts, but it
has been able to bring some pressure to bear on issues such as tax
havens. Its impact may be difficult to measure, but it does contrib-
ute to providing information and hence reducing information asymmetries, lowering transaction costs and reducing uncertainty. The
successful performance of such roles enhances the possibilities for
cooperative behaviour between states and expands the range of
possible deals between nations (Goldstein, 1998, pp. 137–8); global
governance would be less effective if the OECD did not exist.

The IMF and the World Bank

These sister institutions complete the trinity of 'Bretton Woods'
institutions alongside the WTO, but they are more clearly international while the WTO and the OECD are essentially intergovern-
mental. One indicator is the relative size of their secretariats (see
Table 3.1). Unlike the WTO, which is reliant on subscriptions from

the most powerful trading countries, the IMF and the World Bank have a financial base provided by paid up capital. The fact that 18 per cent of the IMF's paid up shareholding is held by the United States does sometimes lead to the IMF being seen as an arm of American foreign policy. Nevertheless, while the OECD has a restricted membership, and the WTO is still recruiting members, the IMF and the World Bank have a virtually universal membership. They have three capacities that are important to effectiveness in international organisations: '(1) an analytical capacity in area where there is need that cannot be met by individual nations or the private market, (2) a way of achieving agreement among their members and implementing those agreements, and (3) sanctions that can be applied if the agreement is violated' (Krueger, 1998, p. 16). Nation states might listen to what the OECD has to say because of its analytical capacity and the quality of its advice. In the case of the IMF and the World Bank, a failure to listen to advice or respect conditions might lead to vital loans being withheld.

The IMF's role in the Bretton Woods era of fixed exchange rates was rather different and less significant than its current one as 'something of a suprastate central bank' (Scholte, 2000, p. 149). Its traditional role was to administer the international monetary system and in particular to stabilize the balance of payments problems that arose under a fixed exchange rate regime. From the 1970s onwards, the IMF 'intervened more intensely with its client governments' (*ibid.*), a process which some critics characterized as 'mission creep' as the IMF has acquired new responsibilities. Nevertheless, it 'emerged in the 1970s and 1980s as perhaps the key international economic institution' (Blake and Walters, 1983, p. 57). What has emerged is an organization that is particularly focused on guiding the economic policies of less-developed countries.

The World Bank's 'distinctiveness and strength derive from the way it bundles together three functions: lending, development research, and development assistance.' From its original role of providing capital to peripheral areas of the world at a time when capital markets lacked liquidity, it has developed into 'a multilateral organization that enables richer countries to assist with the development of the poorer countries without entering into direct bilateral political power relations with them' (Vines, 1998, p. 68). Some of its critics take a less benign view of its activities, and are critical of the 'Washington consensus' embraced by the Bank and the IMF: free markets, global integration, macroeconomic stability. They consider that all too often the institutions seek to impose it on developing countries in a 'one size fits all' mode, leading to increased inequality. They see them as perpetuating an unjust world economic order that causes widespread poverty, inequality and suffering. Whether these injustices would disappear if the institutions did is open to question. The international financial institutions may be seen as reflections of the existing distribution of power rather than prime causes of it, and, given that distribution, demands for radical transformation of the institutions seem unlikely to succeed.

Even looking at the Bank's role in its own terms, it is open to the criticism that its 'core activity is outdated product'. Emerging economies 'no longer need or want the World Bank: they dislike the conditions attached to its loans – about policies the country should pursue (for example, about the environment) – and have little difficulty in borrowing from other sources.' Moreover, 'too many of the Bank's projects and programs appear to fail or underperform' (Vines, 1998, p. 69). More generally, 'the revival of international capital markets has put in question the role and purpose of the Bank' (Henderson, 1998, p. 106).

The aftermath of the Asian financial crisis saw calls for the creation of a new international financial architecture in the form of a world financial authority or at least a merger between the IMF and the World Bank. Elite opinion in the United States would like to see the IMF take a narrower role focused on financial emergencies, especially those that threaten the stability of the international financial system. This perspective would see the IMF move away from providing long-term support for ailing economies. The IMF would revert to its original role of providing short-term financing for countries facing balance of payments difficulties, although extended to cover financial contagion or market panics. The IMF could not expect its financial capacity to grow in parallel with the growth of private-sector capital flows and the private sector should have a greater role in providing finance to poorer countries. The IMF 'should not be a source of low-cost financing for countries with ready access to private capital, or... that cannot break the habit of bad policies' (*Financial Times*, 15 December 1999).

The IMF's role may undergo yet another change, but in some ways it is the World Bank that is in the weaker position despite its larger secretariat. The Bush administration has been pushing for changes at the World Bank, particularly a narrowing of its focus from reducing income poverty to promoting growth. Finance ministries and central banks are regarded as having substantial influence on the activities of the IMF, but as being less influential at the World Bank whose views on development are often different from theirs. The IMF

> has powerful friends in national capitals, since the ministers and officials who deal with it, and feel responsible for it, all come from ministries of finance and central banks. For them, the Fund is their agency: its attitudes and beliefs, its institutional and professional concerns, are theirs. (Henderson, 1998, p. 106)

The IMF has been much more successful at carving out a clear role as a global governance agency than the Bank, but this does not mean that the future of the World Bank is necessarily threatened. Once a major international agency is established, it is difficult to get rid of it, although it may be pruned or given a new mission. Some of the momentum behind the creation of a new international financial architecture has been lost as memories of the 1998 crisis recede. Although there have been modifications, the global governance agencies are largely those established as part of the postwar international settlement which was conceived and designed in a very different world.

G7/G8 summits

The institutions that emerged in the immediate postwar period can be seen as part of what might loosely be described as an 'international Keyesianism'. The obligations of domestic governments to defend fixed exchange rates, maintain reasonably full employment and avoid a resort to protectionist remedies were reinforced by the creation of a set of international institutions to facilitate the achievement of those objectives. In terms of power politics, these institutions provided an international cooperative cloak for the exercise of American hegemony.

These arrangements worked reasonably well for 25 years, but the early 1970s saw the collapse of their cornerstone, the Bretton Woods system of fixed exchange rates based on the convertibility of the dollar into gold. The sharp rise in oil prices, but also in other commodity prices, ushered in a period of 'stagflation' (low growth and high inflation) in western economies. The United States, weakened by the economic and political strains of the Vietnam War, seemed ill-equipped to offer leadership. The sense of crisis induced a mood of cooperation among political leaders:

> During the monetary crisis of February–March 1973 . . . the finance ministers of the United States, Britain, France and Germany began what was to become a series of informal, initially secret meetings, generally on the margins of larger international bodies. (Putnam, 1984, p. 53)

These meetings, which were limited to the ministers plus one senior aide and occasionally central bank governors, eventually included Italy and Japan as well. They became known as the 'Library Group' after one of the early meetings held in the library of the White House. Two of the participants in this group, Helmut Schmidt of Germany and Valéry Giscard d'Estaing of France, became leaders of their respective countries in 1974. Both had been impressed by the informal, relaxed 'fireside chat' atmosphere of the Library Group meetings which led to a considerable feeling of solidarity among those involved (Putnam, 1984, p. 54).

The success of these meetings led to a suggestion by President Giscard d'Estaing of France at a lunch attended by world leaders at Helsinki in July 1975 that they should hold a summit later in the year. The first meeting was held (without Canada) at Rambouillet in November with a focus on the subject of monetary reform. Summits have been held since then on an annual basis each summer. The Russians started to be involved in 1994 and at the Birmingham Summit in 1998 the G7 officially became the G8:

> Nonetheless, the G7, after Birmingham, remains very much alive . . . during and after the Fall 1998 meetings of the IMF and the World Bank, the G7 – both at the finance ministers' and the leaders' level – produced important and high profile initiatives. (Hajnal, 1999, pp. 15–16)

The G7 summits appear to have been more successful in the 1970s, and perhaps the most successful, at least in terms of producing outcomes that led to policy changes, was the Bonn summit in 1978: 'The Bonn agreement is considered by a majority of commentators the most successful instance of economic policy harmonisation produced by Western summitry' (Garavoglia, 1984, p. 17). The participants negotiated a wide-ranging package of economic measures in an effort to stimulate the world economy; West Germany agreed to expand its economy in accordance with the then fashionable 'convoy theory', but 'the worsening of the economy in 1979 provoked much criticism of the country's adherence to the Bonn understanding' (Garavoglia, 1984, p. 18).

The Bonn summit was also the first to make non-economic policy decisions. Subjects such as Afghanistan, Euromissiles and terrorism increasingly appeared on the agenda. 'The summit is no longer just economic: political questions and various global issues have taken on increasing importance for a number of years' (Hajnal, 1999, p. 4). Perhaps this was unavoidable:

> It is worth noting that Giscard d'Estaing and Helmut Schmidt were former finance ministers who understood monetary and other economic issues well and were eager to discuss such issues with their opposite numbers from other major industrialised countries. The subsequent generation of G7 leaders did not share this background; some of them were, therefore, more inclined to broaden the scope of their discussions to political and other non-economic topics and to entrust economic issues to their finance ministers. (Hajnal, 1999, p. 5)

The success record of the summits is not that impressive. Hajnal's table setting out the cooperative achievements of summits suggests that at five of them 'nothing significant' was achieved (Hajnal, 1999, p. 68), which is not impressive given the investment of time and effort by world leaders. His review of literature assessing the level of compliance with summit undertakings by the countries involved suggests an overall level of one-quarter to one-third (Hajnal, 1999, pp. 67–71). One might draw the inference that countries comply when it suits them to do so.

The participants in the summits often did not find them very worthwhile occasions. Lamont recalls of the Washington finance ministers meeting (1999, p. 154) that much of the time was spent

> arguing about the communiqué which, as always at international meetings, was stretched to cover several different positions. A cynic might have said we had spent several hours deciding to do nothing about the world economy, and half an hour deciding to do nothing about the Soviet Union.

John Major recalls (1999, p. 117), 'the only thing I enjoyed less than banquets were G7 summits'. He was not alone among international leaders 'in questioning the value of such an event in an overcrowded international calendar' (Major, 1999, p. 525). In September 1992, Major put forward a number of proposals to reinvigorate the summits, prompted by his disappointment at the failure of two consecutive summits, London in 1991 and Munich in 1992, to achieve a breakthrough in the GATT Uruguay Round negotiations. John Major and the foreign secretary, Douglas Hurd, considered that the summits had become too stage-managed and too concerned with pomp and circumstance. Detailed preparations reduced the talks among heads of governments to carefully rehearsed statements of previous positions. However, although some summits might be better organized to facilitate informal discussion than others, nothing changed fundamentally.

It is therefore not surprising that EU finance ministers decided to limit their attendance at the 2000 summit in Japan to just 24 hours (*Financial Times*, 7 July 2000). The journey together on the same aircraft might have been more significant in terms of interchanges than those at the meeting itself. There is a sense that the summits have become somewhat ritualistic occasions that may generate useful media publicity for the leaders involved, but little of substance, and questions are increasingly being asked about whether they continue to perform a useful function. This debate intensified after the rioting, leading to one death, which accompanied the Genoa summit in 2001. Perhaps some of the most important work is done by bodies that have spun off from the G7/G8 process such as the Financial Stability Forum. Set up in the aftermath of the Asian financial crisis, it brings together financial regulators, finance ministries and central banks from the G7.

Putnam (1984) identifies five positive consequences that might flow from summits:

- They can help to foster personal understanding between leaders, although one might question whether more might be achieved in that respect through bilateral meetings.
- They can 'energise the policy process, allowing central executives to overcome bureaucratic and political obstacles that would be more obdurate under normal circumstances' (Putnam, 1984, p. 75). There is potential in this area, although often it is not realized, for example in terms of unlocking trade talks.
- Summits may also justify internationally desirable policies. 'As a rule, national leaders go to summits to get international legitimation for their existing policies, not to discuss changing those policies' (Putnam, 1984, p. 76). This function was probably more important in the 1970s and 1980s when countries were still adjusting to the breakdown of the old economic orthodoxies and seeking to legitimize their replacements.
- The task of accommodating divergent policies may be more effectively performed by the markets than the summits. The experience of the 1970s and the early 1980s 'showed that

international money markets react so sharply to national policy divergences that most deviants are forced back towards the international median policy mix' (Putnam, 1984, p. 77). Given the widespread acceptance of globalization, it is probably less useful than it once was for summits to strengthen internationalist factions within each government (Putnam, 1984, p. 79).

• Finally, Putnam suggests that summits may help to overcome prisoners' dilemma problems; solutions may be found but, as noted above, they are not always implemented. Summits have not been very successful at making 'mutual commitments more credible' (Putnam, 1984, p. 80) as was anticipated.

The summits had a more clearly defined role in the management of the upheavals taking place in the international economy in the 1970s. In an era of globalization it is the markets that enforce fiscal and other forms of economic discipline. This is not to say that the weakness of political coordination arrangements is not a problem, but it is questionable how far the G7/G8 process really offers the solution. Efforts are being made to make them less bureaucratized, but it is doubtful whether the 'fireside chat' atmosphere of the 1970s can be recaptured.

Other mechanisms have emerged to complement G7/G8. The Transatlantic Declaration of 1990 was 'the first attempt to establish a broad framework for the conduct of EU–US bilateral relations' (Smith, 1998, p. 567). It led to twice-yearly bilateral summits between the USA and the EU, which were able to tackle difficult questions such as trade relations. With Japan afflicted by prolonged economic difficulties, the two major economic powers in the world got together to try to resolve the issues that divided them. One spin-off of this process was a series of transatlantic dialogues, of which the most important was the Transatlantic Business Dialogue. This enabled chief executive officers of companies on both sides of the Atlantic to work together to devise solutions to current problems which they then presented to the USA and the EU. The most important outcome of this process was a bilateral Mutual Recognition Agreement dealing with regulatory standards in six sectors which was estimated to produce savings of as much as one billion dollars a year for private investors (Coen and Grant, 2001).

G2 (US–EU) arrangements of this kind meet some needs, but there has also been an increasing recognition of the need to involve emerging countries in attempts to manage the global economy. *Ad hoc* groupings emerged during the Asian financial crisis such as G22 and G33, which led to the launch of G20 that brings together G7 with selected emerging market countries including Brazil, China, India and Russia. The EU, the IMF and the World Bank also participate in meetings. The first meeting in Berlin in December 1999 produced the kind of unstructured and constructive debate typical of the early days of G7. G7/G8 may therefore become one of a number of both more narrowly and more widely based coordination arrangements. Apart from anything else, G7/G8 seems more of an anomaly as the EU becomes more integrated.

There is a clear imbalance between an increasingly integrated global economy and the often weak or incoherent political arrangements designed to manage crises and continuing problems. Some of the more effective arrangements seem to be relatively unstructured arrangements that bring together global firms such as the Transatlantic Business Dialogue (TABD), the annual World Economic Forum in Davos, Switzerland, or the work of the Trilateral Commission. This was set up in 1973 as an organization of domestic elites in Japan, Europe and North America against the background of declining American hegemony and increased international economic interdependence. Organizations of this kind are often the subject of speculation by conspiracy theorists seeking to identify a shadowy world leadership. Nevertheless, there are legitimate concerns that need to be addressed about the privatization of public policy and the reinforcement of imbalances between the rich and the poor in the world. Forms of world government remain a utopian dream, but effective political arrangements may be constructed at a regional level which offer a mechanism for making a political response to globalization. The most successful example of such a regional arrangement is the EU, but political opposition to its further development remains strong in Britain.

3

Economic Theory and Economic Policy

Introduction

This chapter reviews some of the theoretical debates that have been influential in the discussion of economic policy, with the underlying assumption that it is important to talk about the ideas that have influenced economic policy. As Keynes argues (1936, p. 383) 'I am sure that the power of vested interests is vastly exaggerated, compared with the gradual encroachment of ideas.'

The market and the state

One of the central theoretical tasks in any discussion of economic policy is seeing whether any principles can be identified that might determine the proper boundaries between the market and the state. The ascendancy of neo-liberalism in the last quarter of the twentieth century saw a shift in the boundary line in favour of the market mechanism. Indeed, as classic interpretations of Marxism diminished in popularity, sometimes seeming to increase the sect-like characteristics of some of the doctrine's adherents, critics of the effects of an unrestrained market increasingly grouped themselves around interpretations of Polanyi's (1944) work. His 'central proposition [was] that a self-regulating market that makes the rational pursuit of economic gain the only maxim of human action, will ultimately destroy its own human, social and natural conditions' (Streeck, 1997, p. 207). As human beings, our roles as producers and consumers are important ones, but we also have other roles which may come into conflict with the logic of an economic analysis based on self-regarding behaviour. At the beginning of the twenty-first century, this is often expressed by reference to Oscar Wilde's comment that 'we know the price of everything, but the value of nothing.'

Given the ascendancy of advocates of organized (sometimes called 'Rhineland') capitalism among academic analysts, it is well to pause to consider some of the benefits of a freely operating market mechanism. The unconstrained market can have many consequences that most people would regard as undesirable. Nevertheless, we should also remember Adam Smith's famous comment (1986, p. 119) that 'It is not from the benevolence of the butcher, the brewer or the baker that we expect our dinner, but from their regard to their own interest.'

Classic economic analysis offers a model rather than a description of reality. Social behaviour is complex and economics seeks to understand that complexity, or one aspect of it, by making some simplifying assumptions about human behaviour. In practice, human beings may not be rational utility maximizers and, even if they were, they may confront conditions such as imperfect information that prevents markets from working as classical economic theory would predict. Nevertheless, markets in practice may approximate to the theoretical model, or at least to an extent that enables us to make non-trivial and verifiable predictions about behaviour.

The price mechanism is an unmatched means of conveying large amounts of complex information between buyers and sellers. 'It is informationally undemanding. Each individual need only know his or her preferences and the relative prices of goods and services available' (Helm, 1986, p. vii). It permits the decentralization of decision-making so that the consumer has a wide variety of choices open to her, even if in practice 'the individual is confronted only with choices on a piecemeal basis and has to take as fixed the conditions of use' (Hirsch, 1977, p. 90).

Advocates of state planning claimed that the arrival of the computer would increase the capacity to transmit and process large quantities of information. In practice, state planning was never able to match the responsiveness of the market mechanism. In state socialist societies, the parts of the economy that functioned best were the small parts left in private hands, or the black market. Even democratic socialists in Britain believed that there was an inexorable tendency for the state's share of gross domestic product to grow. While private firms might be tolerated, their relationship with the state should be regularized through planning agreements. Profits were seen not as a measure of economic efficiency, but of the exploitation of labour and consumers.

It required a heroic effort to restore some acceptance of the role of the market mechanism. In a sense, what happened was that Durbin's insight that the arrival of democracy undermined capitalism by removing the dynamic of *laissez-faire* (Dell, 2000) was turned on its head. *Laissez-faire* was restored to its earlier primacy so that 'The market is now considered by a majority of managers and politicians as the coordinating mechanism "par excellence"' (Boyer, 1997, p. 57). Nevertheless, not everyone accepted that 'the role of government is confined to allowing the market economy to work well' (Heffernan, 2000, p. 81). Polanyi postulated (1944, p. 132) a double movement in society between the organizing principle of economic liberalism 'aiming at the establishment of a self-regulating market', and 'the principle of social protection aiming at the conservation of man and nature as well as productive organization'. Thus, in the nineteenth century when a series of global developments 'under the aegis of the gold standard gave an unparalleled momentum to the mechanism of markets, a deep-seated movement sprang into being to resist the pernicious effects of a market-controlled economy. Society protected itself against the perils inherent in a self-regulating market system' (Polanyi, 1944, p. 76).

The dilemma we face as individuals or as a nation is this: if we do not succeed economically, we may not be able to achieve many of our individual or collective goals, but in pursuing those goals without restraint, we may damage the social fabric beyond repair. There is a difficult balance to be drawn between material success and social well-being and there are those who would argue that the balance has been disturbed in a way that is morally unacceptable and socially self-defeating. Against this, it could be argued that if a market economy is to function properly, there have to be losers as well as winners. In order to assess these concerns, it is necessary to consider in more depth the issues of market failure and government failure.

Market failure

Market failure is perhaps an unduly dramatic term as it suggests some type of catastrophic collapse. In fact reference is being made to a sub-optimal outcome that may be capable of remedy. In general what is being talked about is a situation in which a competitive market made up of agents pursuing their self-interest leads to an outcome that is judged socially inefficient. In particular, this refers to allocative inefficiency. This covers both what is known as X-inefficiency which might be regarded as what we conventionally regard as efficiency (the production of a good or service using the minimum of inputs), but also 'whether the commodity concerned meets the wants of its consumers as effectively as possible' (Le Grand, 1991, p. 425). The problem of market failure can be analysed in terms of the assumptions and language of economics or a broader moral and social critique.

First we shall discuss five common market failures discussed in the economics literature. This is not an exhaustive list, but it covers the most important cases. First, there is a monopoly and the consequent absence of competition. Market domination allows the monopolist to set a monopoly price to the disadvantage of consumers. The policy response to this has been to develop a competition policy that seeks to break up monopolies or prevent their formation. Such policies have enjoyed variable success (see Chapter 6).

A special subset of monopoly is the natural monopoly where it is claimed that the most efficient outcome is secured by having only one producer. This was the classic justification of public-utility nationalization where it was argued that duplicating transmission systems was manifestly inefficient. However, some natural monopolies have been eroded by technological change as in the case of telecommunications where landline systems face competition from mobile phones. It has been shown that it is possible to have a monopoly owner of the transmission system or basic infrastructure but to allow access to a variety of operators with a system of regulation to ensure that access is not unduly restricted and is charged for on a fair basis.

An important part of economics is the study of the divergence between private and social costs (or benefits), referred to as externalities. They are called externalities because they are external to the price system in the sense that no transaction takes place between the affected parties. An externality arises when an economic activity imposes a cost on a third party that may not be recovered from the provider of the activity. In principle, these may be external goods, although most of the attention is understandably concentrated on external bads. In general:

> Markets with self-interested agents will tend to underprovide activities with external benefits relative to the allocatively efficient level because the agents undertaking the activity concerned cannot capture those benefits ... For similar reasons, markets will tend to overprovide activities with external costs. (Le Grand, 1991, p. 426)

Classic examples are a factory polluting a river, or the air pollution and noise created by motor vehicles.

The general preference of economists is to deal with such problems through the price mechanism or surrogates for it. Thus, one might impose a tax on certain kinds of polluting activity, tolls on roads or permit polluters who have substantially reduced their polluting activities to trade permits with those who have not been able to achieve such a reduction. This still achieves a net welfare gain because the existence of the tradeable permit encourages the first polluter to secure larger reductions than might otherwise be the case.

In environmental problems, which are one of the most important classes of externality, there has been a shift to market-based measures in recent years. This is because traditional 'command and control' regulatory measures are seen to impose high transaction costs both on government, which has to set up inspectorates, and the regulated firms which have to complete the necessary paperwork. Moreover, such systems of regulation often seem to be ineffective in securing the desired environmental benefit.

Problems arising from incomplete or asymmetric information have received considerable attention from economists in recent years. Asymmetries of information arise when one party to the transaction has more relevant information than the other party. For example, a secondhand car dealer may have more information about the history of the car than the purchaser who may not have the knowledge and skills to identify evident defects. One way of overcoming asymmetries of information in markets is to have intermediaries between buyers and sellers – for example estate agents in the housing market – although this approach does not always command consumer confidence. Another approach is to impose legal requirements and codes of conduct on buyers and sellers. These, however, require adequate enforcement mechanisms if they are to be effective.

A public good (not to be confused with a publicly provided good or service) is defined to have three distinctive characteristics, non-exclusion, non-rivalry and non-rejectability. If a good is made available to one person, then it is also available to all the other members of the relevant group. The other feature is that one person's consumption of the good does not reduce the amount available for consumption by others. National defence and breathable air are classic examples. However, the range of pure public goods is perhaps more limited than is sometimes supposed. In any event, analysts writing from a social market position accept that the provision of public goods is a legitimate role for governments, if only to overcome the 'free-rider' problems to which they are prone.

Agricultural markets have special difficulties in reaching equilibrium. Supply may be substantially affected by weather and there are long time lags between decisions to plant crops and their arrival on the market. Agricultural economics has developed as a distinctive branch of economics analysing distinctive phenomena such as 'cobweb cycles'. Attempts to stabilize agricultural markets have, however, led to costly and large-scale government interventions which often fail to achieve such objectives as closing the gap between rural and urban incomes.

Outside economics, analysts emphasize the extent to which the successful functioning of the market depends on the social fabric and institutions created by government action. A more fundamental critique is that economics tends to encourage self-regarding behaviour which may be in the individual short-run interest but is contrary to the general long-term interest. What we have learnt from evolutionary biology is that animals benefit from cooperation when engaged in tasks such as hunting. For humans, 'Grassland hunting was more productive when groups of hunters pooled their knowledge of animal spoors and shared their catch . . . So genetics favour co-operative man over rational economic man' (Kay, 2000).

The problem is that an unrestrained market economy tends to encourage self-regarding behaviour: 'Economic liberalism is in this sense a victim of its own propaganda: offered to all, it has evoked pressures and demands that cannot be contained' (Hirsch, 1977, p. 11). The strengthening of self-regarding objectives and the weakening of socially-oriented ones is not accidental: 'The reason is that interests of self-concern and self-regard can be enlisted much more effectively in support of commercial sales efforts' (*ibid.*, p. 82).

Economists themselves are sometimes accused of being prone to rent-seeking behaviour and giving priority to their own individual advantage. Marwell and Ames (1981) set up an experiment that gave participants the choice of participating in a 'group exchange' or an 'individual exchange', the former being an operationalization of a public good and the latter of a private good. They found that 'Economics graduate students contributed only an average of 20% of their resources to the group exchange. They were more likely to free ride than any of our other groups of subjects' (Marwell and Ames, 1981, pp. 306–7). Moreover, 'the economics graduate students were about half as likely as other subjects to indicate that they were "concerned with fairness" in making their investment decisions' (*ibid.*, p. 309). Marwell and Ames suggest that these results are not accidental, but may reflect both the type of person recruited to study economics and their occupational socialization. Thus 'they may start behaving according to the tenets of the theories they study. Confronted with a situation where others may not behave rationally, they nevertheless behave the way good economic theory predicts' (*ibid.*).

Social capital

The notion that the social fabric is necessary for the successful functioning of the market economy has been developed through the concept of 'social capital'. For example, the presence of high levels of mutual trust in a society helps the economy to function successfully just as physical infrastructure such as a reliable transport network is also important. The work of Putnam (1995, 2000) on 'bowling alone' which he used as a metaphor for America's declining social capital has been particularly influential in this debate. 'Put simply, Putnam's thesis is that dense networks of civic engagement produce a capacity for trust, reciprocity and co-operation which in turn produces a healthy democracy' (Lowndes and Wilson, 2001, p. 629).

Pretty (1998, p. 8) identifies 'four central elements of social capital...trust; rules and sanctions; reciprocity; and connectedness'. Trust is one of the most important and most vulnerable elements of social capital. Trust in those whom we know is built up by repeated social interactions; trust in those we don't know helps an economy to function effectively and 'arises because of our confidence in a known social structure' (*ibid*). Rules and sanctions 'place group interests above those of individuals' (*ibid.*) and facilitate investment in collective activities. Diffuse reciprocity is particularly important as it 'refers to a continuous relationship of exchange that at any given time is unrequited, but over time is repaid and balanced.' (*ibid.*, pp. 8–9). Hirsch speculates that the extent of geographical mobility in modern economies reduces 'the chances of social contacts being reciprocated directly on a bilateral basis. A casual favour or gesture is less likely to be returned' (Hirsch, 1997, p. 80).

When Pretty refers to connectedness he is particularly referring to the roles of various associations and non-governmental organizations in society, sometimes encapsulated in the umbrella term 'civil society'. The role of associations in society is particularly stressed by the group of scholars who emerged from neo-corporatist theorizing, the so-called 'corporatist international' (Hollingsworth and Boyer, 1997; Crouch and Streeck, 1997, offers classic expositions of this position). The work of Maloney, Smith and Stoker (2000, p. 803), however, argues that the classic social-capital approach derived from Putnam's work 'neglects the role played by political structures and associations in shaping the *context of associational activity* and hence the concept of social capital'. Thus, 'The role of social capital may be better understood in the context of a *two-way* relationship between civil society and government' (Lowndes and Wilson, 2001, p. 631). If the state is not brought back in, the concept of social capital may be stretched too far. It would, however, be difficult for a society in which the stock of social capital had been badly depleted to have a successful economy.

Another influential argument has been that markets are in part institutions, created by government through interventions to restrain what otherwise might be capricious, destabilizing or unpredictable behaviour. Thus

> most markets are not the result of random interactions of buyers, but rather structures that have been systematically created by government through regulation and which inhibit autonomous or random actions by the participants. (Peters, 1999, p. 15)

Emphasis is placed on the social embeddedness of markets. The 'new institutionalist' school within political science has been influential here (Hall and Taylor, 1996, 1998; Peters, 1999), challenging economic and other approaches that emphasize the role of the individual as an autonomous actor and drawing attention to the cultural construction of institutions (which are more broadly understood than formal organizations to encompass, for example, networks). Crouch and Streeck (1997, p. 5) claim as a 'fundamental fact that economic action is always and inevitably social action, and for this reason depends for its successful conduct on a supportive social context.'

Once again the influence of Polanyi on this school can be noted. Hailing his work as 'prophetic', Boyer (1997, p. 61) argues that Polanyi

> has convincingly demonstrated that most markets call for highly sophisticated institutional arrangements for their coordination, if their efficiency and self-adjusting property [*sic*] are to be obtained in really existing economies.

An important part of Polanyi's analysis was his treatment of commodities 'empirically defined as objects produced for sale on the market' (1944, p. 72). He argued that labour, land and money should be treated as fictitious commodities. In the case of labour, it 'cannot be shoved about, used indiscriminately, or even left unused, without affecting also the human individual who happens to be the bearer of this peculiar commodity' (Polanyi, 1944, p. 73). In the case of land, which he treats as a synonym for nature, he anticipates modern environmental arguments by arguing that its treatment as a mere commodity would produce 'neighbourhoods and landscapes defiled, rivers polluted . . . the power to produce food and raw materials destroyed' (Polanyi, 1944, p. 73). Unregulated money markets would lead to a boom and bust cycle which 'would prove as disastrous to business as floods and droughts in primitive society' (Polanyi, 1944, p. 73).

Although he does not extensively refer to Polanyi, Fred Hirsch (1977) in *Social Limits to Growth* writes in the broad tradition of the need to control capitalism to prevent it destroying itself and society. Hirsch argues that such social controls perform three broad functions. First, it is necessary to have a distributional corrective to 'soften the burdensome impact of capitalist market forces on those individuals or groups with least economic power' (*ibid.*, p. 120). Most of us placed behind a Rawlsian veil of ignorance where we did not know what our own position in society would be would choose a more egalitarian society than that which exists. Skidelsky notes (1999, p. 282) that 'the social market approach is perfectly consistent with boosting life-chances by targeting help on the least well-off. Indeed, this should be the main aim of "social policy" '.

Second, Hirsch argues that 'controls are needed to make the market process efficient in its own terms – to ensure that private market choices reflect social benefits and costs as far as possible' (Hirsch, 1977, p.120). In principle, this is correct. In practice, as was noted in relation to externalities, selecting the most effective policy mechanism to achieve this end is not easy. Third, 'informal social controls in the form of socialized norms of behaviour are needed to allow the market process to operate' (*ibid.*, p. 121). This comment anticipated the debate on social capital referred to earlier.

Some measure of agreement therefore emerges. Pure market capitalism would bring about its own destruction: 'It was the marriage of market capitalism with state regulation that produced a hybrid politico-economic system with the necessary resilience and plasticity to survive' (*ibid.*, p. 118). Skidelsky (1999, p. 279) admits as much when he refers to 'social goods, whose absence or under-supply in the past led to revolts against the capitalist market order'. Thus, as well as supplying public goods, there should also be public provision of those goods 'whose under-supply leads to dissatisfaction with the market economy' (*ibid.*, p. 290). The provision of such goods is not a straightforward matter, however, as one then runs up against the problem of government failure.

Government failure

The 1930s in the United States and the 1940s in Britain saw the development of a widespread belief that only government could solve the problems produced by the interwar depression. Analysts like Galbraith presented 'an idealized model of an informed, efficient and humane government, able to identify and remedy failures of the market' (Wolf, 1993, p. 3). The ungovernability debate in Britain in the 1970s suggested, however, that government's reach had exceeded its grasp, that it could not efficiently meet all of the expectations that the electorate had of it. By the end of the century, faith in the problem-solving capacity of government had been severely dented; government intervention was often seen as creating new problems rather than resolving the difficulties it was intended to tackle. It was either ineffective or created new problems: 'Government failures tend to be as preoccupying as market failures' (Boyer, 1997, p. 60).

Writing in the context of the relative economic decline debate, Crafts (2001, pp. 4–5) suggests that three aspects of government economic decline are particularly relevant to policies designed to improve economic performance:

- Policies may be badly designed or misconceived. 'For example, the effect of subsidies which only give a weak stimulus to productivity performance may be outweighed by the impact of the discretionary taxation used to finance them or a failure to recognize the importance of agency problems within firms might result in an inappropriate balance between industrial and competition policy.'
- 'Second, interventions aimed at correcting market failures are vitiated by agency problems within the public sector. For example,

nationalization might be intended to deal with abuse of market power or under-provision of public goods but lead to low productivity/high cost outcomes because of inadequate monitoring and/or incentivizing of managers.'

- 'Third, a central aspect of the incentive structures facing politicians is that votes may often be lost by pursuing policies that promote economic efficiency and higher productivity.' Protectionist policies offer a classic example. Concentrated interests such of those of business outweigh diffuse interests such as those of consumers and taxpayers. Olson's (1965) work shows that it is easier for smaller groups representing particular interests to form and succeed.

What are the factors that might lead governments to fail? Modern government requires a large bureaucracy to put its plans into effect. Weber's insight was that a bureaucracy organized on lines of rationality, hierarchy and so forth would prove superior to older forms of government organization. Subsequent writing on bureaucracy tended to emphasize its dysfunctional characteristics and the tendency of means to displace ends. One explanation that has been popular with public-choice theorists has been to focus on the aggrandizing behaviour of bureaucrats who want to maximize the size of their agencies so as to improve their career prospects. Rather than being a disinterested provider of public policies, the bureaucracy was seen as a collection of individuals seeking to maximize their own utility. Such an approach overlooks the powerful occupational socialization provided by the British civil service that emphasized the importance of public service. In part, this model was influenced by American experience where administrative agencies have significant autonomy and are engaged in turf battles with potential competitors. This analysis was 'undermined by manifest evidence that bureaucrats satisfied rather than maximized' (Deakin and Parry, 2000, p. 63). Dunleavy's (1991) bureau-shaping model came to be influential, suggesting that 'size and aggrandisement were not ends in themselves' but that 'bureaucrats would calculatedly "shape" their task to obtain the optimal mixture of rewarding and achievable work' (Deakin and Parry, 2000, p. 63).

There is also a problem about the gap between output and outcomes. At one time it was assumed that passing legislation would bring about the required change in behaviour. An extensive literature on implementation problems then demonstrated that policies were often put into effect in a haphazard fashion, policy goals were distorted and unintended consequences were frequent. The pressure on politicians to 'do something' about a problem often leads them to announce policies which have inadequate resources for effective implementation and enforcement.

Some of these problems simply reflect bad management and are in principle capable of remedy. There are, however, more systemic explanations of government failure. 'Markets link, however imperfectly, the costs of producing or sustaining an activity to the income that sustains it' (Wolf, 1993, p. 65). This link is removed in the case of non-market activity. If there is no link between the value of an output and the cost of producing it, the scope for the misallocation of resources is greatly increased:

> [More] resources may be used than necessary to produce a given output, or more of the non-market activity may be provided than is warranted by the original market-failure reason for undertaking it. Inefficiencies are encouraged because the costs of producing the activity are disconnected from the revenues that sustain it. (Wolf, 1993, p. 65)

Le Grand provides a more nuanced analysis, arguing that it is necessary to distinguish between different types of government activity. Provision, subsidy and regulation may all give rise to inefficiency and inequity, but the form and magnitude of the failure will vary with the type of activity. Government provision may be affected by problems of monopoly, although it need not be a monopoly and empirical evidence on the relative performance of public and private provision is inadequate. Government subsidy policies

> drive a wedge between prices and demand and supply such that the role of prices as conveyors of information is reduced or even eliminated. In consequence, the government will find it very difficult to assess the overall efficient level of production of a commodity. (Le Grand, 1991, p. 436)

Government regulation may stifle incentives for innovation and 'create both dynamic and allocative inefficiency' (Le Grand, 1991, p. 439).

A challenged paradigm: relative economic decline

The relative economic decline debate can be traced back to the late nineteenth century (see Williams, 1896), but developed its greatest intensity after the Second World War (English and Kenny, 2001). 'The 1970s was, perhaps, the period of high declinism, with the issue of Britain's comparatively poor performance having become prominent during the past decade' (English and Kenny, 2000a, p. 294), and 'Paradoxically, the period of greatest anxiety about decline has coincided with the greatest prosperity in British history' (English and Kenny, 1999, p. 262). As was noted in Chapter 1, Britain's rate of economic growth, particularly during the early part of the post-war period (the so-called 'Golden Age' from 1950 to 1973), was far superior to its record in the interwar period. No doubt the economic decline debate was fuelled by broader concerns about the decline of Britain's importance in the world. Rising expectations may also have helped to underpin the emphasis on relatively poor performance (English and Kenny, 2000a, p. 295).

Because the decline paradigm dominated discussion of British economic policy for so long, it is worth outlining its main features. Before doing so, it is worth noting that there was some confusion in the debate about causes and effects. To some extent it is possible to separate out the debate into economic, cultural and political aspects, although clearly these were all intertwined. The economic case really centred on the ineffective use of factors of production (reflected in poor levels of productivity compared to competitor countries). A recurrent theme of the debate was the suggestion that there was insufficient investment in British industry, which was then explained by the nature of the financial system that was seen as stockmarket-driven with its emphasis on short-run returns. It was also partly explained by a historical reliance in Britain on relatively unskilled (and therefore cheap) labour that was less attractive to substitute by capital.

Too much can be made of the level-of-investment point; relative economic decline in Britain 'has stemmed from weak productivity performance rather than simply from low investment' (Crafts, 2001, p. 19). In relation to machinery and equipment 'the gap relative to other countries is quite small... relative to German manufacturing the UK investment rate throughout the post-war period has been fairly similar, and the main UK problem has appeared to be the incremental capital to output ratio' (Bean and Crafts, 1996, p. 136). In other words, the problem has not so much been the quantity of investment, but the returns obtained from it. 'Investment received a lower rate of return and produced a lower capital stock growth because of poor capital productivity' (Crafts, 1988, p. 21). Investing in marginal projects might have actually decreased the overall rate of return.

This problem of poor rates of return on capital invested leads us to look at the organization of the production process in industry itself. A series of detailed comparisons of particular economic sub-sectors in Britain and Germany by the National Institute for Economic and Social Research showed that performance in the British factories was generally less satisfactory. The issue of inadequate training of workers, and particularly supervisory staff, was one theme emerging from this work. However, it was also evident that there were deficiencies in British factories in simple but important matters such as the maintenance of machinery and the physical layout of the plant.

This is in part explained by the fact that British factories are often older, and less susceptible to efficient organization, but it also reflects the lower status granted to production management in Britain compared with Germany (Lawrence, 1980). Accountancy skills have a much higher status in Britain than Germany and offer a reliable route to senior management and the board. This reinforces within the firm the emphasis on short-term financial indicators of performance to the detriment of long-term investment and planning.

These problems were compounded by the organization of the British union movement. Unlike Germany, many unions could be found in one factory, which led to the rigid preservation of lines of demarcation which were seen as means of protecting jobs, but in the longer run placed them at risk. 'Unofficial' strikes were a considerable problem in the 1960s and 1970s, often arising from issues about differentials between different groups of workers, a problem compounded by the effects of successive incomes policies. There was often collusion between weak managements and workers to maintain outdated systems of pay and work classification that perpetuated inefficiencies in operation.

A further problem was that Britain devoted smaller proportions of its GDP than its competitors to research and development. Although basic scientific research was often highly successful and made major breakthroughs, these were not always translated into commercial innovations exploited by British companies. Part of the problem was that a large proportion of research and development was devoted to military research with less good arrangements for civilian 'spin offs' than had been made in the United States. The defence industrial base was a significant slice of the industrial economy and has tended to recruit some of the best skilled workers and technicians as the way in which contracts were awarded meant that it could offer higher rates of pay.

Britain was seen as lacking a developmental state that could construct successful partnership relationships between government and industry in areas of training and research and development. This was not surprising when one considers that industrialization had occurred within a pre-modern state. The individual entrepreneur was seen as the hero of the industrial revolution, creating a persistent attitude that the state was an external force that inhibited enterprise rather than an entity that worked with industry to facilitate its continuous modernization. One might nevertheless become too impressed by the dignified outward forms of the state (Gamble, 2000). The real question was whether government and industry could work effectively together, and this did appear possible for short periods of time, perhaps most successfully after the First World War and again after the election of a Labour government in 1964, but a longer-term partnership proved difficult to construct.

Much of the ire of critics of the state was directed against the Treasury, particularly for its use of aggregate demand-management techniques and their adverse effects on investment. An attempt was made under the Labour government of 1964 to construct a rival (the Department for Economic Affairs, DEA) with a different perspective, but this ended in failure. The Treasury is in some ways an easy target because any department which has the task of saying 'no' to demands for increases in public expenditure is not likely to be popular. Nevertheless, policy errors were made in economic management, particularly in the period from the 1950s to the 1970s. 'The interventionist policies and outmoded institutions of early postwar Britain were costly in an era of strong growth opportunities' (Crafts, 2001, p. 35). In terms of the themes of market and government failure outlined above, both types of failure occurred.

A more subtle but perhaps more serious problem was the excessive political displacement exercised by the more mature industries, particularly those developed in their modern form in the early period of industrialization such as textiles, coal and shipbuilding. They were notoriously slow to modernize their methods of production and had developed a dense institutional network of defences against change. Their political displacement enabled them to extract production subsidies from the state that both slowed down the pressures on them to change and imposed an opportunity cost on other, more vigorous industries. The consequence was an ossification of an outdated industrial structure.

Cultural explanations of decline were particularly influential, especially Wiener's (1981) book on *English Culture and the Decline of the Industrial Spirit*. 'In some respects it was the first major "declinist" text to be taken up by both an academic and a wider audience' (English and Kenny, 2000b, p. 25). The essence of the argument was that the British upper class turned away from industry, in part because of values transmitted by the education system, and towards an arcadian vision of a rustic England. But there are a number of problems with this analysis. First, it confuses the symbolic manipulation of particular kinds of notions of 'Englishness' by politicians with their actual decision-making preferences. Second, much of the evidence produced is 'impressionistic and selective and ignores the prevalence of anti-industrial and anti-bourgeois cultures in countries which are supposed to have been much more successful at building industrial economies' (Gamble, 2000, p. 11). Third, Britain has 'more than a single economic culture' (English and Kenny, 2000a, p. 291); Scottish culture, for example, cannot be equated with English culture, and many firms have created their own internal cultures. The cultural explanation is difficult to reconcile with the considerable variability of British economic performance, both between sectors and between firms. The best performing British sectors and the best British firms have been highly competitive internationally.

In Chapter 1 the importance of the imperial legacy was discussed. An often neglected but nevertheless important factor has been the persistence of an outdated imperial mindset:

> Imperial preference locked Britain into an archaic, nineteenth-century trading pattern; in doing so it also reinforced archaic, nineteenth-century attitudes to Britain's place in the world and to her relationship with the European mainland. (Marquand, 1988, p. 135)

More generally, 'The Empire ... acted as a cushion which avoided the need for too much innovation and creative development' (Gamble, 2000, p. 13). In political terms, it distracted Britain's attention in the 1940s and 1950s away from the moves towards greater economic cooperation taking place in continental Europe.

The decline paradigm produced a large literature, but it has been criticized as less relevant to a contemporary understanding of British economic policy for three main reasons. First, it is constructed around an assumption that the nation state is a key actor in economic power, an assumption increasingly challenged by processes of inter-nationalization or globalization. Second, it has been argued that it reflects a particular way of constructing British experience in terms of ideological narratives, rather than a representation of some objective economic reality (English and Kenny, 2001, p. 267). Third, it has been argued that some of the problems identified in the decline literature have been tackled and resolved. 'Since 1979, relative eco-nomic decline against OECD countries has largely ceased', although there is still a large labour productivity gap in relation to leading competitor countries (Crafts, 2001, p. 35). After losing ground in the 1970s

> living standards have largely caught up [with] Germany, France and Italy since the mid-1980s, albeit not against the United States. As a result, GDP per capita is now only slightly below the levels of France and Germany, but remains about one-third lower than the United States. (OECD, 2000, p. 7)

English and Kenny (2000a, p. 293) have suggested that 'perhaps attention should be directed less at decline than at declinism: a state of mind relatively autonomous of the actual historical decline of Britain as a world power'. There is something in that point that the search for 'the causes of, and remedy for, decline has, for a long time, represented a kind of "holy grail" for historians and political commentators in Britain' (English and Kenny, 1999, p. 264). As they suggest, the extent of the problem has been exaggerated and the phenomenon is more complex and requires more nuanced explan-ations than is acknowledged in much of the decline literature. Nevertheless, British performance on a number of indicators has given rise to well-based concern. The UK continues to 'suffer from a substantial and longstanding productivity gap compared with other advanced economies' (OECD, 2000, p. 15), and the Blair government has identified this poor record of productivity growth as a central policy challenge, although its resolution may require tackling deeply-rooted problems of market and government failure.

Keynesianism

In assessing Keynesianism, it is always important to bear in mind the distinction between the ideas set out by Keynes in his *General Theory of Employment, Interest and Money* and the way in which

these were interpreted after his death by his disciples and by politicians and the Treasury. Tomlinson has argued (1985, p. 7) 'that the
whole notion of a "Keynesian revolution" in twentieth century
economic policy-making has been based on a great exaggeration
of the role of economic theory in policy changes'. In contrast, the
account provided by Keynes's biographer, Skidelsky, very much
emphasizes the role of ideas, but such an approach can lead to a
neglect of structural changes in the economy both domestically and
internationally. The position taken here is the significant fact that
policy-makers, both politicians and officials, thought of themselves
as 'Keynesians', even if many of them did not really understand the
General Theory.

Keynes was an economist of centrist (Liberal) political views who
set out to save capitalism from itself by providing a means of escape
from the severe recession that had posed a threat to both capitalism
and democracy in the interwar period. For a political scientist,
Keynes' chapter 24 is the most interesting, somewhat tentatively
entitled 'Concluding Notes on the Social Philosophy towards which
the General Theory might Lead'. Keynes freely admits (1936, p. 379)
that 'The central controls necessary to ensure full employment will,
of course, involve a large extension of the traditional functions of
government.' Nevertheless, this did not mean that Keynes believed
in the relentless expansion of the state. He goes on to argue (1936,
p. 380) that 'there will still remain a wide field for the exercise of
private initiative and responsibility'. He outlines 'the traditional
advantages of individualism' including 'the advantages of decentra-
lisation and the play of self-interest' (*ibid.*).

For Keynes the publication of the *General Theory* was the culmin-
ation of 'a long struggle of escape . . . from habitual modes of thought
and expression' (Keynes, 1936, p. xxiii) represented by the classical
economists. Keynes himself had been educated in the tradition influenced in particular by Alfred Marshall and his *Principles of Economics* (1890). There was a widespread belief in a self-balancing economy;
Say's Law held that supply created its own demand – by producing an
article, just enough purchasing power was also created to ensure that
the good was sold. 'Say was implicitly assuming that the economic
system was always operating up to its full capacity, so that a new
activity was always in substitution for, and never in addition to, some
other activity' (Keynes, 1936, p. xxxv).

Keynes was interested in explaining the behaviour of the economy
as a whole, the behaviour of aggregates of output, employment,

investment and so forth, rather than that of individual firms. A central idea was that output depended on effective demand that could be broken down into two streams, consumption and investment. His theory made possible the creation of the systems of macroeconomic management that became widespread in advanced western industrial countries in the postwar period. As a theoretical perspective, it was ultimately undone by its inability to cope with inflation. However, even as a theory of employment it had its limitations and 'was not quite as general as he believed. For one thing, it left out the many causes of unemployment apart from demand-deficiency, particularly those to do with labour immobility and slowness of adaptation to change' (Skidelsky, 2000, p. 499). His theory focused attention on 'frictional' (Keynes, 1936, p. 6) rather than structural unemployment.

Keynes regarded his theory as having four key elements: effective demand, the multiplier, the theory of investment and the theory of interest. Effective demand was 'the substance of the General Theory of Employment' (Keynes, 1936, p. 25). Technically, it was defined in terms of the value of the proceeds received by employers from selling a quantity of output at the intersection of the aggregate supply and demand functions. 'Keynes contends that the economy can be in equilibrium, with expected proceeds equal to expected costs, at less than full employment. This is the essence of the *General Theory*' (Skidelsky, 1992, p. 550). It led Keynesians to advocate an active fiscal policy to revive investment and demand in the private sector.

The multiplier (originally developed by Kahn) 'is an integral part of our theory of employment, since it establishes a precise relationship, given the propensity to consume, between aggregate employment and income and the rate of investment' (Keynes, 1936, p. 113). If the government spends additional money on public works, there will be a multiplier effect as the additional wages are spent on consumption, benefiting the economy as a whole. The increase in real aggregate demand is considerably larger than the increase in government spending. These effects would be even greater in a period of severe unemployment. Indeed, 'public works even of doubtful utility may pay for themselves over and over again at a time of severe unemployment, if only from the diminished cost of relief expenditure' (*ibid.*, p. 127). Such a recommendation is an attractive policy prescription for politicians who can then hope to reduce unemployment, reduce public expenditure and provide 'pork barrel' benefits all at the same time. Keynes and the Keynesians underestimated the extent to which political biases could be overcome by economic modelling and the more effective use of statistics.

In his discussion of investment, Keynes' interest in psychological factors and his own successful experience as an investor in the stockmarket come up against his desire to specify rules for a central authority to manage a capitalist economy. Many decisions are not taken on the basis of a careful calculation of advantage, but in response to 'animal spirits', a form of intuition. Depending on how one interprets chapters 11 and 12 of the *General Theory*, it is in Skidelsky's view either too easy or too difficult to stabilize capitalism. Between these different perspectives, 'the Keynesian Revolution eventually became unstuck' (Skidelksy, 1992, p. 558).

The important new insight that Keynes contributed in this area of interest rates was to challenge the prevalent conventional wisdom that favoured thriftiness. In a depressed economy, saving did not lower the rate of interest and hence increase the incentives to invest: 'A decreased readiness to spend will be looked on in a quite different light if, instead of being regarded as a factor which will ... increase investment, it is seen as a factor which will ... diminish employment' (Keynes, 1936, p. 185).

The problem of inflation

A central flaw of Keynes' thinking was that he had no real answer to the problem of inflation resulting from upward pressure on wages and earnings in a full-employment economy. Indeed, this can be a problem even where there is not full employment, but shortages in the supply of particular skills. A central premise of Keynesian thinking was that economies were 'sticky', they adjusted slowly to shocks. As Samuel suggested, Keynes might have made 'the simple statement that he found it realistic to assume that modern capitalistic societies had money wage rates that were sticky and resistant to downward movements' (Quoted in Skidelsky, 1992, p. 580).

The index of the *General Theory* has just seven references to inflation. Keynes recognized that 'When full employment is reached, any attempt to increase investment still further will set up a tendency in money-prices to rise without limit ... we shall have reached a state of true inflation' (Keynes, 1936, pp. 118–9). Challenged by Durbin that his policy would lead to inflation, he replied that he would be prepared to relax his expansionist measures before technical full employment had been achieved (Skidelsky, 1992, p. 603). When

Keynes thought about an attainable level of unemployment, the figure that usually came into his mind was 5 per cent.

When Keynes entered the Treasury in the Second World War, it was his 'anti-inflationary perspective which reconciled Keynesian economics to Treasury orthodoxy' (Skidelsky, 2000, p. 20). He came up with practical ideas such as compulsory savings to deal with the threat of wartime inflation. Nevertheless, he was inclined to see keeping wages reasonably stable as 'a political rather than economic problem' (quoted in Winch, 1989, p. 107). Commenting on the Australian White Paper on full employment, he remarked, 'One is also, simply because one knows no solution, inclined to turn a blind eye to the wages problem in a full employment economy' (quoted in Jones, 1977, p. 53).

Policy-makers could not, however, turn a blind eye to what became an increasingly urgent problem in the postwar period. The solution they adopted was incomes policy, policies which took a variety of forms: voluntary or compulsory; fixed rate or percentage increases; various prices and incomes boards to adjudicate on diffi-cult cases and implement the policies; or no accompanying insti-tutional mechanisms. Emergency policies such as the Labour £6 a week pay rise limit of 1975 might have helped to avert an eco-nomic crisis, but although policies were able to achieve short-term reductions in earnings growth, they proved impossible to sustain in the long run. Moreover, by narrowing differentials, they distorted the labour market and increased industrial unrest.

The Keynesians

The overwhelming majority of postwar economists defined them-selves as Keynesians. However, converting theory into policy was not easy:

> Although by 1953 the general principles of a counter-cyclical policy to stabilise the economy had been common ground among economists for a decade or more, there was no experience in Britain of putting such a policy into effect and hence little detailed knowledge of the rate at which various components of demand were likely to change and the size and speed of the impact on the economy that measures of economic policy would bring about. (PRO: T267/12, p. 34)

In practice, however, being a Keynesian certainly involved macro-economics being seen as a superior activity to microeconomics. The demand side of the economy was more important than the supply side: 'This meant that little attention was paid to "supply side problems" in the golden age; and they tended to cumulate' (Skidelsky, 2000, p. 499).

There was a clear, if limited, role for government in managing the economy. Government should 'by using monetary and fiscal policy instruments, try to regulate the level of aggregate demand, and hence output and employment...the government had a responsibility to manage the economy, intervening continuously to stabilise demand' (Britton, 1981, p. 85). In policy terms, neo-Keynesianism was interpreted as a strategy of cheap money and fiscal surpluses.

Over time, the theoretical apparatus and the policy instruments became more refined, although the outcomes did not necessarily improve. In 1958 Phillips published an article which established a relationship known as the Phillips Curve which became a central orthodoxy of neo-Keynesianism. Phillips appeared to have found a trade-off between inflation and unemployment in terms of a stable relationship between the annual rate of change of money wages and the annual percentage rate of unemployment. This seemed to offer governments a menu of policy choice between high inflation and low unemployment or vice versa. Thus, if the economy became 'overheated' and inflation rose, measures such as increased taxes could be used to choke off demand. As unemployment rose to unacceptable levels (which could mean around three-quarters of a million), demand could once again be stimulated.

This might need to be done outside the annual budget cycle so the 1961 Finance Act gave government an additional lever called the 'regulator', named after the device used to control steam railway engines. The regulator can be seen as the apotheosis of neo-Keynesian policy instruments, although in practice it did not work well (Bretherton, 1999, pp. 76–82). It was introduced just as the policy paradigm was entering its phase of terminal decline, and allowed the Treasury to impose a surcharge or rebate of up to 10 per cent on duties on tobacco, alcohol, betting and so on, and on purchase tax (the forerunner of valued added tax). A number of other new instruments for controlling demand were introduced at this time as the struggle to maintain an acceptable equilibrium continued. All these stops and starts did little for the sensible forward planning of investment, and hence the industrial economy, but they did offer the Treasury the prospect of fine-tuning the Keynesian model.

'Keynesianism' thus provided a broadly acceptable intellectual underpinning for the pursuit of the generally accepted goal of full employment. Keynesian techniques appeared to be a rational system of economic management and for much of the 1950s and 1960s they appeared to deliver the goods in the sense that a return of recession was avoided. 'Full employment proved much easier to maintain than most people had expected at the end of the war' (PRO: T267/12, p. 34). In practice, this 'golden age' of low unemployment, reasonably stable inflation, and higher rates of growth than in the interwar period probably had more to do with 'catch-up' effects than with the efficacy of Keynesianism. A long postwar boom was fuelled by reconstruction funded by American aid, a young and expanding population, and growing consumer demand.

In the early 1970s, the golden age came to an end. 'Stagflation' characterized the economy. Without the first oil shock, the end of Keynesianism might have been delayed, although its theoretical contradictions were becoming more apparent. It limped on as the dominant paradigm throughout the 1970s, partly because its adherents in the Treasury and the Bank of England were so used to operating within it. New monetarist ideas were, however, gaining ground in the City and the media.

Thatcherism

Thatcherism was intellectually legitimized by a revolution in economic thinking in which the key figure was Milton Friedman. Friedman was very much an economist's economist, although in many respects the ideas put forward by Hayek, the leading representative of the 'Austrian' tradition, were more innovative and fundamentally challenging. Central to Hayek's approach was the notion of the economy offering a form of 'spontaneous order'. His interest was in 'markets as examples of human institutions . . . which have evolved without any conscious plan on anyone's part'. While he accepted that inflation was a monetary phenomenon, he did not believe in the existence of *the* quantity of money. Hayek's criticism of Keynesianism was much more fundamental than that of Friedman as he denied the validity of macroeconomics as such:

> The experience of the Thatcher government, which overshot its monetary targets by miles but, nevertheless, presided over a sharp fall in the inflation

rate in its first few years, was much less puzzling to a Hayekian than a Friedmanite. (Brittan, 1995, p. 115).

Nevertheless, Hayek was perceived as more of a guru who had made a strong case for individual economic freedom, notably in the much reprinted *Road to Serfdom* (1944), while Friedman was seen as the 'practical' economist who could advise on the conduct of current policy. Mrs Thatcher considered herself to be influenced by Hayek (Thatcher, 1993, pp. 12–13), but his radical solution of eliminating money supply growth at a stroke regardless of the cost in unemployment was rejected in favour of a more gradualist approach.

Friedman advanced two main propositions: that 'market economies were much more cyclically stable than Keynes had believed' (Skidelsky, 2000, p. 506) and that monetary interventions do not cure but rather increase instability in the real economy. His work was underpinned by three theoretical propositions: the permanent income hypothesis, the stable demand for money function, and, perhaps most influential of all on policy-makers, the 'natural rate of unemployment'.

Keynes saw consumption as a function of current income, but Friedman argued that what was important was whether the income is expected to be permanent or not. This finding upset the theory of the multiplier and there was no stable and predictable relationship between changes in current income and changes in household consumption plans. Friedman also restated the quantity theory of money, arguing that the demand for money was relatively stable. Economic instability was associated with interventions by the authorities that caused erratic movements in the supply of money.

In work published in 1966, Phelps had already suggested that there was not one unique Phillips curve, and Friedman argued in 1968 that the short-run Phillips curve is highly unstable. This implied that the menu of policy choice between inflation and unemployment only existed in the short run. The long-run tendency is towards an equilibrium rate of unemployment that he called the natural rate of unemployment. No fiscal or monetary policy could keep the economy away from this natural rate, except for short periods. The focus of attention in employment policies thus shifts from the demand to the supply side. The only effective way to reduce unemployment is by reducing the natural rate of unemployment by promoting labour mobility, enhancing skills acquisition, and so forth. A closely related idea was the non-accelerating inflation rate of unemployment

(NAIRU), with much of the rise of unemployment in the 1980s being attributed to a rise in the NAIRU, explained to a large extent in terms of 'a supply-side increase in the number of work-shy unemployed' (Layard, 1982, p. 45).

Policy design was also influenced by rational expectations theory, according to which any government economic policy will be anticipated by economic actors. Unless producers or consumers are misled, stabilization policies can only make matters worse, leaving no useful role for government intervention at the macroeconomic level.

The early 1980s saw 'the heroic or dogmatic phase of monetarism' (Dimsdale, 1991, p. 97) centred around the Medium-Term Financial Strategy which concluded with the suspension of the sterling M3 target in the autumn of 1985 (for a fuller discussion, see Chapter 5). The effective end of monetarism left a vacant space in the ideological shop window, but it was filled by privatization and by substantial cuts in direct taxation. Both of these policies were entirely consistent with Thatcherite principles, as was the continuing emphasis on controlling the Public Sector Borrowing Requirement (PSBR) that became a Public Sector Debt Repayment for a while in the late 1980s. Nevertheless, economic management lacked a central guiding principle now that the monetarist guiding light had 'abandoned us' (Lawson, 1992, p. 987). Lawson was clear that he wanted to pursue an exchange rate objective, but this meant membership of the Exchange Rate Mechanism (ERM) that Mrs Thatcher opposed. Tensions between them increased, leading ultimately to Lawson's resignation. His legacy was an unsustainable boom and higher inflation.

Thatcherism: an assessment

Thatcher did not succeed in her objectives of permanently reducing inflation or substantially reducing the tax burden or public expenditure. Those who view Thatcherism favourably think that her governments led to a transformation of British economic performance; those who take a more critical view would see her strategy as being one of running down Britain's industrial economy.

There was 'a large reduction of the manufacturing productivity gap with Germany between 1979 and 1989, much of which occurred in the first half of the 1980s' (Bean and Crafts, 1996, p. 150). Some of this might be attributed to a 'batting-average' effect whereby the least efficient plants or enterprises went out of production in response to high exchange rates in the early 1980s. There was also more efficient use of existing factors of production 'linked to the conduct rather than the structure of industrial relations, with changed working practices and manning levels contingent on reduced trade union bargaining power' (*ibid.*, p. 151). Some of these gains promised to be long-lasting as 'the gains from future technological improvements are less likely to be diluted than in the past by workers' resistance to new working arrangements' (*ibid.*, p. 153). On the downside, 'British weaknesses in technology and capital accumulation, both human and physical, continued throughout the 1980s' (*ibid.*, p. 151).

Thatcherism should ultimately be judged as a political rather than an economic strategy; the emphasis was as much on strengthening the state as freeing the economy. In these terms, it reasserted the control of the core executive and restored the Conservative Party as a governing party. However, this latter gain was not a permanent one and the Conservative Party was left ideologically divided and ill-equipped for the task of opposition.

The depoliticization thesis

Thatcherism may be the last period during which economic policy in Britain was governed by an overarching orthodoxy. The Third Way is a much looser and less coherent set of propositions. The 'debates centring on "Keynesianism" and "monetarism" have been replaced by a form of technocratic managerialism emphasising the constraints imposed by "global capital"' (Burnham, 2001, p. 129). The lesson learnt by the Blair government is that key policy objectives are not best achieved by '"politicised" forms of management . . . regardless of whether they are wrapped in "Keynesian" or "monetarist" garb' (Burnham, 2001, p. 130).

Burnham's depoliticization thesis provides a useful means of encapsulating some of the points made in Chapters 1 and 2 and also in setting the scene for the rest of this book. Although it has been developed within an 'open Marxist' tradition, the conclusions it reaches are palatable to the most unreconstructed Weberian pluralist. It should also be emphasized that although depoliticization places at one remove the political character of decision-making, it 'is understood . . . as a governing strategy and, in that sense, remains highly political' (Burnham, 2001, p. 136). In particular, 'the state continues to play a permanent and direct role in the reproduction of capital accumulation on both domestic and global levels' (Burnham, 2001, p. 145). The gain for state managers from depoliticization is that they 'retain arms-length control over crucial economic processes while benefiting from the distancing effect of politicisation' (Burnham, 1999, p. 21).

Burnham sees a politicized or discretion-based management of economic policy prevailing at least until 1976 and to some extent into the 1980s. Economic policy management from 1945 onwards was increasingly centred on elaborate forms of government intervention to persuade business and trade unions to moderate wage demands. This politicized form of management was characterized by:

1 government publicly adopts primary responsibility for economic management;
2 an emphasis on direct intervention in the management of labour, capital and finance;
3 government takes immediate credit if policies are successful but a perceived 'economic' crisis can quickly become a more general 'political' crisis of the state (Burnham, 1999, p. 43).

By the 1970s it was becoming clear that this strategy had not been successful, and there was a need to prevent economic crises becoming crises of the state. Depoliticization took three main forms:

1 The reassignment of tasks from the party in office to 'non-political' bodies as a means of demonstrating to the markets the commitment to pursuing inflation targets, e.g., greater independence for the Bank of England.
2 Efforts to increase the accountability, transparency and external validation of policy, e.g., the Blair government's Code of Fiscal Stability.
3 A general emphasis on binding 'rules' which limit government room for manoeuvre in the area of economic policy, e.g., WTO's Dispute Settlement Mechanism (Burnham, 1999, p. 44).

The Blair government's economic model looks rather like the social market model defined as 'one that combines a rule-based macroeconomic policy (subject to override in emergencies) with the promotion of flexible product and labour markets and targeted investment in human capital' (Skidelsky, 1999, p. 287). In other words, this is a model with a strong supply-side emphasis in terms of the role of government, but a more activist supply-side role than Thatcherites would have envisaged. Keynes, however, reformulated the way that we think about economics; his influence persists and may yet revive. Of one thing we can be certain: controversies about the proper role of the market and the state will continue and can never be finally resolved.

4

Monetary Policy

Introduction

> Monetary policy is undertaken by the government in order to affect macro-economic variables such as output, employment and inflation. It involves controlling the quantity of money in existence, or its rate of growth, either by controlling the supply of money or the demand for money via the interest rate, i.e. the price of money. (Griffiths and Wall, 1993, pp. 401–2)

Part of the story in this chapter is of the increasing domestic ascendancy of monetary policy relative to fiscal policy. Monetary policy came to be seen as a better mechanism for economic stabilization, given that it is easier to reverse than spending increases or tax cuts. It is easier to cut taxes than to raise them, and, in addition, fiscal policy can be slow to deliver results and they can be unpredictable. Attempts to tackle a short-term demand deficiency may lead to long-term problems:

> Whereas in general in the 1950s and 1960s changes in fiscal and monetary policy were not closely related, the adoption of targets for monetary aggregates led to explicit co-ordination in the 1980s and the increased importance of exchange-rate considerations dominating monetary policy. (Burnham, 2001, p. 132)

A second part of the story is the increasing importance of the EU in relation to monetary policy, first through the Exchange Rate Mechanism (ERM) and then through the euro. If Britain joined the euro, there would not be a distinct British exchange rate and control of interest rates would pass to the European Central Bank (ECB).

Monetary policy in the 1950s and 1960s

The emphasis in this period, particularly up to 1965, was on demand management through fiscal policy with monetary policy performing a subordinate, supporting role. From a Treasury perspective:

Of all the methods used to influence the level [*sic*] demand in the 1950's,
monetary policy was the most controversial. Indeed, the revival of monetary policy as a means of checking inflation has sometimes been
regarded as the most notable feature of economic policy during the
period. (PRO: T267/12, p. 26)

In opposition, the Conservatives were attracted to 'the view that if
more use was made of monetary policy, inflation could be controlled without much extensive use of direct controls or very large
Budget surpluses obtained through high rates of taxation' (PRO:
T267/12, p. 26). After they entered government, monetary policy
became more activist (Cairncross, 1999, p. 1); ministers raised the
bank rate (the prevailing rate of interest) first to 2.5 per cent in
November 1951 and then to 4 per cent in March 1952. The ministerial view was that 'the deflationary effect of monetary policy had
been much stronger than was generally expected. The Bank of
England held a similar view' (Cairncross and Watts, 1989, p. 217).

Increased reliance on monetary policy offered an opportunity for
enhancing the influence of the Bank of England, although the Treasury dismissed its initiatives in monetary policy as 'usually of the
nature of money market management rather than major steps in
general economic policy' (PRO: T267/12, p. 4); 'The Bank of England
itself blew hot and cold on the effectiveness of monetary policy' (Dell,
1997, p. 198). Opinion within the Economic Section of the Treasury
was divided, but more sceptical about the potential contribution of
monetary policy. In so far as economists viewed it as effective, it was a
means of restricting demand rather than expanding it.

Monetary policy was nevertheless used quite extensively in the
1955–57 period, not because of its merits, but because of the absence
of other policy instruments. Direct controls had been withdrawn
'and the effectiveness of fiscal policy [was] reduced by Ministers'
unwillingness to see direct taxes raised' (PRO: T267/12, p. 35).
'Probably the main lesson learned from experience with policy to
control demand in 1953–58 was that monetary policy was of much
limited effectiveness than most of the hopes held at the beginning of
the decade had implied' (PRO: T267/12, p. 35).

Tensions between the Bank and the Treasury over limitations
on bank lending, which annoyed the banks but failed to squeeze
out inflation, led to the appointment of an official committee of
inquiry under Lord Radcliffe in 1957. Its report in 1959 offered a
wide review of the role of monetary policy and the techniques
of monetary control. It reinforced the prevalent conventional

wisdom by concluding that 'monetary policy should play a subordinate role to fiscal measures in the context of demand management policy, aiming to achieve full employment with reasonable price stability' (Dimsdale, 1991, p. 108). Monetary policy was also used to pursue two external objectives, 'to peg the spot exchange rate for the dollar by official transactions in the foreign exchange market and to discourage excessive capital outflows' (Tew, 1978, p. 218).

Nevertheless, there was some attempt by ministers in the early part of the 1958–64 period

> to shift the emphasis of control from fiscal to monetary measures... But fear of discouraging long-term investment, as well as of making Government borrowing more expensive, limited the use of monetary measures when restraint was required; and as stimuli to expansion they were admittedly slow to act. (Bretherton, 1999, p. 87).

Thus, by the time of the change of government in 1964, 'the budget remained the Government's chief and most effective instrument for the control of demand' (*ibid.*).

'Managing the economy with an overvalued exchange rate led to an increasing reliance on monetary restraint in the mid-1960s.' This constraint was removed by devaluation in 1967 but 'Increasing reliance was [then] placed upon monetary policy because of the need to contain the rising trend in inflation in the later 1960s' (Dimsdale, 1991, p. 109). In general, however, 'the main impact of monetary measures was on external flows as short-term interest rates were regulated in order to maintain the fixed exchange rate. On the domestic side, monetary policy acted as a support for fiscal policy in demand management, chiefly through restricting credit to borrowers' (*ibid.*, p. 115). Given the Keynesian challenge to the quantity theory of money, it is not surprising that there was little emphasis on the money supply:

> In the 1960s monetary policy had only a limited contact with the monetary policy discussed in textbooks. It was largely a collection of administrative devices intended to improve the balance of payments and moderate excess demand. It was neither aimed at controlling the stock of money nor was it much relied upon to combat inflation. (Cairncross, 1996, p. 243)

With fiscal policy used to control demand, and incomes policy relied on as the principal instrument to restrain inflation, there was little room for attention to the money supply. 'Until late in the

[1964–70] period the money supply...was widely regarded in the Treasury as the more or less *incidental result* of credit policy and of no great importance as a dynamic force on its own for either demand or prices' (PRO: T267/22, p. 92). Control of the money supply was, however, attracting some attention in the broadsheet and specialist press, and an official seminar on the subject was held in London in October 1968 for Bank of England and Treasury officials and IMF representatives (Tew, 1978, pp. 246–7).

The 1970s: a period of transition

A widespread reform of the monetary system known as Competition and Credit Control was introduced in 1971. This removed lending ceilings on banks that had disadvantaged banks compared to other providers of finance; the system of direct quantitative restriction on lending was replaced by the use of short-term interest rates. The clearing banks in London were no longer to fix interest rates through a cartel, and their rates ceased to have an automatic relationship to the Bank Rate. The Chief Economic Adviser at the time regarded it as 'an inherently inflationary scheme' (MacDougall, 1987, p. 190). Its successful operation required a willingness to raise interest rates to control the money supply, but MacDougall suggests that political resistance delayed this from happening. Thus, an unintended and unfortunate consequence of the reforms, aided by a deliberate expansion of demand, was a very rapid growth in the money supply, reaching 25 per cent on average for a year under the Heath government (Britton, 1991, p. 97). As Dell observes (1991, p. 35), 'There was no need to be a monetarist to be concerned at the rate of monetary expansion under Barber.' Even so, the link between expansion of the money supply and high inflation seemed to lend support to the monetarist position.

  However, although the 'monetarists were winning over the press, the city and the Conservative Party...they had as yet scarcely a toehold either in the Treasury or the Bank' (Britton, 1991, p. 24). An alternative analysis was provided by the 'New Cambridge' school of Keynesians who were influential in the Treasury in the mid-1970s; they proposed using fiscal policy to target the balance of payments rather than full employment. This was of itself not a very radical idea, but their advocacy of import controls was more controversial.

The Labour Chancellor, Denis Healey, was deeply sceptical of monetarist nostrums, arguing that

> no one has yet found an adequate definition of money, no one knows how to control it, and no one except Friedman himself is certain exactly how the control of money supply will influence inflation, which is supposed to be its only purpose. (Healey, 1990, p. 382)

Nevertheless, 'My years at the Treasury had taught me that the neo-Keynesians were wrong in paying so little attention to the monetary dimension of economic policy' (*ibid.*, p. 491). Even before the agreement with the IMF in 1976, he had decided to publish the undisclosed monetary targets that had been in use since 1973 in order to placate the markets.

In a speech to the Labour Party conference in October 1976, Mr Callaghan made it clear that the traditional neo-Keynesian remedy of coping with a recession by cutting taxes and increasing spending was no longer available as a credible policy option. In his Mais Lecture in 1978, the Governor of the Bank of England redefined the traditional goals of economic policy, to place '[g]reater emphasis ... on the control of inflation in the medium term through monetary measures rather than the maintenance of full employment through an active policy of demand management' (Dimsdale, 1991, p. 127). Incomes policy was, however, to remain as a policy instrument, but would be reinforced by the framework for economic stability provided by monetary targets. A key decision was to introduce a system of rolling six-month targets for M3 (a broad measure of money supply including bank deposits held in sterling by UK residents) announced in the 1978 Budget, a statement that 'was notable for the emphasis laid on monetary policy' (Browning, 1986, p. 112).

Ministers and leading officials at the Bank of England and the Treasury had not been intellectually converted to monetarism; 'Most of the senior officials were still unsympathetic to monetarism' (Britton, 1991, p. 39). By the end of the 1970s, they were treating it with more respect, 'but with the detached respect of non-believers' (Britton, 1991, p. 39). The period from 1974 to 1979 saw a new recognition of the value of monetary targets, accompanied by a greater emphasis on the inflation rather than unemployment objective. After 1976 fiscal and monetary policy was tightened as unemployment increased. These changes do not, however, represent a conversion to full-blown monetarism, although the Labour government did make the use of monetary targets more familiar and acceptable.

The 1980s: the disappointments of monetarism

The election of the Thatcher government in 1979 saw an end to incomes policies as a policy instrument while the reduction of inflation through 'reduced monetary growth over the medium term became the dominant feature of macroeconomic policy' (Dimsdale, 1991, p. 131). The economic world had been turned upside down with monetary policy given precedence over fiscal policy.

The framework for policy in the first period of the Thatcher government was provided by the Medium-Term Financial Strategy (MTFS). This specified the government's objectives over a four-year period in terms of targets for growth of the money supply, public sector borrowing, public expenditure and taxation. The MTFS was intended to influence public attitudes and expectations by convincing employers and unions 'that inflationary wage demands would not be financed: strict control of the money supply would mean that the money to finance such rises would not be forthcoming, hence the cost would be lost jobs' (Thain, 1985, p. 268). The broader political purpose of the MTFS was 'to confirm and consolidate the complete change of direction' (Lawson, 1992, p. 69) that Thatcherism involved, not least moving away from 'the commitment to full employment, come what may' (Lawson, 1992, p. 70).

One of the principal difficulties with implementing money supply targets was choosing which measure to use. An unfortunate lesson was drawn from the apparent reliability of M3 in the early 1970s when officials from the Treasury and the Bank of England came to make their choice. 'Subsequent events in the early 1980s were to confirm that the explanatory power of M3 for inflation had been greatly exaggerated by the particular circumstances of the early 1970s' (Britton, 1991, p. 97). In fact, there is evidence to suggest that M3, with its curious emphasis on bank deposits, was the least stable of the target aggregates available. As Lawson admits (1992, p. 987), 'The main practical problem with the MTFS was that the domestic monetary guideline that we inherited, known as Sterling M3, proved treacherous.' In this respect, the incoming Conservative government proved to be surprisingly reliant on the choices of its predecessors and the advice of officials. A narrower definition of money such as M0 or M1 might have offered greater success, but it lacked market credibility.

Whichever target had been chosen, the intentions of policy-makers were likely to be confounded by Goodhart's law which 'states that any monetary indicator becomes distorted as a guide to monetary conditions once it is selected for target purposes' (Brittan, 1983, p. 149). In practice the central emphasis of the policy moved to control of the Public Sector Borrowing Requirement (PSBR) by 1982 and the M3 target was suspended in 1985. Nevertheless, Lawson defends the MTFS as a political success, even though the monetary targets were missed. He considered that

> the spirit of the strategy was observed, as a result of which inflation fell far more than our supporters – let alone our critics – would have believed possible; and... the framework was useful in resisting calls for 'reflation'. (Lawson, 1992, p. 413)

After 1985 the Chancellor focused on the exchange rate which he saw as 'clear and unequivocal' (Lawson, 1992, p. 1023), a stance which drew the ire of a group he called the 'sectarian monetarists... united only by a detestation of any emphasis on the exchange rate' (Lawson, 1992, p. 482). From 1987, Lawson began to 'shadow the deutschmark' within a range between DM2.75 and DM3.00, although Mrs Thatcher initially claimed to be unaware of this policy.

Fuelled by financial deregulation, but also by the government's own cuts in taxes and interest rates, the economy developed an unsustainable boom that led eventually to higher inflation and a collapse in the housing market. Lawson admits (1992, p. 989) that 'my central mistake was undoubtedly to underestimate the strength and duration of the boom of the late 1980s and thus of the inflationary forces it unleashed'. He concludes (1992, p. 991) that 'although monetary policy during my tenure of the Exchequer was tight, with the benefit of hindsight the conclusion can only be that it was not tight enough'.

Even M0 started to exceed its target range in 1988 and it was evident that monetary policy was too relaxed. Lawson 'was forced to abandon the exchange-rate policy and raise interest rates' (Thomas, 2001, p. 59). Base rates increased from 7.5 per cent in June 1988 to 13 per cent by November. Monetary policy 'had to bear the main burden of correcting the... overheating of the economy, since fiscal fine tuning remained out of favour with the government' (Dimsdale, 1991, p. 139). The Chancellor's reliance on interest rates led to him being described in golfing terms by Edward Heath 'as a one-club man and that club is interest rates'. The phrase stuck, although Lawson's defence was that he was using a range of different instruments, not least tax reform, to influence the economy. 'But interest rates are the essential means of curbing inflation, just as a golfer confines himself to the use of his putter for putting' (Lawson, 1992, p. 848). Over the decade as a whole, monetary policy which started 'as a formal exercise in monetary targeting, ended as discretionary policy relying on adjustments in short-term interest rates with little support from fiscal policy' (Dimsdale, 1991, p. 139).

The 1990s: the ERM episode

When John Major became Chancellor in 1989, there was no anchor for economic policy:

> One after another, the possibilities had been knocked away. Following the Boom of the late 1980s, the monetarist orthodoxy and the Medium Term Financial Strategy had lost credibility. The money-supply targets were no longer credible: we could hardly shadow the deutschmark as Nigel [Lawson] had done – even he had abandoned this approach. (Major, 1999, p. 153)

The answer was to join the EU's Exchange Rate Mechanism (ERM), once Mrs Thatcher's opposition had been overcome. This was achieved in October 1990 at a high central rate of 2.95 marks against the pound sterling. It was accompanied by an ill-judged cut in interest rates at the insistence of Mrs Thatcher to make entry politically palatable in the run-up to the Conservative Party conference. 'The ERM was to provide a totally new framework for monetary policy, in which a fixed exchange rate became the main anti-inflation instrument and domestic interest rates became subordinated to it' (Johnson, 1991, p. 69). By maintaining sterling within the ERM bands, it was hoped that UK inflation would move into line with the best inflation performance of its competitors in continental Europe. Indeed, inflation did drop from just under 11 per cent when Britain joined the ERM, to less than 4 per cent when Britain suspended its membership in September 1992. As the Budget Red Book explained, ERM membership was the central discipline underpinning UK macroeconomic policy in the medium term, providing the framework for monetary policy and the operation of the UK economy.

This acknowledgement of the centrality of ERM membership makes the events of 'Black' or, as it is sometimes called, 'Golden', Wednesday (16 September 1992) one of the most extraordinary events in postwar British economic policy. The Major government was forced to leave the exchange rate mechanism in humiliating circumstances. Although the consequent devaluation was beneficial for the British economy, the Conservatives lost one of their most precious electoral assets, their lead in perceptions of economic competence over Labour.

Many readings are possible of this event, depending in large part on whether the observer is a Eurosceptic or a Euro enthusiast. A reading of the various accounts does suggest, however, that the Germans were preoccupied with their own domestic inflationary problems resulting from reunification and were not predisposed to be very helpful to other countries in the ERM. The Ecofin meeting at Bath in September 1992 may or may not have been mishandled by the British Chancellor, Norman Lamont, but the Germans were reluctant to make any concessions on their domestic interest rates. Incautious remarks by the president of the Bundesbank, Dr Schlesinger, produced the ultimate crisis, but forces were building up for such a crisis anyway.

One argument that is sometimes made is that Britain entered at too high a rate against the deutschmark. Certainly, the economic circumstances of 1990 were a less-favourable time for entry than an earlier opportunity in 1985. However, the ERM was supposed to act as a constraint on inflation and it could not fulfil this function if the rate was set too low. In any case, 'the central rate was close to the current market rate and the average of the previous decade' (Lamont, 1999, p. 210).

It became increasingly apparent over the summer of 1992 that the rate was unsustainable. Why, then, did Britain not seek a realignment within the ERM? Major claims that the French were not interested in a realignment (Major, 1999, p. 324), but the British never seemed to have pushed very hard on the issue. Lamont's account is that devaluation within the ERM was unacceptable as it would have meant higher interest rates. Base rates had edged down from 14 per cent in the autumn of 1990 to 10 per cent just before the ERM crisis, after which they fell rapidly to 5.25 per cent by February 1994. The groups most affected by high interest rates, such as mortgage payers and small business owners were at the heartland of Conservative support. Lamont takes the view that raising rates might not have made much difference and that at most all it would have achieved was the postponement of the crisis until the following summer when France was not able to sustain its participation in the ERM (Lamont, 1997, p. 257). Against that, it could be argued that the crisis of September 1992 made that of the summer of 1993 more likely.

It has been argued

> that the UK government had not accepted the full implications of participation in the ERM . . . when they joined in 1990. According to this view, participation in the system required a commitment to follow German interest rates, however harsh the consequences for the domestic economy. (Wincott, Buller and Hay, 1999, p. 103)

This strategic argument has more weight than the disputes about the correctness of the tactics followed on Black Wednesday itself. However, its economic strength has to be placed against the political weakness of a government faced with a party that was increasingly hostile to anything which appeared to transfer power to the EU.

The adoption of an inflation target

An inflation target with an initial range of 1–4 per cent was the pragmatic response to the void in policy left by Britain's departure from the ERM. The inflation target was supplemented by a target range for M0 of 0–4 per cent. Lamont recalls (1999, p. 276) that 'Some monetarists would have liked us to have had only a series of targets for the money supply'. While he attached considerable weight to M0, notably as a proxy for retail spending, he saw it only as a means of tracking the current state of the economy. While there was no exchange-rate target, this pragmatic mix was completed by giving some weight to the exchange rate.

Lamont argues (1999, p. 389) that these events represent the 'real, decisive break in Britain's inflation record'. In his view, they permitted an export-led recovery and a long period of sustained growth. Labour redefined the 2.5 per cent medium-run target of 2.5 per cent or less set by the Conservatives in 1995 as a symmetric 2.5 per cent target in 1997, and the Bank of England was given operational independence in the conduct of monetary policy. Thus 'the operation of monetary policy is based on the same approach as that of the previous Conservative governments except that they rejected the notion of an independent central bank' (Thomas, 2001, p. 66).

By the end of the century, fiscal and monetary policy were not seen as competing alternatives, but as different aspects of policy that needed to be consistent. The extent to which coordination has suffered because the two policies are no longer in the hands of one individual has been discussed. The Chancellor's stated view is that coordination is important and involves a flow of information between the fiscal and monetary authorities (House of Lords, 2001, para. 20). The House of Lords committee was not sure whether this system of coordination would always be effective and expressed surprise at the lack of discussion between the Governor and the Chancellor on the balance between fiscal and monetary policy (House of Lords, 2000, paras 21 and 22). Whatever difficulties arise in the future, external observers have felt able to compliment the UK for 'sound fiscal and monetary policies, underpinned by transparent medium-term policy frameworks' (IMF, 2001, p. 2). A problem that may arise if Britain joins the euro is 'that policy coordination under EMU is not as intense as it was prior to EMU within individual countries between the fiscal and monetary authorities' (Smaghi and Casini, 2000, p. 388).

The development of EMS and EMU

The crucial monetary policy decision that will face Britain in the future is whether to surrender domestic control of interest rates and a flexible exchange rate for the single European currency. Such a sacrifice of policy instruments is an unavoidable consequence of euro membership as 'The euro and Monetary Union are based on a credible monetary policy' (Trichet, 2001, p. 1). It is first necessary to consider how EMS and EMU developed and why Britain did not participate.

When the Bretton Woods system start to fall apart in the early 1970s, it ran up against a strong preference for a fixed rate exchange system in Europe and an unsuccessful effort was made to create a zone of regional monetary stability through the 'snake' mechanism. There was already a blueprint for monetary union in the Werner Report of 1970, produced by a committee of experts established following the Hague Summit in 1969 which recommended that it should be achieved by 1980. There were two broad differences in the Werner proposals from what was eventually adopted in the Maastricht treaty. Werner did call for a common fiscal policy and an enlarged budget that many commentators saw as essential to the successful completion of EMU. His plan did not, however, include any model of a central bank and did not provide for a sufficient constraint on national policies.

General dissatisfaction with floating exchange rates and with 'Eurosclerosis' led the Commission President, Roy Jenkins, to suggest the revival of monetary union in a speech in Florence in October 1977. He presented monetary union as a means of lowering inflation and unemployment and increasing investment. The key event in the revival of EMU was, however, the conversion of Chancellor Schmidt of Germany in February 1978 who was able to secure French participation. This development 'reflected the emergence of Germany as a major player in international economic relations during the 1970s and the country's new developed self-confidence in responding to and initiating changes in the arena of world politics' (Zis, 1999, p. 44). In Britain, Healey's view (1990, p. 439) was that joining would involve unacceptable levels of intervention to keep sterling down. Politically, the Labour Party remained ambivalent about Europe.

The European Monetary System and the Exchange Rate Mechanism

Although it was made possible by the economic disorder of the 1970s, the formation of the European Monetary System (EMS) in January 1979 was a highly political act, something that would be characteristic of the continuing evolution of EMU. As Tsoukalis emphasized (1993, p. 187), 'It was clearly a decision of high politics.' The notion of the EU as a counter against American hegemony is never far from the minds of continental European leaders, and EMS was a means of strengthening Europe in relation to the United States. It was also evidence of the growing importance of the Franco-German axis as the driving force behind European integration. The main feature of the EMS was the Exchange Rate Mechanism (ERM), which had three key elements:

1 A grid of central parities of the participating countries.
2 A choice of narrow (2.25 per cent) or broad (6 per cent) bands of fluctuation. Italy, and Britain when it eventually joined, made use of the broader bands.
3 The ecu, a weighted basket of currencies based on share of GNP.

The EMS experienced an early test as a result of the expansionary policies undertaken in France from 1981 to 1983, possibly the last attempt by a major country to attempt to solve unemployment problems through a traditional Keynesian reflation. The franc was devalued in October 1981, June 1982 and March 1983, by 27 per cent in total. Germany was prepared to bail out the French, but at a price; insisting on budget cuts at the time of the 1981 devaluation and a new austerity plan following the 1982 devaluation.

Important changes in the operating rules for the EMS occurred with the Basle–Nyborg agreement in September 1987. This strengthened the very short-term credit facility, allowing central banks to borrow Community currencies for intramarginal interventions. These new arrangements underwent an early and successful test in October 1987 when a fall in the dollar put pressure on the French franc. Against a benign economic background, the ERM became a quasi-fixed rate system with no realignments between 1987 and 1992 (other than Italy moving to the narrow band). Spain joined in 1989 and Britain in 1990. The ERM appeared to be a success, with converging inflation rates for the narrow band states, although these were affected by a number of different factors.

Meanwhile, the internal market project was setting up a number of new dynamics within the European Community that led to 'spillover' effects on policy. If one is seeking to have a true internal market, its successful functioning could be undermined by competitive devaluation by member states. There was also a risk of more volatile and unstable exchange rates following the decision in June 1988 to remove all exchange controls that impeded capital movements. An important paper by the German foreign minister, Hans-Dietrich Genscher, in February 1988 'took the position that, if monetary union was to happen at all, it should be fully institutionalised around a single currency and a European central bank' (Levitt and Lord, 2000, p. 45). The Delors Committee, with a majority of central bankers, was set up and reported in 1989, providing a blueprint for a three-stage process for achieving EMU which was largely incorporated into the 1992 Maastricht Treaty. Stage one would see all member states joining the ERM. Stage two was a transitional one with convergence of economic performance and the establishment of the precursor of the European Central Bank (ECB), the European Monetary Institute. Stage three would see the establishment of the ECB and the single currency.

The Maastricht Treaty provided convergence criteria that set entry rules for stage three. These provided that the rate of inflation should be no more than 1.5 per cent above that of, at most, the three best performing member states. The public-sector deficit should not be more than 3 per cent of GDP and the total public debt not more than 60 per cent of GDP. Given that this criterion could prove difficult for some member states, there was a let-out clause if it was declining substantially and continuously. Entrants should have been in the narrow band of the ERM for two years, and their interest rates should be no more than 2 per cent above the, at most, three best performing member states.

The collapse of the ERM and the route to EMU

Unfortunately, while this architecture was being carefully assembled, the economic and political climate was deteriorating. German reunification in 1990 produced higher inflation and led to a sharp tightening of the monetary stance in the anchor country; deflationary pressures were created through interest rate rises and the appreciation of the deutschmark against other currencies; and a weakening of the US dollar increased competitive pressures on European currencies, in particular sterling. Southern member states were suffering from declining competitiveness with interest rates above the EMS average, and a negative referendum result in Denmark and a close one in France undermined the political credibility of EMU. A series of crises ensued in 1992–93. As Levitt and Lord note (2000, p. 65):

> the old ERM collapsed in a two-stage crisis between September 1992 and August 1993. The first wave attacked the 'soft underbelly of the system': that is, the countries that had still not achieved full economic convergence – the UK, Italy, Spain and Portugal. The second afflicted the core itself, notably the Franco-German parity.

These events alarmed those supporters of EMU who had seen the ERM as offering a 'glide path' route to EMU which would provide a mechanism for convergence on low inflation rates and a 'one-size-fits-all' interest rate. A more optimistic interpretation was that a better economic environment would be created with falling interest rates and more realistic exchange rates. This would in turn facilitate easier achievement of the convergence criteria. The virtual collapse of the ERM also undermined the advocates of any kind of 'halfway-house' arrangement. The political supporters of EMU realized that they had to back full monetary integration; the price of not doing so would be to undermine the whole integration process. However, the immediate outlook was bleak. 'Thus in the mid-1990s, EMU seemed an unlikely prospect' (Dinan, 1999, p. 466). In 1995 the European Council abandoned the goal of launching stage three in 1997.

The political imperative for EMU remained, particularly in Germany. Nevertheless, Germany had to do something to counter domestic opposition and reassure the Bundesbank. They therefore developed the Stability and Growth Pact that provided for surveillance of budget deficits and fines for countries running excessive deficits. At the time this was interpreted as a signal to discourage Italy and other southern countries from becoming participants in the euro. Despite demands by the new socialist government in France which led to the adoption of a separate resolution about growth and employment, the Stability and Growth Pact was adopted at the 1997 Amsterdam Council. The ECB came into existence in June 1998 and stage three of EMU commenced in January 1999 with the irrevocable fixing of exchange rates. Euro banknotes and coins came into circulation in January 2002, with national banknotes and coins losing their legal tender status by July 2002.

Getting 11 states across the finishing line (later 12 with the addition of Greece) was a considerable achievement; it reflected the political determination of Germany and France to ensure that the project was a success. The leaders of France and Germany had invested a considerable amount of political capital in EMU that they were reluctant to write off. Failure to achieve the launch of the euro would be damaging both to them and the EU and their leaders were determined to make their mark on history, even if it involved a little creative accounting to meet the convergence criteria. Economic recovery also helped with the economic cycle turning at the right moment. Euro-zone currencies depreciated against the pound and the dollar, making it easier to satisfy the convergence criteria. Outside of Britain, there was really very little organized opposition to EMU.

The case for economic and monetary union considered

In this section the general case for EMU as it affects the EU as a whole is considered; there are special considerations in relation to

British participation in the euro which are discussed in a subsequent
section. The economic and political arguments that apply to Britain
are somewhat different from those that relate to the EU as a whole.
Supporters of EMU argue that 'while the benefits are significant,
cumulative over time and reasonably uncontroversial, the costs are
much more uncertain, widely exaggerated and almost certain to
diminish with the period of time' (Healey, 2000, pp. 19–20). Perhaps
the single most important benefit of EMU is that

> Greater nominal exchange rate stability will occur, which reduces the risk
> associated with fluctuating exchange rates and is therefore assumed to
> encourage greater trade and investment which, in turn, should result in
> higher growth and employment in the longer run. (Baimbridge, Burkitt
> and Whyman, 2000, p. 4)

While there are means of hedging against exchange rate uncertainty,
there are costs associated with their use, and they are more readily
available to large than to small and medium-sized enterprises.
If greater growth could be realized as a result of EMU, this alone
would serve to outweigh many of the disadvantages. However, the
benefits of reducing exchange-rate uncertainty may be exaggerated.

Popular presentations of the arguments for EMU make reference
to the elimination of transaction costs. For example, it is possible to
illustrate that a person who started with a sum of money in one
country and changed it successively in each member state would
end up with a very small sum of money. For frequent travellers
within the EU, this can be a real irritant. In economic terms the
benefits of reductions in the transaction costs of currency exchange
are more limited. Many large firms already denominate their internal
transactions in one currency. As with greater exchange rate stability,
'SMEs which lack sophisticated treasury departments are likely to
benefit more from the Euro than larger multinational companies'
(Healey, 2000, p. 23). After early ambitious estimates of the impact
of reducing currency transaction costs, 'it is now widely agreed that
the likely savings will be between 0.25 per cent and 0.5 per cent of
GDP' (*ibid.*).

Because goods, services and labour are priced in the same currency, price transparency should increase under the euro. This
should exert 'a downward pressure upon prices to the benefit of
European consumers' (Baimbridge, Burkitt and Whyman, 2000,
p. 5). Supporters of EMU also argue that the priority given by the

ECB to price stability should lead to lower inflation and hence lower interest rates in the long run. This would give a further boost to investment and economic growth beyond that provided by nominal exchange-rate stability. Critics of EMU argue that there are credible national mechanisms for pursuing objectives such as price stability (Minford, 2000).

It is also important to consider the consequences of continuing to have competing currencies within what is supposed to be a single European market. It can be argued that the price transparency provided by EMU 'is a precondition to the final completion of the single market' (Baimbridge, Burkitt and Whyman, 2000, p. 5). More generally, 'The danger with non-cooperative policymaking is that it can become dangerously competitive.' A classic prisoner's dilemma situation arises in which countries 'have an incentive to engineer competitive devaluations, even though the net result is simply higher inflation' (Healey, 2000, p. 37). In order to prevent such destructive competition, one has to go beyond the voluntary arrangement represented by the EMS from which it was easy to withdraw when the going got difficult. 'EMU provides an alternative, more robust framework within which policy co-operation could be orchestrated' (*ibid.*, p. 38).

Opponents of the euro point to its fall against the dollar since its launch despite a coordinated intervention in the market in September 2000, followed by three further interventions in November 2000 intended to put a floor under the euro. However, in early April 2001, the euro was around the level at which the US Federal Reserve had intervened the previous September, below $0.88. There seem to have been a number of reasons for this fall, including the slowness of structural reform in Europe and the capital outflow which occurred to fund the US demand for savings to finance its investment boom. This seemed to be continuing early in 2001 despite the slowdown in the US economy. There were also continuing market uncertainties about the credibility of the new framework. At one time, weak European growth relative to US growth was seen to be a factor, but this was a less credible explanation for the strength of the dollar by 2001 as US growth slowed. The fall of the euro is a matter for concern if one adhered to the belief that its creation 'would establish a major world currency capable of rivalling the US dollar and Japanese yen, which could confer certain economic advantages as well as providing political prestige' (Baimbridge, Burkitt and Whyman, 2000, p. 5).

While such an argument might appear attractive to European élites, especially those with an anti-American bias, it was always one of the more politicized and less convincing arguments in favour of EMU. It is perhaps time to try and move beyond the language of describing currencies as 'strong' or 'weak'; using terms like 'over-valued' and 'undervalued' presents an alternative picture of the situation. German manufacturing interests, for example, were quite pleased to see the euro fall against the dollar.

One of the key arguments advanced by opponents of the EMU is that the EU does not fulfil the conditions for an optimal currency area. There is an extensive literature about optimal currency areas (OCAs) in economics, although perhaps it is less influential than it once was. A number of criticisms have been made of OCA theory (Artis, 1999, pp. 163–4), but nevertheless it suggests that there are four criteria for deciding whether regions should form a currency area:

> [mobility] of factors of production, flexibility of prices and wages, open-ness to trade and diversity of production. Regions that have relatively closed economies, narrow product ranges, strong wage and price rigid-ities, and low external mobility of labour and capital should not join monetary unions but should instead retain exchange-rate flexibility. (Taylor, 1995, p. 25)

'If the EU – or even the hard core of the EU – is not an OCA, the loss of the exchange rate instrument as a macro-stabilizer will create significant costs to the Member States which form the monetary union' (Apel, 1998, p. 96). Given the commitment to price stability, this is most likely to appear as higher levels of unemployment than would otherwise be the case. Even 'the US may not be an optimal currency area' (*ibid.*, p. 95). Supporters of EMU argue that it is sufficient if the EU is a feasible currency area 'in the sense that it could survive, but it might not be optimal' (Taylor, 1995, p. 36). In other words, it does not matter whether or not the EU satisfies the theoretical parameters of OCA theory: the key question is whether EMU can be made to work. As the history of EMU shows, its creation has been more a matter of political commitment than of economics.

There is concern that 'The lack of prior cyclical and structural convergence amongst the participating member states will create strains within EMU' (Baimbridge, Burkitt and Whyman, 2000, p. 6). In making comparisons with the USA, there is a tendency to overlook the extent to which there are substantial regional discrepancies within the US economy, as indeed there are within EU member states such as Italy (Trichet, 2001, p. 5). However, the USA does have certain advantages in operating a single currency, leaving aside the fact that it has been in place for a much longer period. Real wages tend to be more rigid in Europe and labour tends to be less mobile within Europe for a wide range of reasons. Perhaps above all else, the EU lacks a federal fiscal policy. Public expenditure remains in the hands of member states and the transfers of funds that are made to the EU represent a very small proportion of total European GDP. Hence, a greater burden is placed on exchange rate flexibility as a means of adjustment.

This does not constitute a case for abandoning EMU, but rather for accelerating efforts started at the Lisbon summit to increase the flexibility of the European economy, although it has to be admitted that there is a tension between this objective and that of a 'social Europe'. It also implies greater harmonisation of taxes and more central redistribution of funds as a necessary condition for the long-run success of EMU and this is just what the British Eurosceptics fear.

The case for and against British membership

As Artis notes (1999, p. 170), 'Overall assessments of the optimality of EMU for its potential members virtually always place the UK in an "outsider" category.' OCA analysis would suggest that 'the UK is a marginal candidate for EMU. It is not in the core and in particular seems to have a different business cycle affiliation from that of the countries in the core' (*ibid.*). As has been noted before, OCA analysis has its limitations. The general position taken here is that the economic case for British participation in the euro is not totally convincing, but the political case may be stronger. Paradoxically, because of the political difficulties of winning popular consent to membership, the case may be argued in economic terms.

One of the key concerns about UK membership is that Britain is particularly susceptible to asymmetric economic shocks. 'The economies at the heart of the EU (Germany, France and the Benelux countries) seem more closely integrated and somewhat less susceptible to asymmetric shocks' (Currie, 1997, p. 10). An asymmetric shock is an external event that has a particular effect on an individual country as distinct from symmetric shocks that affect all countries equally. Inducing a variation in the exchange rate is one way of responding to such a shock. If such an option is not available, adjustment may have to take place in other ways – for example higher unemployment. Indeed, 'Where the exchange rate cannot be devalued, the whole burden of adjustment to an external shock . . . will fall on labour markets, either in the form of reductions in real wages . . . or higher unemployment' (Levitt and Lord, 2000, pp. 20–1).

There is a body of empirical evidence that suggests that the UK is more vulnerable to external shocks, which is not surprising given its high degree of integration into the global economy. One study found that 'whereas supply shocks affecting the EC are highly correlated between Germany and its four neighbours, the correlation is much lower between Germany and "the periphery" ' (Taylor, 1995, p. 33), including the UK. The UK's 'experience of both demand and supply shocks has tended to be very different from that of the EC core' (Taylor, 1995, p. 37). This is clearly a consideration that has to be taken into account in assessing the costs and benefits of British membership of EMU. However, it does not of itself lead to the conclusion that the UK should not be a member. It is not the case 'that countries with greater exposure to asymmetric shocks should not participate in EMU, only that they will face greater problems in adjusting to shocks that affect them and the core in different ways' (Levitt and Lord, 1995, p. 22).

The UK has been a major site for investment into the EU, particularly for Japanese companies. One of the attractions of Britain is that it offers a relatively highly-skilled workforce but at a lower total overall labour cost than in most European countries. However, these benefits have been significantly eroded by the high value of the pound and the transaction costs that arise from Britain being outside the euro. There have been suggestions that some investments may be delayed or cancelled or that plant closures have been influenced by the fact that the UK is not in euroland. Opponents of EMU argue that investment is booming, but EMU supporters maintain that the full effects of non-membership have not yet been seen as it is generally anticipated that Britain will eventually join EMU.

Another concern that applies particularly to Britain would be the effect of non-membership on the role of London as an international financial centre. The City has generally been seen as being in favour of membership, although as Talani's (2001) analysis shows, the actual balance of costs and benefits is more complex. Currie's (1997, p. 18) judgement is that

> while some business may be lost, London's strong competitive position is unlikely to be appreciably undermined in the forseeable future whether or not the UK joins EMU, although it may be harmed if the UK stands aside permanently. Unless London plays its hand very badly, the reinforcing virtuous circles are likely to prove just too strong.

A robust line on the question has also been taken by the Governor of the Bank of England, Eddie George: 'There were those who argued that the City would suffer if the UK failed to join from the outset. This clearly has not happened so far – quite the reverse' (*The Economist*, 17 June 2000).

The UK economy has particular structural features that make it more sensitive to interest rate variations. UK households tend to borrow more money (mainly in the form of mortgages) at a variable rate of interest. Changes in interest rates could thus have a much stronger and more immediate impact on the UK economy. Although interest rates in Britain and Germany converged from a four-point differential in 1997 to a one-point differential in 2001, lower interest rates could stimulate consumption and lead to an inflationary boom. The difficulties of cooling the Irish economy within EMU illustrates the limitations of a 'one-size-fits-all' monetary policy. Currie argues that the greater sensitivity of the UK household sector to changes in monetary policy is likely to persist for some time. 'There is a good argument for the UK remaining outside EMU so that it can apply an independent monetary policy appropriate to its particular economic circumstances' (Currie, 1997, p. 10). Healey predicts (2000, p. 33) that 'increasing integration in the financial sector is likely to lead to convergence in borrowing and saving behaviour over time'. Layard points out (2000, p. 63) that 'If we wait for major institutional change, we could wait a long time.'

Thus, even if one accepted that EMU was not working well, it might not work as well for Britain. The economic arguments are more evenly balanced than one is sometimes led to believe. Whether one is in favour of membership or not therefore comes down in large part to a value judgement about the broader political benefits of full participation in the EU. EMU is at the heart of the EU as a political project. If EMU collapsed, the future path of integration would be in serious doubt. In the long run, a situation in which the UK is not part of the EU's major project is not sustainable, and Britain's influence within the EU would be severely diminished. Markets might be placed at risk by 'some sort of "unofficial" protectionism preventing the free passage of UK goods and services across the rest of the EU' (Baimbridge, Burkitt and Whyman, 2000, p. 5).

From the perspective of the Eurosceptics, signing up to EMU would mean the beginning of the end of an independent economic policy. There is no doubt that in general terms and in the long run their analysis is correct. For example, 'National central banks will simply become the regional agencies of the ECB, with no independent power to alter local monetary conditions' (Healey, 2000, p. 32). As has been suggested earlier in this chapter, the limited nature of EU fiscal policy does undermine the chances of success of EMU. The pressure for an increased proportion of taxation to be disbursed by the EU will increase, and pressure for greater harmonization of taxes and for the introduction of qualified majority voting on tax issues will also be maintained. In the short run, it may be the case that 'in EMU national governments will retain considerable powers to operate national fiscal policies to balance the economy', although 'The stability and growth pact will... set constraints on the use of these powers in EMU' (Currie, 2000, p. 126). In the longer run, EMU implies a move towards a common economic policy although, just as in the United States, local and regional variations in taxation would be permissible.

Entry into EMU would undoubtedly reduce the autonomy of UK domestic economic policy-making, even if there could be room for argument about the extent to which this would happen. However, one may question whether an autonomous economic policy pursued by a nation state is really an option under conditions of globalisation. As Currie comments (1997, p. 4) 'The globalisation of financial markets has... constrained the value of an independent currency as a tool of economic policy... With more than a trillion dollars trading across the foreign exchanges daily, the powers of the markets are manifest.'

The position argued here is that joining EMU is predominantly a political choice, a choice that is in practice irreversible and will have important long-run consequences both for the economy and the way in which decisions about it are taken. A particular analysis of the processes of globalization and regionalization can lead to a position in favour of entry on the grounds that sovereignty has to be pooled if globalization is to be controlled. It has to be recognized that that analysis is deeply political and highly contested.

The management of entry

The Blair government attempted to manage the economic and political uncertainties surrounding entry by setting up five economic tests which would have to be satisfied before a recommendation for the UK to join the single currency would be made (see Box 4.1). Many observers see these tests as a convenient smokescreen behind which a decision can be delayed until it is politically convenient. Indeed, it is has been suggested that there is a sixth test imposed by Chancellor Gordon Brown, which requires that the referendum on entry would have to be winnable by a significant margin. Otherwise, Labour's chances of securing a third term would be damaged, as would Gordon Brown's chances of ever becoming prime minister.

There is real substance to the tests, although it is the first one that is really important. The second test is rather vague, although it may be a way of referring to the asymmetric shocks issue. The answer to three and four is almost certainly 'yes', although the satisfaction of either criterion is not of itself a reason for membership. If EMU cannot meet the fifth test, there isn't much point in bothering, although how one measures the achievement of 'stability' or 'a lasting increase in jobs' is open to question, while 'higher growth' as a criterion leads to the question 'relative to what?'

It is the first criterion, that dealing with convergence, that is both important and difficult to satisfy. Indeed, all the tests are placed within the context of a need for 'sustainable and durable' convergence with European economies. It has to be demonstrated that Britain has converged with Europe and that this convergence can be sustained. As Thain comments (2000, pp. 234–5):

> The fear is that the UK economy is on a different economic cycle to the Continental European economy, and that interest rates prevailing in the euro-zone will thus be inappropriate for economic conditions in the UK. The criteria could be viewed as a permanent block to UK membership if the UK economy continues to be at a different stage in the economic cycle, and if the UK inflation level demands a different level of interest rates from that set by the ECB.

Box 4.1   Tests for UK membership of the single currency

The five economic tests are:

1 Are business cycles and economic structures compatible so that we and others could live comfortably with euro interest rates on a permanent basis?
2 If problems emerge, is there sufficient flexibility to deal with them?
3 Would joining EMU create better conditions for firms making long-term decisions to invest in Britain?
4 What impact would entry into EMU have on the competitive position of the UK's financial services industry, particularly the City's wholesale markets?
5 In summary, will joining EMU promote higher growth, stability and a lasting increase in jobs?

Sustainable and durable convergence is the touchstone and without it we cannot reap the benefits of a successful EMU. It means that the British economy:

• has converged with Europe;
• can demonstrably be shown to have converged;
• that this convergence is capable of being sustained;
• that there is sufficient flexibility to adapt to change and unexpected economic events

Source: HM Treasury (1997, p. 5).

The evidence in terms of short-term interest rates, output gaps and unemployment (after account has been taken of structural factors) all 'suggests that cyclical convergence at least is greater than three years ago' (Wolf, 2001). The biggest outstanding difficulty is that a prospective member's currency is supposed to remain within the normal fluctuation bands of the ERM for two years before membership. However, 'sterling is not in the ERM and has been quite unstable against the euro' (Wolf, 2001). 'The "killer fact" in the convergence story remains the current strength and past volatility of the pound' (*The Economist*, 17 June 2000). According to where you stand in the debate, this can be seen as either a strength or a weakness of the British economy. The failure to meet the exchange-rate test may, however, suggest that Britain is not ready for membership.

The politics of British membership

Anyone with some ingenuity and a basic knowledge of economics could write a recommendation for or against membership when the decision point arrives. The decision remains essentially a political one. The key problem here is that opinion polls consistently show a low level of support for membership. For example, the question used by the British Social Attitudes series 'has revealed clear and consistent hostility towards the introduction of a single currency' (Curtice, 1999, p. 182). Given such figures it is interesting that polls also usually show a majority of respondents taking the view that Britain will eventually join. 'For example in September 1998 MORI found that over four in five believe that Britain will have joined the single currency in ten years' time' (Curtice, 1999, p. 191). Focus groups also suggest that many electors are open to persuasion on the issue, which may reflect evidence that suggests that 'opposition is not rooted in a high level of knowledge' (Curtice, 1999, p. 191). Curtice suggests (*ibid.*, p. 198) that 'a sustained campaign of advocacy' may be necessary to change public opinion, but that carries with it political risks such as opening up internal party divisions and giving opportunities to the opposition to inflict political damage. Indeed, Curtice goes on to suggest that even a successful campaign may not be a sufficient condition of success; there would also have to be some restraint shown by other member states on the pace of integration and an absence of bad news from Europe (*ibid.*). Given these political difficulties, it is not surprising that the return of the Blair government for a second term with an overwhelming majority saw a further delay to the launch of any campaign to prepare Britain for membership.

Economic and political logic may suggest that the UK will eventually join EMU, but politics has an unpredictable emotional and symbolic dimension, especially when it comes to issues like a nation's currency. A prudent government would therefore have economic and political contingency plans to deal with a British failure to join.

The role of the European Central Bank

'In a democratic society, elected politicians should decide on the explicit *definition and ranking of the objectives of monetary policy*' (De Haan and Eijffinger, 2000, p. 397). In Britain, government specifies the inflation target. In the EU, the ECB is given a legally binding but imprecisely specified objective of price stability: 'In the current setting it is left to the ECB to provide an operational expression of its primary objective' (*ibid.*, p. 398).

The ECB has a broadly federal structure. In broad terms, the relationship with the national central banks is that they are the implementing arm of the ECB. The governing council of the ECB undertakes such key tasks as formulating monetary policy, setting interest rates and issuing bank notes. As constituted in 2001, the ECB's policy-making governing council has 18 members made up of an executive board of six members based in Frankfurt (appointed for a single term of eight years), plus the governors of the euro-zone's 12 national central banks. All have a vote on interest-rate policy at the council's fortnightly meetings. Pringle and Turner (1999, p. 233) suggest that 'the Executive Board appears in practice to be turning out to be much stronger than expected ... the six only need to gather the support of three governors to prevail if it should come to a vote on any specific issue'. In practice, however, in common with other EU institutions, the preference seems to be to arrive at decisions by consensus. Although central bankers from smaller countries can 'punch above their weight' by using the greater time at their disposal to study relevant data, it is difficult to see a coalition of smaller countries overruling the Bundesbank and the Bank of France. If the Bank of England became a member, it would presumably be in a position of substantial influence as well.

The ECB has adopted a two-pillar approach to its monetary policy, targeting both inflation and money supply growth. It monitors the harmonized index of consumer prices to ensure that it stays within a 0–2 per cent annual growth rate and seeks to keep the growth of M3 ('broad money') close to a 'reference value' of 4.5 per cent. In principle, this is viewed as a sound strategy but there are doubts about whether it is applied in a consistent way.

These doubts are compounded by difficulties that the markets might experience in 'reading' the ECB's intentions compared with those of the US Federal Reserve. This might seem curious given that the ECB has an inflation strategy, has explained its monetary policy strategy and holds monthly on-the-record press briefings. However, the Federal Reserve has a strong leader in Alan Greenspan 'who has managed to steer markets' expectations skilfully. Mr Duisenberg is more a "moderator" of the ECB's 18-strong governing council' (*The Economist*, 6 January 2001). He is also supposed to stand down in 2002 as part of an informal agreement that resolved a controversy in 1998 about who should become ECB president; he was supposed to be succeeded by his main rival at the time, Jean-Claude Trichet of the Bank of France. However, 'no formal written agreement has ever been made public to that effect' (*Financial Times*, 9 April 2001). The exact status of any agreement is a matter of dispute between France and Germany and this uncertainty does not enhance the credibility of the ECB president.

The problem of accountability

There are some difficult and still largely unresolved issues about the relationship of the ECB to other European institutions, particularly its accountability to the European Parliament. Taylor (2000, p. 181) notes that the treaties offer a 'sparse' treatment of ECB accountability. The key features of the ECB:

> the strength of its mandate and independence, the weakness of its accountability, and the assignment of monetary policy to price stability, derive from the German model of central banking and reflect the extent to which it dominated the treaty architecture. (Taylor, 2000, p. 183)

There is a potential inherent conflict between the ECB's emphasis on fiscal rectitude and price stability, and the understandable desire of politicians to boost employment and economic growth. These tensions came to the surface in the autumn of 2001 when a number of politicians, including Chancellor Schröder of Germany and the French Finance Minister, Lauren Fabius, criticized its cautious monetary stance and its reluctance to cut interest rates more rapidly in the wake of the terrorist attacks in September 2001.

The position is complicated by the existence alongside the Economic and Financial Affairs Council of Ministers ('Ecofin') of the informal but influential meeting of ministers from countries participating in the euro (Euro-12). Any proposals to strengthen the role of Euro-12 relative to Ecofin, such as a Franco-Belgian plan advanced in the summer of 2000 to extend the informal meeting from two hours to a full day, usually serves to revive anxieties about a 'two-speed' Europe. France has always been interested in using Euro-12 as a kind of political counterpart to the ECB. At the very least it could 'provide for a more structured monetary–fiscal dialogue between the Council and the ECB, including a mechanism for conflict resolution. Any idea that such a body could give orders or even propose policy guidelines to the ECB was anathema to countries such as Germany and the Netherlands' (Levitt and Lord, 2000, p. 159). What is evident is that the status and importance of Ecofin within the EU's decision-making machinery has been enhanced, not least because of its responsibilities under the Stability and Growth Pact. It can 'provide a setting in which the economic and monetary outlook can be debated by central bankers and finance ministries with a view to reconciling differences in their forecasts or policy responses' (*ibid.*).

In an era in which a belief has grown in the desirability of 'all power to the central bankers', questions about accountability are always going to be difficult to resolve. However, 'democratic accountability may reinforce the credibility and performance of central banks, rather than threaten their independence' (*ibid.*, p. 225). The European Parliament might be thought to have a role in securing accountability and 'has sought to turn its right to be consulted on the appointment of the ECB executive into a power akin to that of the US Senate to "hear" and confirm nominees for the Federal Reserve' (*ibid.*, p. 232). The fundamental difficulty here is that the ECB and the European Parliament may be operating in terms of very different conceptions of accountability:

> For a start the ECB is almost certain to insist that it should only be held politically responsible in a manner that acknowledges its narrow focus on price stability, as well as the core theoretical assumption of independent central banking that there are no long-term trade offs between inflation and the real economy... Another way in which the ECB and the Parliament may differ in their concept of accountability is that the ECB has shown signs of taking a Bundesbank-like position is that it is answerable to the public as a whole and not to any one political institution. In the eyes of the ECB the Parliament is just one element in a wider strategy of communication and legitimation with the public. (Levitt and Lord, 2000, p. 238)

The ECB has been given extensive powers to both formulate and implement monetary policy. This is not simply a technical matter, but has potentially far-reaching economic and social effects. Trade-offs remain between inflation and the level of employment, and it is not easy to deal with the relevant value judgements when 'the EMU area includes countries which still differ markedly in their structures, institutions, and objectives' (Taylor, 2000, p. 186). Adverse economic circumstances could lead to member states pursuing fiscal policies at odds with the monetary policy being followed by the ECB. Indeed, both France and Germany were considering economic stimulus packages in the autumn of 2001, although Chancellor Schröder of Germany emphasized that these would have to be delivered within the limits imposed by the stability and growth pact. One possible conclusion is that the euro will produce severe strains in the conduct of policy which were initially masked by a relatively benign policy environment. Alternatively, it could be argued that handling monetary policy at a European level and fiscal policy at a member-state level is inherently unsustainable in the long run, but member states are likely to be unwilling to give up more policy instruments.

5

Public Expenditure and Taxation

Introduction

It is sometimes remarked that British citizens want European levels of public service and American levels of taxation. The results of some research on public attitudes towards taxation carried out by the Fabian Society, using both focus groups and social surveys, make disturbing reading for decision-makers. On the one hand,

> The process of being taxed is unpleasant, and the taxpayer's mental picture of what it buys in public services is inevitably far paler than their vision of what they might have done with the money foregone. (Hedges and Bromley, 2001, p. 2).

On the other hand, 'There is a very powerful perception that most public services in Britain have got into an unsatisfactory state – and are still declining' (*ibid.*). The majority of survey respondents said that taxes were 'much too high' or 'too high': 58 per cent in the case of income tax, 75 per cent for petrol, alcohol and cigarette duty and 76 per cent in the case of value added tax (VAT) (*ibid.*, p. 29). When respondents were shown a table that placed Britain fourteenth out of 20 advanced countries in terms of total tax in terms of GDP (35 per cent in 1997), the initial reaction of many respondents was disbelief (*ibid.*, p. 14).

Raising and spending public money is a task that remains largely in the hands of the British government; it is ultimately an intensely political process because it is about who benefits from government activity, and who pays for those benefits. It is difficult for governments to make substantial shifts in the level or composition of public expenditure in the short run. Approaching three-fifths of public expenditure is devoted to social security (nearly 30 per cent of all expenditure), health and education. Within the social-security category, approaching half is spent on the elderly, a quarter on the sick and disabled and nearly a fifth on the family. Less than 10 per cent goes on the unemployed.

Most of these categories of expenditure are politically popular and substantially affected by demographic and other factors that are beyond the control of politicians. For example, health spending takes place in the context of an ageing population, continuing advances in medical technology and treatments and rising public expectations. Moreover, there is no guarantee that increasing expenditure will actually lead to higher standards of service or improved levels of public satisfaction.

Politicians have to find ways of raising funds that are, at least, not actively resisted by citizens, something which led to the end of the community charge or 'poll tax' and the fuel-duty escalator. The search for new ways of raising funds has led to an increasing reliance on 'stealth taxes' and has produced an increasingly more complex tax system that is itself the subject of increasing public complaint. During the 1980s and 1990s, the conventional wisdom, established by Mrs Thatcher and endorsed by New Labour, was that income tax, or at least the standard rate, should be reduced. Hence there was a shift from direct to indirect taxation, but increasing reliance on indirect taxes finally ran up against public resistance in the petrol protests of the autumn of 2000. Even the Conservatives have abandoned their long-term commitment to reducing the basic rate of income tax, realizing that it is no longer a vote winner with sceptical electors who realize that such cuts have to be recouped elsewhere.

The latest fashion is for hypothecation, linking particular taxes to particular aspects of spending, thus hopefully 'reconnecting' payments and services in the public mind. After a careful review of the debate, which acknowledged the competing arguments and difficulties, the Commission on Taxation and Citizenship set up under the auspices of the Fabian Society recommended a hypothecated NHS tax. The main argument in favour was that such a tax would 'make a significant contribution to making people feel more "connected" to the tax system' (Commission on Taxation and Citizenship, 2000, p. 184). There are, of course, limits to how far this process can go. Different voters cannot have different levels of provision to suit their personal preferences; there is a balance to be struck between individual choice and the public good. Finance ministries have never liked hypothecation, and it has consistently been opposed by the Treasury:

In each individual case, hypothecation looks attractive. In the round, however, it has the potential to prove disastrous. By the time revenue has been hyptothecated slice by slice in this way, the Treasury would have none left to pay for services for which no one wants hypothecation, such as defence. (Lipsey, 2000, p. 144)

The difficulties of decision-makers are enhanced by the fact that it is notoriously difficult to accurately forecast revenues and expenditures; this has been a long-standing problem. The Treasury's survey of the 1958–64 period refers to 'the inability of the forecasters to make a correct appraisal of the level of the economy at the time of the forecast ... This weakness was mainly due to the fact that most sources of information then available were wholly inadequate' (PRO: T 267/20, p. 11). Forecasts of the extent and timing of economic upturns and downturns are still unreliable, and the condition of the economy has a substantial effect on flows of taxation and expenditure. If anything, levels of revenue are more difficult to predict than patterns of expenditure. For example, during the first Blair government, revenues were higher than forecast, even allowing for the buoyant state of the economy. In part this was attributed to the new self-assessment system of taxation which seemed to be more efficient in collecting revenues, but no one really knew.

Long-term trends in public expenditure and taxation

The twentieth century saw a massive expansion in the role of government in advanced industrial countries. Starting from its 'night watchman' role of providing defence against external enemies, internal order and a reliable currency, government became increasingly involved in the provision of education in the nineteenth century. This role was expanded in the twentieth century, along with a new range of responsibilities in health, housing, pensions and social welfare. Both the First and Second World Wars led to substantial increases in public expenditure, and the reductions after each war saw public expenditure settle at a new plateau. However, it was 'particularly the period between 1960 and 1980 [that] saw an unprecedented enthusiasm for activist expenditure polices coupled with rapid growth in the involvement of the government in the economy' (Tanzi and Schuknecht, 2000, p. 10). After 1980, not least in Britain, there was an attempt to drive back the boundaries of the state. This may have at least prevented a further increase in the public expenditure share of GDP, the achievement of which had been seen as a positive goal by Labour in the 1960s.

If we look at public expenditure aggregates in terms of total managed expenditure (TME) as a percentage of GDP, as measured by the Treasury, the level in 1963–64, the last full year of the long period of Conservative government was 38.4 per cent. It then increased quite rapidly, reaching a peak of 44.1 per cent in 1967–68. As the post-devaluation measures started to bite, it started to fall again, bottoming out at 41.5 per cent in 1972–73. Economic circumstances then saw it rise sharply again, reaching a postwar peak of 49.9 per cent in 1975–76. As the IMF measures started to impact on public expenditure, it fell back again to 44.8 per cent in 1979–80. The initial recession under Mrs Thatcher saw it rise again to a peak of 48.5 per cent in 1982–83, after which it started a long fall to 39.2 per cent in 1988–89, still above the 1963–64 level. As recession took hold it rose again, reaching a peak of 44.2 per cent in 1992–93. It then started to fall back again, dropping to 38.3 per cent in 1999–00, the first time it had fallen below the 1963–64 level. Even the projected increases in the following years would only take it up to 39.6 per cent in 2001–02.

What is evident from these figures is that there is no apparent correlation between the party in office and the public expenditure share of GDP. The state of the economy appears to be a more powerful predictor of short-term fluctuations. Over the long run, however, the public expenditure share of GDP remains remarkably stable, leaving aside the high peak of the mid-1970s. The level at the beginning of the twenty-first century was remarkably similar to that in the early 1960s. Of course, these aggregate figures concealed some changes in the utilization of expenditure; defence and housing had fallen sharply as shares of the public expenditure total.

Despite the extent to which it is politicized, the long-run share of net taxes and social security contributions in GDP has remained remarkably stable. Between 1978–79 and 1999–2000 the range was between 33.3 per cent and 38.9 per cent, the peak being achieved in 1982–83. When Mrs Thatcher came into office in 1979–80, taxes accounted for 34 per cent of GDP and in her last full year in office (1989–90) they accounted for 36.3 per cent. The figure fell away to a low of 33.3 per cent in 1993–94, but then climbed again to reach 35.2 per cent in the last full year of the Major government (1996–97).

These relatively stable aggregates conceal the fact that the tax system in 2000 was 'very different from the one that existed' in 1979:

The income tax rate structure is transformed, the taxation of saving has been repeatedly adjusted, the National Insurance contributions system has been overhauled, the VAT rate has more than doubled, some excise duty rates have risen sharply while others have fallen, the corporate income tax system has been subject to two wholesale reforms and many smaller changes, and local taxation is unrecognisable. (Chennels, Dilnot and Roback, 2000, p. 17)

There has been a doubling of the share of revenue coming from VAT, offset by a fall in excise duties and other indirect taxes. 'This is a pattern mirrored across the developed world as there has been a shift away from indirect taxes levied on specific goods towards general consumption taxes such as VAT' (*ibid.*). The share of revenues accounted for by income tax dropped from 29 per cent in 1978–79 to 26 per cent in 2000–01 and was offset by a rise in the share of corporation tax. However, the overall balance between direct and indirect taxes has changed very little: 'The shift from direct to indirect tax, which was central to the declared strategy of the 1979–97 Conservative Government, seems not to have been achieved' (*ibid.*, p. 18).

What has disappeared is the very high rates of taxation which applied to incomes in 1979, with an effective top rate of 98 per cent. Such very high rates can encourage elaborate avoidance schemes, so that they collect very little additional revenue; they may, arguably, discourage entrepreneurship, and they may encourage people to live abroad. The Fabian Society survey found that 'There is fairly widespread acceptance of the idea that people with very large incomes should pay higher taxes than at present' (Hedges and Bromley, 2000, p. 2). An idea that is often floated, and which has some support, would be a rate of 50 per cent on taxable incomes above £100 000 a year. Acceptance or rejection of such a proposal can be seen as one litmus test that distinguishes old from new Labour.

What is often not realized is the relatively low point at which the higher 40 per cent tax band starts to apply. An income of above £33 000 a year in 2001, little more than 1.5 times average income, makes a taxpayer liable to the higher rate. As a consequence, 'the number of higher-rate taxpayers has grown substantially, from less than 3% of the taxpaying population in 1979–80 to nearly 10% [in 2000]' (Chennels, Dilnot and Roback, 2000, p. 19). This top 10 per cent of taxpayers 'now pay half of all the income tax paid, and the top 1% pay 20% of all that is paid. These shares have risen substantially since 1978–79, despite the reductions in the higher rates' (*ibid.*, p. 20).

The control of public expenditure

Efforts to control public expenditure have been a central theme of British economic policy-making over the last 40 years. Control is necessary for a variety of purposes, including ensuring that the aggregate public expenditure target is not exceeded; that money is spent for the purposes for which it was allocated; and that money is used as effectively as possible so that 'value for money' is achieved. Failure to control public expenditure may undermine the government's credibility, not just with the electorate and media, but more importantly with the international financial institutions and markets.

Plowden and the PESC system

The system of public expenditure management and control was changed fundamentally by the Plowden Report of 1961. This led to the establishment of the Public Expenditure Survey Committee (PESC system) which introduced a comprehensive and centralized examination of public expenditure plans within a multi-year framework (initially five years, later three). Although this system was subsequently to encounter considerable difficulties, it should be remembered how inadequate the arrangements were before the reforms were introduced:

> The report of the Estimates Committee (1958) which preceded the establishment of the Plowden investigation convinced most observers and participants that the procedures inherited from earlier generations with a minimal public sector were now chaotic and inadequate. Decisions were taken within a framework which stressed a single financial year without regard to the momentum or profile of expenditure commitments. (Heald, 1983, p. 174)

The general political context in which the new arrangements were introduced was not conducive to effective control of public expenditure:

> The tighter five-year programming machinery introduced by the Treasury from 1962 onwards for public expenditure as a whole was intended to bring better order to this field; but it in fact coincided with the most rapid and ill-timed growth of public expenditure during this period. (PRO: T 267/20, p. 62)

Post-devaluation measures reflected in the 1968 Public Expenditure White Paper ushered in a more effective implementation of the system. Quantitative targets over a five-year period were now published and taken more seriously by ministers. 'More effort was now given to ensuring that the planned reductions were achieved, and that pressures for additional expenditure were contained' (Thain and Wright, 1995, p. 40).

The breakdown of PESC and the introduction of cash limits

The PESC system broke down in the mid-1970s. In particular, there was a public debate about 'the missing £5 billion' that referred to the way in which actual expenditure in 1974–75 could not be explained in terms of the plans made in 1971. A number of defects in the PESC system came to the surface: 'The main problem was the use of volume terms planning in a time of high inflation' (Deakin and Parry, 2000, p. 37). The crisis gave the Treasury the opportunity to reassert control of public expenditure, with 'The imposition of cash limits in 1976 [marking] the end of the classic PESC regime' (*ibid.*, p. 39).

Cash limits placed a limit on the net amount of cash that could be spent on a given service within a financial year. They thus helped to overcome the problem of a lack of information and monitoring over the way in which money was actually being spent, and in particular the lack of control over local-authority expenditure. One of the political attractions of cash limits was that they pushed decisions about cuts in public expenditure down to programme managers and then to line managers who deliver the services. Cash limits can be changed during the course of the financial year to meet political pressures on particular programmes, but they are particularly helpful in enabling the Treasury to curb spending above projected totals because 'underspending on the aggregate of cash limited programmes is a persistent and consistent phenomenon' (Thain and Wright, 1992, p. 201).

The new measures introduced in 1976 include a tightening of rules relating to the Contingency Reserve. This was an unallocated pot of money that allowed flexibility in increasing public expenditure without revising the planning totals. It was therefore tempting for ministers to try and 'dip into' it, particularly if they had been disappointed during the public expenditure round. After 1976 it was used much more as a control device, and more emphasis was given to 'the desirability of funding additional spending through savings on other programmes. The Reserve became a fund of last resort' (*ibid.*, p. 343).

The Thatcher government's framework

The general framework for the Thatcher government's approach to public expenditure was set by the Medium-Term Financial Strategy (MTFS) announced in 1980. In particular, it set targets for the public-sector borrowing requirement (PSBR), and it was this aspect of the MTFS that was the most successful. The 'PSBR declined as a proportion of GDP from the crisis levels of the mid-1970s and the generation of a budget surplus in the four financial years from 1987–8 to 1990–1 had last been achieved by Roy Jenkins in 1969–70' (Thain and Wright, 1995, p. 23).

Another important turning point was the introduction of cash planning in 1982. One of the reasons why it is difficult to control public expenditure is that inflation affecting the public sector is generally higher than that in the private sector. This reflects the fact that public-sector activities are more labour-intensive. It may also be more difficult to secure productivity gains in the public sector because many of its activities tend to be technologically non-progressive, offering little scope for economies of scale, capital accumulation and innovation, a phenomenon known as Baumol's disease (Baumol, 1967). An alternative explanation is that there are fewer incentives for efficiency in the public sector, suggesting that one solution can be found in contracting out as many services as possible to the private sector. Whatever the cause, the tendency of public-sector costs to rise faster than private-sector costs posed significant problems for the control of public expenditure.

The original system of volume planning operated up to the mid-1970s, in effect, indexed public-sector expenditure. If the cost of goods and services being provided by the public sector 'rose at a higher rate than the rate planned, additional cash was provided to buy them' (Likierman, 1988, p. 12). This was unworkable in conditions of high inflation, so that after the mid-1970s an inflation assumption was built into public expenditure plans. If this was exceeded, cuts had to be made. However, each type of expenditure had its own 'survey price' so that departments were able to recoup fully any increase in prices and costs in their own area of activity relative to the general price level. 'Cash planning provided a means to exert continuous downward pressure on costs, especially pay and jobs' (Thain and Wright, 1992, p. 54).

In practice, many public expenditure decisions under the Thatcher government were thrashed out in bilateral meetings between the

Chief Secretary to the Treasury (the minister for public expenditure) and each spending minister which began in July each year and were often completed during the party conference in October. 'It was a matter of virility for spending ministers to put in bids well above anything remotely consistent with the overall envelope agreed by Cabinet' (Lawson, 1992, p. 288). Spending ministers tried to win popular support by leaking stories to the press. If the Chief Secretary and the spending minister could not arrive at a compromise, then there might be a meeting with the Chancellor or even one involving the Prime Minister. The final resort was to the 'Star Chamber', a committee of non-spending ministers chaired until 1988 by Willie Whitelaw. Viewed as a whole, the process was rather messy and highly politicized. 'Unsystematic bargaining during the autumn became the norm' (Deakin and Parry, 2000, p. 41). Matters were not helped by the fact that the Chancellor, Nigel Lawson, was preoccupied with other issues such as taxation reform.

Reforms under Major

The Major government thus faced a situation in which the system of public expenditure control was again not working properly. The extent to which this was the case in the late 1980s was masked by rapid economic growth that enabled the ratio to GDP to fall. Major 'was clear that we needed a "top-down" system in which the Cabinet agreed the maximum sum the economy could afford, and the public expenditure round allocated this sum between departments' (Major, 1999, p. 666). The government devised a new arrangement, the Expenditure Committee of the Cabinet (known as the EDX committee), which is generally agreed to have worked quite well, although perhaps less so towards the end of the government's term of office. The EDX committee was different from the 'Star Chamber' as it was chaired by the Chancellor and serviced by Treasury officials. It was meant to offer regular scrutiny of departments rather than operating as a 'court of appeal'. When ministers appeared before it 'the discussion focused on conformity to the control total rather than the merits of departmental bids' (Deakin and Parry, 2000, p. 49). Bilateral discussions with the Chief Secretary became much less important. It should be noted that Ken Clarke kept 'a large contingency reserve which he could release for spectacular new announcements each year' (Lipsey, 2000, p. 165). Nevertheless, 'The 1992 pre-election spending spree was probably the last of the line of departmentally driven incremental relaxations for which a price had to be paid afterwards' (Deakin and Parry, 2000, p. 60).

Golden rules?

Trends in public expenditure and taxation under the Blair government are discussed more fully later in the chapter. Here the discussion will be confined to the structure of the new arrangements for controlling public expenditure introduced by the new government. The overall framework for fiscal policy is set by the two rules referred to in Chapter 2 that are designed to enhance its credibility. The 'golden rule' requires the public sector to borrow only to invest; current spending must be financed from tax receipts. To achieve this, there must be a surplus on current budget over the economic cycle. The 'sustainable investment' rule requires net public-sector debt to be kept stable as a share of GDP, which the government has judged should be no more than 40 per cent. It should be noted that

> The government has provided no justification for a net debt target of 40 per cent of GDP – it could just as easily have chosen 38 per cent or 42 per cent. The Maastricht Treaty, for instance, allows UK gross general government debt of no more than 60 per cent of GDP, which is consistent with net public debt being considerably higher than 40 per cent. (Emmerson and Frayne, 2001, p. 2)

The debt rule imposes a limit on public-sector net borrowing which, for any given surplus on current budget, places a constraint on public investment.

These rules are not uncontentious. As Emmerson and Frayne comment (2001, p. 2), 'There is nothing sacrosant about these two rules, nor are they necessarily optimal.' One problem is that it is not easy to precisely determine what constitutes current spending and what counts as investment. For example, is spending on various forms of training current spending or does it count as an investment in human capital? The golden rule also implies levels of borrowing that are historically very low and might lead to lower levels of public investment than are desirable, given evident deficiencies in the country's infrastructure. Public-sector net investment as a percentage of GDP was 0.6 per cent in the three years from 1997–98 to 1999–00. It is also by no means clear that the rules promote intergenerational equity since each generation pays for its current spending as the government claims. Spending may benefit taxpayers differentially according to their age and the benefits received are sensitive to life expectancy.

Some commentators thus consider that the rules are too stringent, while others regard them as too loose. IMF economists have for some time questioned the rule which allows a deficit to be run to fund investment, 'arguing that it does not sufficiently restrain government spending. An IMF working paper critical of the golden rule was drafted [in 2000] but never published' (*Financial Times*, 28 February 2001). The IMF returned to the attack in its annual 'Article 4' health check on the UK economy in 2001, recommending 'that it would be preferable to fund all public investment through higher public saving, i.e., to maintain a surplus or broad overall balance over the cycle' (IMF, 2001, p. 2). The low level of private savings in the UK reinforces the case for higher government savings. 'The chancellor apparently takes the view that no more need be demanded of fiscal policy if his rules are met. A more sensible position would be that meeting the rules is a necessary, but not a sufficient, condition for a sound fiscal policy' (Wolf, 2001, p. 23).

New Labour effectively abolished the annual public expenditure cycle. Public expenditure (now to be known as Total Managed Expenditure TME) was divided into two halves. One half was to be managed through three-year Departmental Expenditure Limits set in cash terms. The other half, called Annually Managed Expenditure (AME), is subject to annual review as part of the budget process and is largely made up of social security expenditure and debt interest. The annual spending rounds and the Fundamental Expenditure Reviews introduced by the Conservatives are replaced by Comprehensive Spending Review (CSRs) which have so far occurred in 1998 and 2000. They are intended to look at government spending as a whole and trade-offs and linkages between programmes. Departments are given measurable targets for their public service objectives in terms of Public Service Agreements. What all this amounts to is a substantial reassertion of Treasury control over public expenditure. If the Treasury can maintain its political and technical strength, it is possible that the battle to secure control over public expenditure may finally have been won.

Devolution and the Barnett formula

One major problem remains unresolved, how the system of public expenditure control can cope with a new political system in which substantial authority is devolved, particularly to the Scottish

Executive and Parliament. Deakin and Parry (2000, p. 177) pose the question, 'We may ask how far the Treasury is a product of the unitary United Kingdom and as such is an obsolescent institution.'

The Barnett Formula was developed in 1978 by the then Chief Secretary to the Treasury, Joel Barnett, as a means of apportioning public expenditure between England, Wales, Scotland and Northern Ireland. Barnett does not mention the formula in his book on life in the Treasury and clearly did not realize its significance at the time. He told the Treasury Committee (1997, Q.1) in evidence, 'At the time, I must confess, I did not think it would last a year or even twenty minutes.'

Essentially, the formula has been a means of depoliticizing disputes about the territorial allocation of public expenditure, given that the territories do rather better per capita than England. Barnett saw it as a means of making life 'a trifle easier' as he would 'have to handle only English departments'. Spending ministers 'could not say anything about the allocation to Scotland and Wales because they, in Cabinet, had agreed it' (Treasury Committee, 1997, Q.1). The depoliticization thesis is confirmed by the Blair government's view that the formula has ' "produced a fair and politically acceptable distribution of funds over a long period", avoided "the need for annual negotiations between the centre and Scotland, Wales and Northern Ireland" and is simple' (Treasury Committee, 1997, p. vii). Perhaps the key features identified here are political acceptability and low transaction costs.

The original formula was based on an 85 per cent (England), 10 per cent (Scotland) and 5 per cent (Wales) population-based calculation of changes in shares of comparable expenditure in Britain. Slightly different formula arrangements were agreed at the same time with Northern Ireland. The formula was not adjusted until 1992,

> ostensibly to reflect the results of the 1991 Census, but of equal importance in the decision to revise it was the Chief Secretary's attempt to keep total spending in line with published targets. This change ... benefited Wales and Northern Ireland at the expense of Scotland. (Thain and Wright, 1995, p. 324)

The formula is a way of 'sharing out changes in public expenditure plans between the countries of the Union. It is not used to determine their overall levels' (Treasury Committee, 1997, p. v). Proposed changes in UK-wide spending are first multiplied by a comparability percentage, intended to reflect the importance of the programme to the devolved administrations. The outcome is then multiplied by the relevant population proportion (which can be expressed as a percentage of the English population, or of that of England and Wales, or of Great Britain). As a result, the budgets available to the secretaries of state were added to, or subtracted from. They could make adjustments at the margin in the allocation of funds, although substantial changes were difficult because of continuing commitments.

The Barnett formula was supposed to lead to convergence of public spending over time, but has not done so because of low inflation and different population growth rates. Thus, in 2001 public spending was about £5270 per capita in Scotland, compared with £4280 in England and £5050 in Wales:

> Moreover, Scotland gets 16 per cent per head more than the north-east of England, even though Scottish gross domestic product per head is more than 20 per cent higher than its closest English neighbour. The evidence is clearly visible in the decaying fabric of Northumberland schools against their Scottish counterparts. (*Financial Times*, 21 April 2001)

The classic defence offered by Scottish officials is that extra spending is justified by Scotland's size and low population density which makes some services more expensive. However, as Professor Arthur Midwinter commented in evidence to the Treasury Committee (1997, Appendix 1):

> [It] is important to recognise that this higher spending is *not* based on any rigorous, systematic appraisal of . . . needs as used in local government or the health service. Rather the differential rests on its political acceptability. It is certainly the case that Scotland has higher expenditure needs than the average of the UK, reflecting its higher morbidity rates; the sparse population in remote areas; or the degree of poverty. The *extent* of this [*sic*] higher needs has never been established with precision, because precision in needs assessment models is impossible.

The Treasury Committee (1997, p. viii) was 'disappointed that no Government studies have been made in relation to the appropriateness of the Barnett Formula and how it relates to needs.' They called for the needs assessment to be brought up to date which 'would help to show whether the Barnett Formula remains the appropriate method of allocating annual expenditure increases (or savings) to the four nations of the Union'. In the context of the introduction of devolution, this intervention was not welcomed. The government did not wish to abandon a politically convenient formula that was popular in Scotland and Wales, nor did they wish to have to engage in awkward annual negotiations about block grants to the devolved parliaments.

However, the issue did not go away and indeed became more prominent as discussion of the possibility of English regional assemblies increased. Resentment increased among northern Labour MPs, while the mayor of London, Ken Livingstone, accused the government of taxing Londoners to fund Scottish spending. In April 2001, John Prescott suggested that the time had come to 'bite the bullet' on the issue, in a statement interpreted as a shot across the Chancellor's bows. A spokesman for Tony Blair quickly announced that the formula was working well and there were no plans to change it. (*Financial Times*, 25 April 2001). Indeed, it can only be changed with the agreement of the Chancellor, the Scottish and Welsh secretaries and the devolved administrations.

A broader issue is that around 8 per cent of public spending is now decided by the devolved governments of Scotland, Wales and Northern Ireland. The Scottish Executive can levy up to an extra 3p on basic-rate income tax, although Labour has promised not to use this power until after the next Scottish elections in 2003. The Scottish Executive and Assembly have shown a propensity to undertake more ambitious spending plans than those favoured south of the border. Abolishing students' tuition fees cost £50 million a year, while the installation of central heating for pensioners and social housing tenants who do not have it will cost £20 million. A generous pay settlement for teachers will cost £350 million by 2003–04, and may have knock-on effects on other public-sector pay settlements. £27 million was also allocated to a decommissioning scheme for Scottish fishermen. After pressure from their Liberal Democrat coalition partners, the Scottish Executive had to make a U-turn and promise free and universal personal care for all Scotland's elderly with an initial cost of £100 million a year.

All this might be seen as an example of the vigour of the new Scottish democracy. After all, there is little point in having a Scottish Assembly and Executive if it can't pursue distinctive policies. The additional spending adopted up to the spring of 2001 can be accommodated within the existing budget envelope; however, it does produce equity arguments that similar provision should be made south of the border. For example, payment for personal as well as nursing care for the elderly would cost £1 billion should it be introduced in England. The British government regards it as a poor use of public funds as it would benefit a lot of relatively well-off elderly people. Scotland may therefore develop an agenda-setting role in relation to public expenditure issues that may disturb the stringent equilibrium established in the 1990s.

Taxation and the budget

There is a much more extensive literature on the politics of public expenditure in Britain than there is on taxation and the budget. No doubt this reflects the secrecy with which the budget-making process has traditionally been shrouded. The process has always started with a series of often rather ritualistic meetings with various pressure groups. 'The most important lobbyists may get to see a minister. Less important lobbyists will see officials, or be confined to written representations' (Lipsey, 2000, p. 126). After spending a long period in 'purdah', during which time he would make no speeches or hold no meetings with lobbyists, the Chancellor arrives at an overall Budget judgement about how much he should 'take out' of the economy or 'give back' to taxpayers. The Budget is a mechanism for achieving general economic objectives, so the Budget judgement has to be made in the light of the ranking of those objectives, the condition of the economy, and forecasts of its future performance (which often turn out to be unreliable). Some major decisions about new taxes, or the abolition or reduction of certain taxes, can be taken at a relatively early stage. In the case of the 2001 budget, this probably happened in the case of the betting tax that was being rendered ineffective by the spread of offshore betting offices. Although much of the Budget may be anticipated in advance, the Chancellor may try to include a 'surprise' element in the package to make it more attractive and to outmanoeuvre the opposition.

Nevertheless, real innovation in tax policy remains difficult. Economists have argued that the most effective way to tackle environmental problems is to use the price mechanism by introducing new taxes. From a Treasury perspective, this offered the opportunity of new, politically correct sources of revenue. In his 1999 budget, the Chancellor mentioned 22 environmental taxes. However, these attracted considerable resistance from business interests. For example, the climate-change levy had to be modified both in terms of the amount to be raised and through offering discounts to energy-intensive industries that offered to negotiate agreements on cutting pollution. A senior Treasury official commented, 'What we needed was fewer stories about threatened steel plants and more about threatened seal pups' (*Financial Times*, 15 March 2000). The raising of taxes is ultimately a highly political business that is constrained by what public opinion and influential pressure groups will accept.

Throughout the process of drafting the Budget, the Chancellor remains in close contact with the Prime Minister. The Cabinet plays a much more limited role in drawing up tax plans than it does in expenditure decisions, and it is informed by the Chancellor of the contents of the Budget speech on the morning before its delivery. The day then proceeds in accordance with the rituals of one of the great days of the parliamentary calendar. The Chancellor leaves No.11 Downing Street, raising the red box containing his Budget speech for the benefit of the photographers. Gordon Brown has often been photographed with his whole Treasury team. The Chancellor reads his speech to an overflowing chamber, while in television and radio studios a host of commentators give an instant interpretation of the Chancellor's pronouncements. In the City, dealers wait in front of their screens to see if there is any reaction from the securities and foreign exchange markets. The evening news programmes and the next day's newspapers will assess its impact on 'typical' families ranging from a single parent to a household in the higher tax bracket.

Norman Lamont tried to change the format of the Budget by introducing a single unified Budget covering both spending and taxation plans (although the first of these was actually introduced by his successor, Ken Clarke). Lamont considered that this separation encouraged unrealistic expectations about expenditure and pressure for gimmicks and special tax reliefs that contributed to the complexity of the tax system. He was opposed by Treasury officials who were concerned that the proposal would intensify workloads and weaken the Treasury's position in Whitehall (Lamont, 1999, p. 166). There was concern that 'taxes would no longer be decided by the Treasury alone. They would become a subject of collective discussion, decision even, by Cabinet' (Lipsey, 2000, p. 123).

These fears do not seem to have been realized. In any event, the unified Budget was abolished by Gordon Brown. He did, however, introduce a green Budget in the autumn that restates the government's economic strategy and gives some, often quite a considerable, indication of his thinking on taxation. It has been argued that this can become a mini-Budget with politically attractive concessions. More generally, 'the Treasury is not as fearful as it used to be that giving details in advance will merely spark opposition and avoidance measures' (Lipsey, 2000, p. 132). This somewhat greater openness, and the use of the mini-Budget, means that the Budget contains fewer surprises than it used to and its presentation is less of a dramatic occasion. If, however, there has been a real move away from a 'boom and bust' economy, there should be less need to make adjustments to the economy in the Budget. Rather, it should be used to further develop agreed microeconomic policy lines such as fostering job-creation, training and research and development. As economic policy has become less macroeconomic in character, this has been reflected in the Budget as well.

Taxation and expenditure under the Blair government

One of the issues for debate about the Blair government is how far its policies represent a continuation of a Thatcherite paradigm. In its first term of office, it offered the curious picture of a 'tax and not spend' government. Looking at the taxation side first, the real annual average increase in taxes was over twice as high as under the Conservatives from 1979 to 1997. Total government spending in the period to 2000–01 increased less rapidly in real terms than under the Conservatives from 1979 to 1997, although at the same rate as in the Thatcher years. If one extends the analysis forward to 2001–02, then the real average annual increase in spending exceeds the average for 1979–87, although it is still below the figure for the Major years (Table 5.1).

Table 5.1   Real average annual increase in taxation and spending

Period	Total taxes	Total government spending
Thatcher years	2.0	1.2
Major years	1.3	2.6
Conservatives, 1979–97	1.8	1.6
Blair to March 2001	4.8	1.3
Blair to March 2002	4.1	1.9

Source: Institute of Fiscal Studies data.

Developments in taxation are open to a number of interpretations: 'It is possible to calculate figures to show that Gordon Brown has either increased taxes by £21 bn a year, or by £6bn a year, or cut them by £1bn a year' (Crooks, 2001, p. 8). The cut of £1 billion is produced by excluding all increases in duty as a result of the escalators on fuel duty and tobacco on the grounds that they were introduced by the previous Conservative government. However, the fact that the Conservatives introduced them did not prevent Mr Brown from abolishing them, as he eventually did with the fuel duty escalator. The £6 billion figure is produced by adding up all the changes in Budgets since 1997 and comparing this figure with what would have happened if the Chancellor had simply increased allowances and duties in line with inflation each year. The £21 billion figure is produced by comparing the share of taxes and social-security contributions in GDP in 1996–97 (35.2 per cent) with the figure in 2000–01 (37.7 per cent): 'That rise of 2.5 percentage points in the tax take is equivalent to about £21 bn a year at today's prices' (Crooks, 2001, p. 8).

Some of this increase in tax revenues is not due to decisions by the Chancellor; the rise in the number of people on higher incomes, for example, has pushed up income-tax receipts. The money raised from the third generation mobile telephone licenses might be regarded as a windfall gain, and in other cases changes in the tax base have led to increased revenues. For example, the phasing out of tax relief on profit-related pay and the abolition of the payment of dividend tax credits to pension funds was estimated to have raised income-tax receipts by £1.7 billion and £5.4 billion a year respectively. Nevertheless, the Chancellor could have offset these increased receipts by tax cuts and chose not to do so. He must therefore take responsibility for the greater portion of the tax increases. In keeping taxes relatively high, however, he was behaving prudently. Given the view that interest rates have been too high and the pound too strong, it is hard to argue that taxes should have been lower. One way to bring down the value of the pound would have been to have even higher taxes. The government claimed at the time of the 2001 Budget that the ratio of net taxes and social security contributions to GDP would fall steadily over the following three years because of factors such as tax cuts announced in that Budget and slightly weaker projections of GDP growth.

'Up until 1999–2000, all of the additional real increase in taxes was used to reduce public borrowing. Public spending in the first three years of the parliament was actually lower in real terms than the Conservatives' plans' (Institute of Fiscal Studies, 2001, p. 11). The Chancellor announced that the government would adhere to the Conservatives' spending plans for their first two years in office. This policy was subsequently criticized by his predecessor, Ken Clarke, who said he would never have adhered to them if the Conservatives had retained power. Mr Brown had imposed a spending freeze on unsuspecting cabinet colleagues who had not thought through their new portfolios. 'The result was that, for no good reason, he squeezed public spending so that it fell to the lowest level since the 1960s. So he began as a public spending-cutting Chancellor when he didn't need to' (*Independent*, 22 February 2001).

The July 1998 CSR planned a significant rise in public spending for the three years starting from 1999–2000; these plans were not fulfilled:

> The significant growth in spending envisaged by the first CSR had, up to the end of 1999–2000, failed to materialise. Compared with initial plans, there has been a considerable underspend on cyclical items of expenditure, such as social security spending and debt interest, as well as on discretionary items across many programmes and departments. Throughout this parliament, public spending in each year has turned out lower than initial plans and forecasts. (Institute of Fiscal Studies, 2001, p. 23)

Admittedly, the biggest undershoot was in AME because of the buoyancy of the economy. 'Within AME, social security spending was £3.3 billion lower than expected despite an addition of almost £900 million to social security spending in Budget 1999' (*ibid.*, p. 24). However, 'there was also a considerable shortfall in departmental spending' (*ibid.*, p. 25); half of this was due to a shortfall in planned net investment. What is of particular concern is that 'underspends may also have arisen because departments have been unable to spend up to the plans set out for them – for example, because of recruitment problems or problems getting capital projects off the ground' (*ibid.*, p. 27). In the financial year to April 2001, government departments spent £6.2 bn less than their budgets, and departments in areas where the government was keen to improve public services undershot their spending targets significantly. For example, the (then) education and employment department underspent its £19 bn budget by £1.4 bn, there was a £860 m shortfall at the Department of the Environment, Transport and Regions and £500 m at the Department of Health (*Financial Times*, 24 June 2001).

The CSR in July 2000 made provision for an increase in public spending of £68 bn between then and 2003. Departmental expenditure was projected to increase in real terms by 5.3 per cent a year, offset by a 0.7 per cent growth rate in AME. However, even by 2003–04, the proportion of public expenditure to GDP would be lower than it was immediately before Labour came into office. 'Even after all the increases, TME will account for only 40.5 per cent of national income, less than in all but three years of the Conservative government of 1996–7, and compared to 41.2 per cent in 1996–97' (*Financial Times*, 19 July 2000). Even these increases caused international doubts about the Chancellor's commitment to prudent policies. The Executive Board of the IMF delivered a magisterial rebuke to the Chancellor, advising 'that it would be prudent to abstain from introducing significant new spending commitments or tax cuts in the March 2001 budget' (IMF, 2001, p. 2).

Brown's strategy encounters problems

The Chancellor's strategy faced two major problems. One was that the economy had not moved from 'boom and bust' to sustained growth, as his comments in April 2001 seemed to acknowledge. The margin for error in his plans was not great and they could be undermined by an economic downturn that depressed receipts and increased AME. Concerns in this area intensified after a prolonged period of economic slowdown seemed more likely after the events of September 2001. Second, there is a difference between spending public money and the expenditure actually making a difference in the delivery of public services as perceived by voters. The government hoped to use the mandate of its second term to put greater pressure on teachers, doctors and otherwise to improve quality of delivery, but there were already signs of increased resistance from the education and medical professions. The Blair government hoped to make greater use of private provision of public services, but there was considerable resistance from the public-sector unions who argued that the efficiency gains were largely illusory and made largely at the expense of driving down wages and working conditions for employees. If voters do not consider that public money is being spent effectively, disillusionment with the government may grow.

Up until 2001, Labour tax and public expenditure policies had been conducted in buoyant economic conditions which allowed Gordon Brown to cut taxes and give additional money to public services. The foot and mouth crisis in that year substantially depleted the contingency reserve. The war against terrorism suggested that further cuts in defence expenditure, which had been reduced from 5 per cent of national income in 1984 to just over 2 per cent in 2001, were unlikely. Nevertheless, the Gulf War only cost about 1 per cent of national income. The real pressure was likely to come from receipts growing less quickly than expected, making it more difficult to sustain average annual spending increases of 3.7 per cent above inflation. The Institute of Fiscal Studies suggested that this implied tax increases of around £5 bn a year (*Financial Times*, 17 October 2001). It is therefore significant that the Prime Minister inserted a section into a speech to public-sector workers that implied that the government might be prepared to make the case for higher taxes. He commented:

> I do believe that people can be persuaded that they have to pay for good public services. I don't believe the public is any longer fooled by the notion of short-term tax cuts at the expense of long-term investment (*Independent*, 17 October 2001)

Given that the government has ruled out increases in the rate of income tax, one possibility would be to raise the national insurance ceiling which would, of course, increase taxes on income.

Nevertheless, Labour's policies may seem to have been more cautious than those of the Conservatives, even allowing for the surge in public expenditure after 2000. However, there is one significant difference and that is in the use of the tax system for redistributive purposes. The Conservatives saw the taxation system as, in principle, a level playing field, but Gordon Brown has been prepared to make 'progressive' use of an increasingly integrated tax and benefits system. He has made it clear that he rejects 'both crude means-testing and old style tax system' in favour of something he calls 'progressive universalism'. This is seen as a modernised tax and benefit system 'under which the tax man can give money as well as take it, and designed to help families who need help most – when their children are young' (*Independent*, 5 February 2000). Reviewing the impact of changes such as the working families' tax credit, the Institute for Fiscal Studies found

> The post-tax income of an average household in the bottom decile of the income distribution is 8.8% higher if we take account of all measures introduced since May 1997. Further deciles gain proportionately less on average and the richest 30% of households experience a fall in post-tax income once all of the reforms are considered. (2000, p. 3)

The policies of Conservative and Labour governments do differ, but there is not such a sharp divide over 'tax and spend' policies as existed in the past, even if politicians would like to claim otherwise in partisan debate. The biggest difference is over whether there should be a distributive element in policy. 'Otherwise . . . and to an extent that previous generations would hardly have believed, the politics has gone out of macroeconomic policy'; Conservative and Labour chancellors 'do not have any real and fundamental differences about macroeconomic policy' (Lipsey, 2000, p. 115). There is, however, still a vigorous bureaucratic politics concerned with decisions about public expenditure in particular. Fiscal policy is 'still widely regarded as the Treasury's core power' (*ibid.*, p. 105).

Any shift of decision-making to the European level would be viewed with apprehension by most of the current participants in the policy process. Hence the sharp reaction in April 2001 to a European Commission proposal that spending on public services should be cut if the economy performed badly in the coming year. The Treasury commented, 'This is entirely a matter for individual member states. We believe the Commission has over-reached itself' (*Financial Times*, 26 April 2001). It would certainly mark the end of domestic economic policy as we have known it if decisions about public expenditure were to be substantially influenced by the EU.

6

The Supply Side and Competitiveness

Introduction

Industrial policy in the 1960s and 1970s was concerned with the management of decline; it sought to prop up declining industries and firms, easing the pain of the transition to a new type of economy. In many cases, the funds made available enabled firms that would have otherwise gone out of business to survive. By the 1990s, a new rhetoric had emerged. Michael Heseltine's Competitiveness White Papers presented a series of supply-side measures intended to improve the ability of British companies to compete in the international economy. This emphasis on a range of supply-side measures has been continued under New Labour, notably in the 2001 joint paper from the Treasury and the Department of Trade and Industry, *Productivity in the UK: Enterprise and the Productivity Challenge* (HM Treasury, 2001).

If anything had been learnt from the decline debate, it was that Britain was handicapped by poor performance in such areas as skill formation and the conversion of research findings into commercial innovations. UK expenditure on research and development declined throughout the 1990s, leading to Britain falling even further behind its competitors in terms of business research and development expenditure as a share of GDP. The UK also remained behind on indicators of innovation such as the number of patents generated by different countries (HM Treasury, 2001, p. 10).

Poor levels of productivity compared to competitor countries remain a central problem for the UK economy, as identified in the Treasury's 2001 paper:

UK productivity, however measured, lags that of other major industrialised countries. The labour productivity gap with the US was 45 per cent in 1999, that with France was 19 per cent and Germany 7 per cent ... If the UK were to match the productivity performance of the US, for example, output per head would be over £6,000 higher.

Another curious and persistent feature of the UK economy is that there is a considerable spread in the performance of the best and worst firms. At the beginning of the 1980s it was noted that

> There is...a particularly wide spread between the best and the worst firms within individual sectors in Britain, whether measured in terms of productivity or of wage levels, with the best firms well abreast of international competition. What is disturbing is the survival of a rather large tail of poor performers which have been neither squeezed out of existence nor forced to adopt best-practice techniques. (Jones, 1981, p. 147)

The recession at the beginning of the 1980s supposedly squeezed many of these poor performers out of business, leading to a 'batting-average' improvement in productivity levels. It is therefore disturbing to find that these discrepancies in performance at the firm level persist:

> Recent research has mapped out the gulf in productivity between the best and the worst manufacturing plants. The best are over five times more efficient than the worst ones...While there are bound to be differences in performance, the disparity between the high-fliers and the stragglers appears to be more pronounced than in other countries. (*The Economist*, 28 July 2001, p. 32)

This feature of the economy does tend to undermine cultural explanations of relatively poor economic performance which have been very influential. An anti-industrial or enterprise culture should have an equivalent effect on all firms. What this suggests is that some firms have been able to create their own cultures that are conducive to superior levels of performance. Of course, if such cultures become too deeply embedded, they may create a resistance to change within the firm which is ultimately self-defeating, Marks and Spencers offering a classic example.

This chapter has selected four aspects of supply-side policy for further examination. Competition policy has been chosen because it 'is at the heart of the Government's strategy to close the productivity gap' (HM Treasury, 2001, p. 19); it has displaced industrial policy at the heart of microeconomic policy. Transport policy is examined because the provision of an adequate transport infrastructure is essential to the success of a modern economy. It is the responsibility of government to provide at least a framework for transport policy and it is an area in which New Labour has been relatively unsuccessful. Skill formation is of central importance to New Labour's enterprise strategy and it will be examined. The privatized public utilities form an important part of the UK economy and the way in which they are regulated will be examined in relation to its impact on competition.

Competition policy

Competition policy is concerned with anything that inhibits the operation of free, fair and open competition between firms: conventionally control of monopolies, mergers, cartels and restrictive practices and, at an EU level, state aid. The Monopolies Commission was established in 1948 as part of the postwar settlement and legislation to control restrictive trade practices was enacted in 1956, followed by the passage of legislation to free up retail prices in 1964. Nevertheless, for a long time competition policy was a Cinderella branch of economic policy. When the Blair government consulted a group of competition-policy experts, they found that only 10 per cent of respondents thought that competition policy was important to the UK public, compared with 83 per cent of respondents in the USA (HM Treasury, 2001, p. 20).

Business persons may say they are in favour of maximum competition but, as Adam Smith warned, any meeting between them is likely to lead to a conspiracy against the public interest. Even if business did not exert a dominant influence on competition policy 'it was accorded a privileged position by officials who recognised the importance of sustaining co-operative relationships' (Wilks, 1999, p. 188). For government, 'Competition policy was the poor relation of industrial policy' (*ibid.* p. 345). Some policies pursued by government, such as the Labour government's attempt to promote mergers in the 1960s, seemed to contradict the key objectives of competition policy, but state-sponsored mergers were welcomed by business as a means of downgrading competition policy (Dell, 2000, p. 366).

Competition policy was largely bipartisan, but in a sense this reflected its lack of salience. 'Since the political parties did not develop strong views on competition, this policy area escaped the doctrinal inter-party conflict that dogged so much of supply-side policy, but it fell by default under the control of the civil service'

(Wilks, 1999, p. 189). This produced in turn an incrementalist approach to policy-making and a failure to face up to the need for change: 'The officials' instincts were to respect company autonomy, to privilege property rights and to conform to the "weak state" attitude that was part of the post-war settlement' (*ibid.*). It is therefore not surprising that 'the longest-standing element of [competition] policy', monopoly control, was 'arguably the least effective'. What prevented more effective control was 'the reluctance of government departments to refer potential problems to the [Monopolies and Mergers Commission]' (*ibid.*, p. 343). Britain developed one of the most concentrated economies in the world, and although concern about this issue diminished as the economy became more internationalized, that is not to say that it should be dismissed as a subject of concern.

Competition policy under New Labour

New Labour has given 'a whole new centrality and importance to competition policy'. It is evident that 'competition and the market are at the heart of the New Labour project' (Wilks, 1999, p. 349), and a stated New Labour objective is that 'competition policy should have a high profile – because of its importance for economic performance' (HM Treasury, 2001, p. 22). The other key operational principles advanced by New Labour were: competition decisions should be taken by strong, proactive and independent competition authorities; the regime should root out all forms of anti-competitive behaviour; there should be a strong deterrent effect; harmed parties should be able to get real redress; and government and the competition authorities should work for greater international consistency and cooperation (*ibid.*, p. 21). It is this last principle that is perhaps the most problematic, as will be discussed later.

New Labour takes the clear position that competition policy has been an historic weakness in a key area that can drive private-sector productivity growth:

> strong competition drives improvements in efficiency and innovation across the economy. Competition reduces prices and improves the quality of service for consumers whilst rewarding companies that innovate and operate efficiently. (HM Treasury, 2001, p. 2)

In reaching this conclusion, Labour is building on the one area where academic research appears to give a clear view about the underlying causes of productivity differences and the ability of governments to influence them: the more intense the competition, the more likely businesses are to innovate and grow. As in other policy areas, New Labour has drawn lessons from the United States that has had a strong anti-trust tradition since the late nineteenth century. Gordon Brown stated that 'I believe a step change in competitive pressures within the British economy is essential if we are to reach for US levels of productivity growth.' Competition policy before 1997 had 'unclear objectives [and] Byzantine procedures with inadequate penalties and was not properly transparent' (*Financial Times*, 19 June 2001).

The 1998 Competition Act introduced a major reform of competition policy, although a broadly tripartite institutional structure of the Office of Fair Trading (OFT), the Competition Commission (CC, formerly the Monopolies and Mergers Commission) and the Department of Trade and Industry (DTI) remained in place. Steps have been taken to improve the resourcing of the competition authorities as part of the government's strategy to enhance their status. The OFT sees its central task as making markets work well for consumers, and the Competition Act gave the OFT significant new powers of investigation, enforcement and punishment against firms that rig markets against the interests of consumers. It prohibits anti-competitive agreements and abuse of dominant market positions, rather than treating them as subjects for agnostic investigation as in the past. 'Dawn raids and encouraging whistle-blowing are now an established part of UK competition enforcement' (Office of Fair Trading, 2000, p. 9). Firms which breach the law face penalties of up to 10 per cent of their turnover in the market in question for up to three years of an infringement.

The OFT advises the Secretary of State for Trade and Industry which mergers should be referred for detailed examination to the CC. The CC is not a policy-making body: it investigates or adjudicates on matters that are specifically referred to it or come on appeal. New Labour policy has been to accept OFT advice in all but exceptional circumstances and the government plans to legislate to remove ministers from decision-making on competition matters, except where issues of national security arise. The current public interest test for determining mergers, which has been seen as both elastic and elusive, will be replaced by a more specific competition-based test, although it will be possible to take account of benefits arising to UK consumers from the merger. Quite what that would mean in practice if, for example, a media company attempted to acquire a football club, remains to be seen. When the CC finds that a merger is against the public interest, the OFT advises the Secretary of State for Trade and Industry on remedies and implements them. The Secretary of State is thus removed from the administrative process as regards actions and remedies.

Further reforms are proposed, including the complex monopoly provisions of the 1973 Fair Trading Act. These provisions have been very important in enabling competition policy to tackle industries which, even if they are not dominated by a single large company, exhibit reduced competition. Examples include inquiries into domestic electrical goods, cars, supermarkets and small-business banking conditions. However, provisions drafted 30 years ago need updating to improve their effectiveness. There will, however, continue to be greater ministerial intervention here than in other areas of competition policy, in effect because these issues could become more politicized or unduly strain the government's relationship with business.

The government also proposed to make engagement in cartels, which is seen as the most important form of competition breach, a criminal offence. The directors of companies engaged in cartels could be imprisoned, a power not available in any other large EU country. There will also be new civil procedures for those harmed by anti-competitive behaviour to seek redress, perhaps before a special competition court or tribunal.

The European dimension

The 1998 Competition Act was closely based on the relevant provisions of the Treaty of Rome, Articles 81 and 82. 'After years of not being European enough, some lawyers are suggesting that the Government has now become too European' (Wilks, 1999, p. 323). Historically, the DTI was often concerned with protecting the interests of British companies in European cartel cases, for example by seeking to reduce the level of fines. Monopolies and Mergers Commission cases increasingly came to be affected by European provisions or actions: 'For its part the OFT is in constant discussion with [the EU Competition Directorate] on a daily basis and on multiple issues. Since 1997 it has also begun to take part in the more substantive and delicate discussions in Brussels' (*ibid.*, p. 306).

Competition policy is very distinctive from many other aspects of EU policy; it is an area in which the relevant directorate-general of the Commission (the Competition Directorate, formerly DG IV) enjoys directive executive authority. In this area of policy 'the centre of gravity lies with the bureaucratic and juridicial institutions of the EU rather than the political and representative institutions' (McGowan, 2000, p. 123). The Competition Directorate's officials approach their task with an almost missionary zeal; they 'see themselves as situated on the moral high-ground, endowed with a mission to establish norms and to encourage working practices that promote competition' (Cini, 1997, p. 86).

'Monopoly policy is perhaps the weakest link in the Commission's competition policy chain' (Cini and McGowan, 1998, p. 80), having been eclipsed by the much more high-profile mergers policy introduced in 1990. It applies to large mergers involving firms operating in more than one member state. In 2001 the Competition Commissioner blocked General Electric's $48 billion bid for Honeywell, a merger that had already been approved by the US competition authorities. The EU may have been influenced by the fact that it cannot re-open investigations and take further action if a merged company 'misbehaves'. The case does illustrate how difficult it is to pursue the British government's stated aim of improved international cooperation in competition policy. The USA and the EU do operate a sophisticated system of competition policy cooperation known as the 'positive comity agreement' which allows each of them to raise concerns about the local impact of competition cases to the counterpart bodies across the Atlantic. That there was such disagreement on the GE–Honeywell case shows how difficult it is to operate and improve bilateral cooperation, let alone create some kind of global governance agency in this area which a globalized economy might eventually require.

The Commission has substantial powers in relation to cartels that it has exercised freely, often imposing large fines on companies, although its decisions are subject to appeal to the Court of Justice. The biggest fine to date was €273 million imposed in 1998 on a group of maritime freight companies. A number of cartels have been discovered in the steel industry and in 2001 the Commission imposed fines of €219 million for price fixing in the mini steel industry. The cement and chemical industries have also been the subject of a number of investigations. Participants in cartels have been discovered holding meetings in anonymous locations such as airport hotels or sending coded messages to one another through trade papers. The Commission's view is that cartels are 'one of the very worst ways of distorting competition' (*Financial Times*, 19 July 2001). However, it is converging its cartels policy with US practice in terms of allowing plea bargaining and reducing fines for firms who cooperate in investigations.

The Commission adopts a very broad definition of collusive behaviour and has, for example, used its powers to investigate and make changes to the European football transfer system, as well as looking into the way in which the television rights for Champions' League matches are sold. Although the Competition Directorate is generally seen as unusually resistant to business interests, it is not totally exempt from the Commission culture of reaching deals with big firms. It is therefore interesting that in the football transfer case, where matters were complicated by tensions between the European football federation (UEFA) and the global federation (FIFA), a key role in brokering a settlement was played by G-14, a grouping of Europe's largest football clubs.

State aid policy is the most controversial and politicized area of competition policy and the one most likely to bring the Competition Directorate into conflict with the member states. It is politically difficult for a member state if they are told that a subsidy that is intended to keep a factory in business, or encourage development in a backward region, is not compatible with competition rules. Nevertheless, overall levels of aid have been falling, although they are still considerable. In 1997 to 1999 state aid totalled €90 billion a year in the 15 member states compared with an annual average of €102 billion in the preceding three years.

Despite pledges by EU leaders to cut state aid, and declarations of a strict approach to its authorization, politics can override policy objectives. Indeed, the EU itself called for temporary aid for the shipbuilding sector in the summer of 2001. Political considerations were also evident in the struggle between member states and the Commission in the autumn of 2001 to limit the amount of aid given to 'national carrier' airlines in the aftermath of the terrorist attacks of September 2001. Many of these airlines were already in serious difficulties and were seen by low-cost airlines as being given an unfair competitive advantage. Ultimately, decisions on state aid matters are taken by simple majority vote in the College of Commissioners where all kinds of national pressures can be influential. 'Whereas on the anti-trust side a pro-competition consensus was visible during the 1980s, on the state aid side this consensus was always more fragile' (Cini and McGowan, 1998, p. 156).

The principles of European competition law jurisprudence are now incorporated into the British approach. The Blair government has welcomed Commission proposals for decentralizing decision-making to national competition authorities. However, it is concerned that some of the proposals might 'undermine the effective operation of key parts of our domestic regime – in particular, the complex monopoly provisions and the existing regimes for utility regulation' (HM Treasury, 2001, p. 24). In practice, however, there is a good working relationship between the national and European authorities. It is becoming more difficult to engage in anti-competitive behaviour and get away with it.

Transport

The importance of transport infrastructure for both getting people to work and transporting goods is recognized in the 10-year plan for transport published by the Blair government in 2000. The report argues that 'Good transport is essential . . . to a strong economy' (Department of the Environment, Transport and Regions, 2000, para 1.2). 'Transforming our transport networks and tackling the legacy of under-investment is vital for this country's economic prosperity' (*ibid.*, para 1.7), and achievement of the plan's objectives would 'sharpen the competitiveness of British industry' (*ibid.*, para 1.9).

Developing effective policy in this area presents a number of challenges. For example, growth in transport tends to run ahead of GDP growth:

> People are choosing to spend more of their increased disposable income in ways that generate transport demand. Households spend 70% more in real terms on transport than they did 30 years ago, even though transport costs have risen even more slowly than disposable income. (Department of Environment, Transport and Regions, 2000, para 3.2)

Transport is dominated by road transport. 'Cars are often the most attractive, and sometimes the only choice. The vast majority of personal travel (93%) and freight movement (90% excluding water and pipeline) is now made by road' (*ibid.*).

The preference for car travel is deeply rooted and influenced by considerations of cost, convenience, control of personal space and cultural considerations. Land-use decisions such as the location of out-of-town shopping centres and new housing estates reinforce the preference to use car travel. 'As a general rule public transport has little or no significance for residents of new estates regardless of the transport opportunities available' (Headicar and Curtis, 1998, p. 237). Difficulties on the railways have reduced already low levels of public confidence, and research suggests that 'simply providing alternatives to the car, or restricting its use, will probably do little to alter the fundamental reasons why most people use cars for most journeys and do not want to change' (Anderson, Meaton, Potter and Rogers, 1998, p. 284).

Total traffic as measured in terms of vehicle kilometres is forecast to grow by over a fifth between 2000 and 2010 (Department of Transport, Environment and Regions, 2000, para 3.5). More traffic will thus come onto roads that are already seriously overcrowded and quickly seize up if there is even a minor accident. Forecasts of traffic growth are subject to a number of uncertainties, not least the rate of economic growth, but one scenario is that 'the cost of using a car is forecast to fall in real terms as fuel efficiency improves over the next ten years. If this happens, the gap between the cost of motoring and public transport fares will continue to widen' (*ibid.*, para. 9.6).

The traditional way of dealing with growing traffic was the 'predict and provide' methodology. Traffic growth was forecast and roads planned to meet the increased demand. This methodology was discredited when it was realized that building new roads such as the M25 stimulated a further increase in traffic demand because people were encouraged to make trips they would otherwise not have made. 'The difficult challenge is how best to influence demand for road space in a way that is efficient and fair' (*ibid.*, para. 9.8). Increasing fuel duties in real terms proved to be politically unpopular and at best slowed down the rate of increase in passenger kilometres by road because of the inelasticity of demand for fuel. Charging for road use is an increasingly favoured way of dealing with congestion, but is likely to take some years to introduce even in London.

Rail transport is especially important for London commuters. Around '75% of those working in central London travel to work by public transport' (Department of Environment, Transport and Regions, para. 3.5). The London Underground operates in a way that presents a danger to the safety and health of its users; overcrowding in the peak travel periods reaches dangerous levels and has to be dealt with by such expedients as temporarily closing stations. The level of small particles that can penetrate deep into the lungs in many areas of the system is a serious health problem, and breakdowns can expose passengers to dangerously high temperatures and risks of dehydration. The system is a disgrace to a world city. Yet when the new Jubilee Line was built the Chancellor described it as a 'fiasco, two years late, massive [cost] overruns' (speech by Gordon Brown at the Transport and General Workers' Union conference, 5 July 2001); signalling problems made it difficult to deliver the promised frequency of service to the rapidly growing complex of offices in the Canary Wharf area.

The Blair government initially published a white paper on integrated transport policy in 1998. In large part this amounted to a miscellaneous collection of ideas, often desirable in themselves but unlikely to solve the overall problem. Its most innovative proposal was that local councils should draw up five-year Local Transport Plans. These introduced the possibility of hypothecation, the dedication of particular revenue streams, such as road congestion levies, to improvements in transport. It seemed likely, however, that there would be a long lag between advancing the idea and its implementation.

Facing criticism that it was doing little to correct the infrastructure problem, the government launched its 10-year transport plan in 2000. This promised £180 billion of additional spending on transport and a 6 per cent reduction in congestion by the end of the period. It was implicitly understood that the transport system would get worse before it got better because of the long lead time in transport projects and the disruption that occurs when they are being constructed. By the summer of 2001 the government's plan was encountering increasing criticism. The CBI complained about 'painfully slow' progress which could alienate the private sector that was expected to provide £56bn worth of investment. The CBI commented:

> Transport 2010 is best described as an overarching strategy rather than a detailed plan. It lacks detail on the prioritisation of investment, the mechanics of physically handling such a heavy workload, and the measures needed to minimise the inevitable disruption while the work is in progress. (*Financial Times*, 16 July 2001)

The difficulties in the rail industry posed particular problems for the government; the rail regulator warned that the senior management of Railtrack was 'a major barrier to improving the industry' (*Financial Times*, 25 June 2001), and the government subsequently intervened to replace the company by a publicly-owned trust, a move that amounted to a *de facto* renationalization. Any restructuring of the industry will, however, take time to bring results. More generally, the government seemed unwilling to contemplate any radical measures that might offend motorists. Congestion seemed likely to increase in a way that both annoyed voters but also undermined economic efficiency.

Skill formation

Deficiencies in education and training in Britain have been a central explanation of relatively poor British economic performance for over a century. Writing at the end of the nineteenth century, Williams gave a central place to differences in standards of technical education between Britain and Germany in his explanation of inferior British performance. He drew the attention of his readers to

> the splendid system of industrial education...in Germany, a system which is an integral factor in Germany's industrial success, and which, compared to anything in the nature of technical education to be found in England, is an electric lamp to a rush-light. (Williams, 1896, p. 156)

In the last quarter of the twentieth century, there was increasing concern about the extent to which the education system was seen to be failing children of average or below average ability, particularly in terms of basic skills of numeracy and literacy. New Labour saw 'Improving the skills base [as] critical to long-term economic growth' (HM Treasury, 2001, p. 33).

Up until the 1960s, governments took a generally *laissez-faire* approach to training with the emphasis being placed on the expansion of the education system. Considerable faith was still placed in the traditional, time-based apprenticeship system that had the support of the unions as a means of controlling entry to skilled trades. One of the consequences of the more interventionist mood that developed after 1960 was the recognition of a need for government involvement in the systematic encouragement of training. The 1964 Industrial Training Act passed by the Conservatives but implemented by Labour created a system of tripartite industry-based training boards with a power to raise a levy on firms in their sector.

In 1973 the levy power was removed and a tripartite Manpower Services Commission (MSC) set up to supervise the provision of training services. The Thatcher government introduced a Youth Training Scheme which was novel in its emphasis on general rather than craft skills, but was seen by its critics as largely motivated by the need to mop up youth unemployment. The majority of the tripartite industry boards were abolished and replaced by employer-led non-statutory training organizations.

From the late 1980s onwards there was a greater, if belated, recognition by the Thatcher government to take action to improve levels of human capital in the economy. A new system of National Vocational Qualification was introduced in 1986, followed by the National Curriculum in the Education Reform Act of 1988. This Act together with the 1992 Further and Higher Education Act is seen by Ainley (1999, p. 83) as framing 'a new settlement for education comparable to that of 1944'. In many respects, the power of the education establishment came to be undermined by a new training policy community; there was a 'development of the "new vocationalism" in secondary schools and in further education, with the Technical and Vocational Training Initiative' (Rainbird, 1990, p. 17). Even within higher education, the value of knowledge came to be challenged by a new emphasis on transferable skills.

At the end of the 1980s the MSC was transformed into a Training Agency in the Department of Employment which supervised a system of centrally financed Training and Enterprise Councils (TECs) set up in 1990/1. These were employer-led bodies with very little trade-union representation. 'The responsibility of TECs for training, business support and economic development policy was confused from the outset' (Bennett and Payne, 2000, p. 143). There was considerable tension between government departments, who had a narrow view of their role, and the TECs themselves who along with the CBI saw them as having a broader role. The Treasury and the DTI took the view 'that the TECs should be completely focused on the unemployed as the target group and that training programmes could not be accessible [to] people already in employment' (*ibid.*, p. 150). The TECs did manage to drive down the unit cost of training, although this created surpluses that could be diverted into business support and economic development. There was also concern about excessively generous pay structures for their managers. Nevertheless, they 'delivered enormous efficiency gains and increases in effectiveness' (*ibid.*, p. 165) up to the announcement of their abolition in 1999, in particular through their flagship modern apprenticeship programme.

The Labour Party has had a long-standing attachment to the importance of education, but New Labour came into office with a belief that globalization demanded considerable investment in human capital. Education was seen as crucial 'to overcoming the low-skill equilibrium of the British economy – low productivity and supply-side constraints to sustained growth' (Kendall and Holloway, 2001, p. 154). In particular, they were influenced by 'new' growth theory which saw human capital as an alternative, or at least a complementary, engine of growth to technological change (Stedward, 2000, p. 171). They found that 'the skills of the workforce in the UK remain below many competitor countries'; in terms of basic skill levels, 'over 20 per cent of the adult UK population lacks functional literacy... with only Ireland and Poland of the thirteen countries surveyed faring worse'; and the UK continued to exhibit another long-run problem of having 'a much smaller number of people with intermediate skills or above than a wide range of countries surveyed' (HM Treasury, 2001, p. 33). In terms of functional literacy and intermediate skills the contrast with Germany was particularly marked, suggesting that not much had changed since Williams wrote on the subject in 1896.

One element of the new approach, initially revived by the CBI, is to convert Britain into a 'learning society'. Such a society 'systematically increases the skills and knowledge of all its members to exploit technological innovation and so gain a competitive edge in fast-changing global markets'; in particular, 'education and training (conceptually united as learning) should no longer be "frontloaded" upon the young, but lifelong' (Ainley, 1999, p. 94). In practice, political pressures from voters will always lead to a considerable emphasis on education up to the compulsory school-leaving age. However, the Learning and Skills Council, which took on responsibility from the Further Education Funding Council for funding post-16 education from April 2001, has been given a mandate to develop learning. The Local Learning and Skill Councils that have taken over the role of the TECs act as subregional arms of the national Learning and Skills Council. The abolition of the TECs was something of a surprise but means that the training system is focused on the single target of training, rather than being mixed up with business support policy and local economic development policy.

Any strategy for improving skill formation, even if it is successful, does not bring results in the short run. Nearly 40 years of attempts to improve skill levels in the British economy have seen a variety of policies, and institutions appear and disappear. There are, however, some signs of improvement, even if they are rather gradual and there are recurrent suspicions of grade inflation. There is now an acceptance of the way in which learning policy is 'integral to economic policy' (Ainley, 1999, p. 94); a high priority has been given to learning policy and there is something resembling a coherent strategy in place. Policy outputs now have to be converted into policy outcomes to solve a set of problems at least a century old.

Utility regulation

When nationalized industries were privatized in the 1980s, the public utilities among them were subject to a variety of forms of regulation, most usually by an individual regulator, supported by an office, and responsible for a particular industry such as electricity, gas and water. At the end of the 1990s there were at least 60 firms under some kind of regulation, accounting for 17 per cent of the London stockmarket's capitalization (Wolfe, J. D. 1999, p. 895). They thus account for a significant portion of the economy in terms of value and provide goods and services that are extensively used by other firms and by domestic consumers such as energy, water and telecommunications. The effectiveness or otherwise of the regulatory arrangements put in place thus has a wider impact on the economy. The purpose of this section is not to provide a comprehensive review of the regulatory arrangements and of all the difficulties that have arisen in their operation; general reviews of their development are available elsewhere (Young, 2001). The purpose of this discussion, in line with the objectives of the chapter, is to focus on the implications of regulation for competitiveness. The available evidence suggests that

> the quality of regulation is a key determinant of performance whether the utility is public or private...Compared to the quality of regulation, ownership seems relatively less important, though there may be more chance of high-quality regulation under private than public ownership. (Newbery, 1999, p. 127)

Many of the motivations for privatization were political or opportunistic in character. They included undermining the power of public-sector trade unions; reducing the decision-making load on ministers; providing a stream of funds that could be offset against the public-sector borrowing requirement; and widening share ownership in a way that might reap political dividends for the party in office. There was also a view that nationalized industries were inherently less efficient than their private counterparts; managers enjoyed less freedom of action because of political controls and ministerial interventions. For example, they could not diversify in a way that private-sector managers could. After the privatization of the airports, BAA became as much a retailer as a provider of airport services. For politicians involved in the process, a fundamental consideration was that 'What public ownership does is to eliminate the threat of takeover and ultimately of bankruptcy, and the need, which all private undertakings have from time to time, to raise money from the market' (Lawson, 1992, p. 202). As will be discussed later, the efficiency imperative provided by these threats may have been less in practice than Lawson supposed.

Making comparisons between the performance of public-sector and private-sector companies is notoriously difficult. For example it is rarely possible to make comparisons between similar companies, one in the private and one in the public sector, because the majority of nationalized industries were monopolies. Lawson was nevertheless influenced by the work of Pryke, originally a champion of the nationalized industries (Pryke, 1971) who then produced a later study in which he took 'a much less favourable view of the nationalised industries' performance, and indeed of public ownership itself, than before' (Pryke, 1981, p. vii). There was good reason to believe, however, that the nationalized industries were overmanned and privatization generally led to substantial reductions in workforce size. Ownership changes can lead to 'structural and managerial changes that can have significant effects on factor productivity' (Newbery, 1999, p. 127).

It should be noted that economic theorists see regulation as a second-best solution compared with competition. Regulation is seen as 'inevitably inefficient because of problems of information and commitment and, more fundamentally, because of inefficient bargaining between interest groups over potential utility rents' (*ibid.*, p. 134). The regulatory process in practice involves considerable bargaining and negotiation between utilities and regulators, and the utilities have developed specialist regulatory affairs offices to handle their relations with the regulators (Coen and Willman, 1998). Not only are the transaction costs involved with the process considerable, but the greater resources available to producers may lead to outcomes which are more favourable to them than to consumers.

The existence of a continued natural monopoly, particularly in network services, in many nationalized industries provided an impetus for some form of regulation. This was particularly necessary given that the Thatcher government was unwilling to subdivide the industries into competing companies, partly to avoid resistance to privatization from the existing managers and partly to maximize the sale price. However, there was no coherent plan about how regulation should be provided. It is evident that 'no coherent institutional design seems to have inspired [the regulators'] creation and it has in general been left to the regulators themselves to develop their own procedures' (Prosser and Moran, 1994, pp. 46–7). The model for regulation was set by the 1983 Littlechild Report on the profitability of BT after regulation. Professor Littlechild 'contended that regulation needed to achieve as far as possible the conditions of competition with a minimum of interference and cost'. His analysis led to 'a distinctive British model, combining the price-cap method of regulation, an autonomous regulator centring on the person of the DG, and the commitment to promoting competition' (Wolfe, J., 1999, p. 897).

The original intention was that, as competition developed, the need for the regulators would disappear. Lawson recognized (1992, p. 202) that governments tend 'to exaggerate the irreducible amount of natural monopoly and neglect ways of introducing competition'. Nevertheless, he held to an optimistic belief 'that it was important to privatize as much as possible as quickly as possible; and this would itself set up pressures for more competition and other structural changes' (*ibid.*, p. 239). Even if competitive pressures did not compel efficiency in the product market, this would happen in the capital market 'where takeover raiders would buy up shares of underperforming utilities, sack the incompetent managers, and reorganize them to increase efficiency' (Newbery, 1999, p. 165). In fact, some of the companies such as BT were simply too big to take over and blundered on until they ran into serious trouble. Takeovers of smaller companies, on the other hand, were often motivated by the prospect of tax write-offs rather than efficiency considerations. Moreover, once utilities 'are acquired by diversified institutions, they are somewhat protected from these takeover threats and may again relapse' (*ibid.*, p. 166).

It has to be recognized that 'The main goal of utility reform in Britain was to transfer ownership to the private sector rather than to introduce competition' (*ibid.*, p. 177). It is therefore perhaps not surprising that utility regulation should grow in scope and resources consumed. Indeed, public-choice theorists would predict that, once created, the main objective of public utility regulators would be to perpetuate themselves. The joint budget of the electricity and gas regulators tripled between 1995 and 2000, while that of the telecommunications regulator doubled. Many of the price controls have been removed with household gas sales freed from control in 2000 and household electricity controls scheduled to end in 2002.

When the government's Better Regulation Task Force reviewed the regulation of the leading utilities, it identified a number of concerns according to its chairman, Lord Haskins. It found that 'competition has not developed as much as might have been expected, so the level of regulatory bureaucracy remains far too high'. In particular

> The terms of reference for the regulators are almost unworkable. They have to establish price mechanisms and formulae to ensure long-term investment, as well as meeting some environmental and social criteria ... The resultant complexity is confusing and easy to exploit. (*Financial Times*, 12 July 2001)

Regulatory bureaucracy flourished in the regulators' offices and the sponsoring departments encouraging a 'culture of bureaucracy and game-playing' which left 'consumers confused and suspicious' (*ibid.*). This last finding is of particular concern given that the admittedly watered-down Utilities Act 2000 set 'The new principal objective ... to protect the interests of consumers, wherever appropriate by promoting effective competition' (Young, 2001, p. 155).

The future of utility regulation

In the 1980s, sectoral regulation compensated for weak competition law. However, since the passage of the 1998 Competition Act Britain has one of the world's strongest competition regimes. It should eventually be possible for much of the market regulatory work to be undertaken by the Office of Fair Trading and the Competition Commission. Safety responsibilities could be transferred to the Health and Safety Commission with environmental regulation given to the Environment Agency.

Three justifications remain for utility regulation. First, there are still natural monopolies such as the electricity grid and the gas network and it may not be possible to dispense with separate regulation of the core natural monopoly. Second, social and environmental issues remain important both for the government and a range of pressure groups. Third, issues of access by entrants to existing networks have not been resolved. Above all, the real agenda for the system of regulation may not be promoting competition, but enhancing new forms of government control. As J. Wolfe suggests (1999, p. 891) 'the privatization programme, in reducing the state's role as direct producer, provider and regulator, appears to have enhanced the efficiency of its control'.

It is widely accepted that 'introducing competition into previously monopolized and regulated network utilities is the key to achieving the full benefits of privatization. Privatization seems to be necessary but it is not sufficient' (Newbery, 1999, p. 386). Competition between vertically-integrated utilities in Scotland has had little impact on productivity growth compared with the unbundling of generation in England and Wales (*ibid.*, p. 411). Substantial changes in the method of generation away from coal towards gas-fired and other stations have seen real fuel prices fall, as well as having an environmentally friendly impact. However, government has intervened to protect what remains of the coal industry, showing that there are political limits beyond which competitive effects are curtailed, for example by imposing a moratorium on new gas-fired power stations. Indeed, the need to protect what remains of the European coal industry is an argument now being advanced at the EU level on energy security grounds. Questions remain about whether new waves of investment can be sustained while keeping prices down and shareholders contented. Some competitive effects have been the result of technological change, as in the challenge offered to fixed-line systems by mobile phones. The promotion of competition by the regulators has had to compete with other objectives and pressures and outcomes are the result of bargaining processes, and it is therefore no surprise that while competition has been enhanced, it has not been maximized.

Conclusions

The recognition of the importance of supply-side problems in the economy does not mean that they will be remedied. The government objective of ensuring that the UK's productivity rises faster than that of its industrial competitors so as to close the productivity gap is an ambitious one. In terms of the areas surveyed here, the most progress has been made in competition policy; a new basis for a much more effective policy with a much higher profile has been created. Progress has also been made in the area of skill formation, although the problems are considerable, particularly where they intersect with issues of social exclusion. Following a review launched by the Chancellor in November 2000, the government is only just beginning to overhaul the system of utility regulation. Ultimately, it will need to be subsumed within the overall competition regime. Transport presents some of the most intractable problems because of deeply-rooted consumer preferences, inadequacies in the railways and the tendency of supply to create demand. It is in the area in which it is unreasonable to expect dramatic improvements in the short run, but uncertainty remains about whether they can be achieved in the long run. What is characteristic of all these areas is the importance attached to economic considerations, particularly in relation to competitiveness. This represents an important shift in the way in which policies that are economic policies in the classic sense, but nevertheless affect economic performance, are made and implemented.

7

The Electorate and the Economy

Introduction

The slogan 'It's the economy, stupid' that was displayed in a campaign room in Little Rock, Arkansas during Bill Clinton's bid for the presidency in 1992 has passed into political folklore. It captures what came to be seen as one of the truisms of modern electoral behaviour. As allegiances to class and other social groupings have declined, electors have come to be seen more and more as consumers, selecting the political brand that is best for them. Establishing and marketing the brand, as was done so successfully with 'new' Labour thus becomes a more central political skill. It carries with it the risk that politicians will follow the short-term preferences of the electorate, as revealed by focus groups, rather than following some longer-term strategic plan based on a coherent set of values (what used to be known as an 'ideology'). It could be argued that the issue of whether Britain should join EMU has been influenced not by considerations of the economic merits of membership, or by longer-term political considerations, but by whether the electorate can be persuaded to support EMU in a referendum. If they cannot, then a political 'sixth test' comes into operation and membership will not be pursued.

It is, of course, possible to exaggerate the extent to which political leaders provided leadership in some golden age in the past, regardless of the state of public opinion. Stanley Baldwin in the interwar years was a master of the art of manipulating public opinion, yet it is arguable that the National government's stance on rearmament in the years leading up to the Second World War was strongly influenced by what it felt public opinion would accept. In a democracy, some weight should be attached to public opinion. However, it is possible that we have arrived at a form of politics where most policies are decided in relatively closed off policy arenas in which

164

epistemic communities of experts have considerable influence. The major issues of high politics are driven by the extent to which the modern arts of political marketing can secure a particular outcome.

There is a more specific implication for the conduct of economic policy if elections are, in fact, influenced predominantly by economic performance. Should that be the case, politicians may seek to engage in short-term manipulation of the economy for political ends, and such manipulations may inflict lasting economic damage. Hence, it would appear that the case is strengthened for the depoliticization of economic policy, for the removal of some decisions from politicians altogether, and the conduct of other aspects of policy on the basis of rules rather than discretion. This is indeed what has been happening with the transfer of interest-rate decisions to the Bank of England and the conduct of fiscal policy under increasingly stringent rules.

The political business cycle

In fact, the evidence that there is a political business cycle is more mixed than is supposed. Since its development in its modern form by Nordhaus (1975), a number of variants of political business-cycle theory have been developed. As summarized by Alt and Chrystal, political business-cycle theory contains three main propositions. First, governments aim to win elections which makes them vote maximizers. Second, voters have preferences about economic outcomes that are reflected in their political behaviour. Third, governments are able to manipulate the economy so as to improve their chances of re-election (Alt and Chrystal, 1983, p. 104)

It is the third proposition that is the most contestable. First, politicians may not always engage in such manipulations. The budget preceding the 1959 election is described by a senior civil servant in a review of the conduct of policy as 'moderate and cautious', and he is magisterially dismissive of the Opposition's 'general cry of pre-election bribery' (Bretherton, 1999, p. 11). In 1964 a budget that 'was politically more courageous than officials had thought possible when they tendered their advice' (*ibid.*, p. 45) increased taxation. The budget introduced by Roy Jenkins before the 1970 general election was a model of prudence, and Labour's failure to win the election has sometimes been blamed on the budget. The budget introduced by Gordon Brown before the 2001 election contained targeted tax concessions, but not a general giveaway, nor any massive boost for public expenditure (indeed, such a boost would have to be provided for some time before the election for its effects to be felt).

One can, of course, produce counter-examples. Lamont even alleges that John Major's conduct of interest-rate policy was influenced by by-elections (Lamont, 1999, p. 325). At least, however, politicians do not systematically manipulate the economy to enhance their election chances. Second, if manipulations do occur, they may not be guaranteed to secure the desired effect. Bretherton drops a rather opaque hint (1999, p. 83) that what he calls 'electoral cycle' effects may be felt more through increases in public expenditure as an election approaches. Such increases may not deliver short-run improvements in service quality, a point the Conservatives tried to make something of in the run up to the 2001 election. Third, political manipulations may be of relatively minor importance compared to other influences on the economy. In so far as there are harmful effects, they might be dealt with by moving to fixed-term parliaments that would allow politicians less scope to vary the timing of an election to suit the electoral cycle.

If the political business-cycle model is less robust than is sometimes assumed, the economic voting model has also seemed less secure:

> In the 1980s, there was a very clear correlation between MORI's [Economic Optimism Index] and voting intention figures, and the academic David Sanders was able to produce models using economic data which were powerfully predictive of the general election results. (Worcester and Mortimore, 2001, p. 25)

The outcome of the 2000 presidential election in the United States might suggest that electors are willing to blame politicians for economic failure (as in 1992) but less willing to reward them for success which might anyway primarily be attributed to Alan Greenspan and the Federal Reserve. The lesson the British Labour Party took from the failure of Gore to win the 2000 election in propitious economic circumstances was that the fruits of economic success could not be claimed automatically, but had to be secured through emphasizing them in the campaign. Even if this worked in Britain in 2001, helped by the opposition's failure to focus on possible areas of government weakness, it still leaves the puzzle of 1992 and 1997 to be explained. In 1992 the Conservatives won despite a recession and in 1997 they lost despite a considerable record of economic success. Before seeking to explain these events which seem to undermine the economic model of voting, it is first necessary to review alternative models of the voting process.

Models of voting behaviour

There was a considerable difference in patterns of voting behaviour in Britain between the middle and the end of the twentieth century. In the early 1950s, Britain was still a very homogeneous society relative to other countries. Religious differences were largely confined to the north of Ireland and the west of Scotland, ethnic minority groups were a tiny proportion of the population and Nationalist consciousness in Wales and Scotland was very weak. The major social cleavage in the population was that of class. In what was one of the most quoted remarks about British politics, Pulzer commented (1972, p. 102), 'Class is the basis of British party politics: all else is embellishment and detail.'

Voting on class lines meant that 96.8 per cent of the votes in the 1951 general election went to the two main parties. The Liberal Party came close to extinction. Voting was, of course, not entirely on class lines:

> In the 1964 and 1966 elections, roughly two-thirds of electors voted for their 'natural' class party, so that class influence was by no means universally decisive, but its influence was none the less impressive. (Sanders, 1997, p. 53)

There was considerable interest in 'class-deviant' voters, especially working-class Conservatives who were numerically a much larger group than middle-class Labour supporters and helped to make the Conservatives the most electorally successful party in the twentieth century.

Even then, upward mobility was enlarging the non-manual group in the population, but social cleavage lines changed slowly. In any case, many voters continued to give allegiance to the party their parents voted for so that political socialization effects tended to slow down the impact of social change. Given the glacial character of change in social party formations, why did movements of votes occur between elections? Interest focused on the 'floating voter'. The view emerged that these voters were often cross-pressured: their social class position might be ambiguous, or upward mobility might conflict with the traditional voting patterns of their family and neighbourhood. It seemed that floating voters were often less interested in, or less knowledgeable about, politics than those who showed a constant allegiance to one party.

The decline of social class and the emergence of new identities

By the 1990s, social class was much less important in British politics, although its effects had not disappeared altogether as was demonstrated by the continued existence of very safe Conservative and Labour constituencies. In 1997, Labour attracted over half the votes of the C2 and DE groups (broadly manual workers), but its share declined to 31 per cent in the professional and managerial (AB) grouping, although only 37 per cent of the votes in this grouping went to the Conservatives (data from Sanders, 1997, p. 49). Nevertheless, the index of absolute class voting shows a clear downward decline. This is calculated by deducting the percentage of working-class Conservatives plus middle-class Labour voters from the percentage of voters who vote in accordance with their class membership (although whether this is why they are voting this way cannot necessarily be assumed). In any event, in 1964 the score was 76 and in 1997 it was 27, a striking difference (*ibid.*, pp. 54–5).

'The 2001 election showed a significant narrowing of class differentials in voting' (Worcester and Mortimore, 2001, p. 197); in particular, Labour led among routine office and clerical workers (C1s) for the first time. In a more heterogeneous and more open society, voters were freer to construct their own identities as, for example, Scottish or gay (or both). Voters had become much less likely to identify with one political party, a process known as partisan de-alignment. They were also less likely to vote: turnout was down from 82.5 per cent in 1951 to 71.4 per cent in 1997, plunging to 59 per cent in 2001, the lowest ever turnout under a modern franchise. A two-party system had been replaced by a multiple party system in Scotland, Wales and Northern Ireland and by a modified two-party system in England where tactical voting was highly significant in the 1997 election. The Conservative and Labour share of the poll was down to 73.9 per cent in 1997, although it recovered slightly to 75 per cent in 2001.

Economic performance models of voting

Given that voters were much less likely to vote on 'tribal' lines, how were they going to make their choice? The most parsimonious explanation seemed to be as consumers in terms of their judgement of the performance of the economy. The conduct of economic policy is what Butler and Stokes (1969) refer to as a 'valence' issue. By this they mean that the goal of economic prosperity is widely shared, so that electors have to make a decision about which party is most likely to achieve economic success. In its simplest form, the economic model of voting suggested that governments that deliver prosperity secure re-election and those associated with economic failure tend to lose office. Voters who are better off (or think they soon will be) support the government. Those who are, or think they will be, worse off tend to support the opposition. Thus, 'to the extent that voters are optimistic about the economic future, they seek to preserve the *status quo* that has created their optimism; to the extent they are pessimistic, they seek to change it' (Sanders, 1999, p. 253).

As far as politicians managing the economy are concerned, they need to know not just that economic performance has a significant impact on voting behaviour, but how it does so. Do voters make an assessment of the past economic performance of governments in arriving at their voting decisions (retrospective voting), or of its likely future performance compared to its opponents (prospective voting)? Economists might expect rational actors to 'make decisions on the basis of forward-looking rational expectations. The [1997] election results indicate that backward-looking adaptive expectations may be as important in motivating decisions within the polling booth' (Wickham-Jones, 1997, p. 117). Moreover, retrospective voting is particularly likely in systems with a limited number of parties, such as Britain, compared with a multi-party system such as Italy (Alt and Chrystal, 1983, p. 159).

Retrospective models are inherently more plausible than models based on what candidates say they will do if elected, particularly given low and declining levels of trust in politicians. It seems unlikely that most voters would be able to, or would wish to, review the economic performance of the government over its whole period in office before deciding how to cast their ballot. Traumatic economic events may, however, be recalled and have a lasting effect. Each of the governments that has devalued in Britain since 1945 has either lost or failed to win an adequate majority at the next election (Labour in 1949 and 1967, the Conservatives in 1992).

The view that voters generally focus on economic performance over a relatively short time period receives some support from Price and Sanders who reviewed the period from 1951 to 1989. They found that 'voters may take several months to assimilate what is happening in the economy, but also have a short "memory", so that current perceptions are given much higher weight than even quite recent events' (Price and Sanders, 1991, p. 22). In other words, voters are generally relatively myopic, but their myopia incorporates a short time lag. Economic improvement may need to be secured some months before the election. Given that there are time lags in the response of the economy to policy changes, and that forecasting methods are still far from foolproof, it can be seen that securing the desired political effect at election time is actually quite difficult.

A further issue is which particular economic indicators voters pay attention to and how these mesh with their perceptions of their own personal well-being. The indicator which preoccupied politicians for long periods of the second half of the twentieth century was unemployment. Thus, in 1959, unemployment rising to 2 per cent was enough for the Cabinet and especially the Prime Minister to take 'fright' (Bretherton, 1999, p. 6). In doing so, the prime minister was probably unaware of the distinction between sociotropic and egocentric forms of voting. The former is concerned with voters' perceptions 'of the *general* condition of the economy', the latter with 'perceptions of the individual elector's *personal* financial circumstances' (Price and Sanders, 1995, p. 460). Aggregate data suggests that 'changes in unemployment did not seriously damage the government's electoral fortunes during the Thatcher years' (*ibid.*, p. 461), and their analysis (*ibid.*, pp. 461n–462n) did not find much evidence that the Thatcher government had managed to shift blame for unemployment on to the private sector. What is evident is that while unemployment may be seen as a general political problem, the number of families affected is a minority of the population (often concentrated in safe Labour seats). Inflation has more widespread effects.

Inflation did displace employment as the focus of government concern, but it may be that electors are as much influenced by, for example, the level of interest rates or the trend in house prices. Indeed, the evidence suggests that voters' subjective economic perceptions are 'far more powerful predictors of party support than objective measures, though economic perceptions were themselves influenced by the macro-economy and in particular by real interest rates' (Sanders, 1999, p. 253).

The median voter theorem

Downs' economic theory of democracy or median voter theorem has proved to be one of the most robust models of electoral behaviour available to political scientists, perhaps because its assumptions and methodology are derived from economics. The central proposition is a simple but important one, 'that the parties in a two-party system converge ideologically upon the center' (Downs, 1957, p. 140). Hay, although critical of various aspects of the model and its explanatory value, notes (1999, p. 77) that the Downs model 'provides a disarmingly accurate (if nonetheless rather simplistic) *description* both of New Labour's electoral strategy and, rather more alarmingly, of the assumptions informing Labour's reprojection of itself as a "catch-all party"'.

The Downs model is constructed on the basis of an assumption of conscious rationality on the part of voters. They are seen as individual actors seeking to maximize their utility. It is also assumed that each individual is selfish so that by rational behaviour is meant actions 'directed primarily towards selfish ends' (Downs, 1957, p. 27); parties are assumed to act rationally in pursuit of a single goal, that of election or re-election (*ibid.*, p. 11). Policies are simply a means for the politician to gain the reward of office that is an end in itself. Thus all the actions of a party 'are aimed at maximizing votes, and it treats policies merely as means towards this end' (*ibid.*, p. 35). Parties are characterized as teams by which Downs means 'a coalition whose members agree on all their goals' (*ibid.*, p. 25). The parties are 'Concerned only to get elected, at any cost in terms of policy output', and it can thus be deduced 'that parties will change their policies in the pursuit of maximising electoral success' (Robertson, 1976, p. 26). Although parties produce platforms and ideologies which help to reduce for voters the costs of gaining information, these areas ambiguous as possible to increase the number of voters to which a party appeals.

Thus in a two-party system, to which the party system in England at least still approximates (particularly given the Liberal Democrats self-definition as another way of voting against the Conservatives), 'each party will try to resemble its opponent as closely as possible' (Downs, 1957, p. 127). They stop short of becoming completely identical because of the fear of reducing turnout and losing votes from the extremes of their support. The model also imposes a limiting condition that 'political parties cannot move ideologically past each other' (*ibid.*, p. 122). This is realistic in the sense that parties are more than just competing brands of toothpaste. In fact, even in consumer markets, very similar products seek to differentiate themselves from their competitors, for example by claiming that they are 'new' in some way, a rebranding exercise successfully imitated by new Labour.

There is evidence that 'in seeking to accommodate electoral preferences, Labour had moved some time before the 1997 election to a position significantly to the right of the median voter' (Hay, 1999, p. 99). Hay provides a number of reasons why this is consistent with the Downsian model; for example, it might be a means of over compensating for the persistence of the 'old Labour' image. It also reflects Labour's emphasis on narrowly-defined target groups in the electorate, exemplified by 'Worcester woman', a geographically middle-England voter with a median income and driving a middle-range car (a Ford Mondeo). Labour had, quite rationally, arrived at a very narrow definition of the electoral battleground in terms of floating voters in marginal constituencies whose views were likely to be somewhat to the right of the median voter (*ibid.*, p. 100). 'The possibility that "Worcester woman" – the archetypal female middle Briton – could decide the results of the [1997] election became more tangible' (Peake, 1997, p. 167).

The standard Downsian model assumes a unimodal and near-normal distribution of voters along a traditional left–right axis, and as a simplifying assumption it is reasonably realistic. Not all voters can be placed along this axis and there may be other, weaker dimensions such as a populist–authoritarian one (Crewe and Sarlvik, 1980, p. 254). However, enough voters can be placed along a higher spending versus lower taxation axis, associated with different degrees of government control of the economy, for the model to be a sufficiently good approximation of reality. The traditional Labour model assumed a bimodal distribution of voters along class lines that implied that the principal objective should be to mobilize the votes of 'our people'. Part of the transformation of old into new Labour involved a rejection of a bimodal distribution for a more classical Downsian model (Hay, 1999, pp. 97–8). While there may be no direct line of influence from Downs' model to new Labour, 'market-research socialism' (Leys, 1990) was susceptible to Downsian thinking:

> [Both] political advertising and political market research rely on an implicit economic theory of democracy. Indeed, their most fundamental

premise is that electoral competition is analogous to the competition for
market share amongst capitalist entrepreneurs. This, we should recall, is
Downs' starting point. (Hay, 1999, p. 101)

The task became not to consolidate the votes of 'our people', but
to search out and win over the median voter. Given the absence of
any viable alternative to the left of the Labour Party, Labour voters
would have nowhere else to go (this assumption may have been less
realistic in Scotland). After 1997, concerns grew that 'heartland'
Labour voters, some of whom were in marginal constituencies,
might simply abstain and this led to policy adjustments designed
to retain their support. In general, however, the gains to be made by
moving to the centre outweighed the losses from disillusioned voters
on the far left. Research by Sanders and Brynin (1999, p. 235) shows
that 'there were simply a lot more voters in the ideological centre
(22.1% of our sample, 1991–95) than there were on the left (3.7%)'.

One of Downs' core assumptions is that 'citizens' political tastes
are fixed' (Downs, 1957, p. 47). By relaxing this rather unrealistic
assumption one can actually increase the interest of the model.
Downs assumes that electors influence parties, but Dunleavy has
suggested that parties can influence electors. He provides a prefer-
ence-shaping model in which parties alter the aggregate distribution
of preferences which results in a shift in the position of the median
voter in favour of one party.

In 1974 Keith Joseph identified what he called the 'ratchet' effect
whereby the centre ground was moved to the left as each Conservative government accepted the new middle ground defined by the
outgoing Labour government. This certainly can be said to have
happened in the ten years after the Second World War. In so far as
one of the objectives of Thatcherism was to reform political opinion
on key issues, it largely failed to do so. As Heffernan points out,
Thatcher's target was as much elite opinion and institutions as the
mass electorate. As far as the electorate was concerned, 'certain
social democratic values retained strong support among the public
even at the height of the Thatcherite boom' (Heffernan, 2000, p. 110).

One of the shortcomings of the Downs model is that it fails to
take account of the extent to which the distribution of the preferences of party activists differs from those of the electorate. Moreover, they may attach a greater value to winning office to implement
a particular package of policies than simply winning office. Hence,
they may pull the party away from the median voter. This is what
happened to Labour after 1979 and also to the Conservatives after

1997. Many Labour activists took the view that it was better to be out of office than to be in office and implement policies which, as they saw it, were not socialist in character. Indeed, it was often argued that if socialist policies were properly explained to voters, they would understand their innate superiority. One consequence was that the political space vacated by the party was filled by the breakaway Social Democrats who, in alliance with the Liberals, gave Labour a close run for second place in terms of votes in 1983.

Successive Labour leaders (Kinnock, Smith, Blair) thus faced the task of moving the party back towards the centre again as the attractions of being out of office but remaining ideologically pure remained. The fact that they moved the party in this way serves as confirmation of the Downsian model. This shift took place within the broad parameters of the new Thatcherite political settlement, particularly in terms of what constituted acceptable state intervention in the economy. Thus:

> In contrast to the classical Downsian model (building upon that of Dunleavy) a model of party competition driven party change suggests that while electors do influence parties, parties influence electors but also separately influence other parties. The ultimate consequences of Thatcherism demonstrate that under certain circumstances successful parties shape the choices other less-successful parties make. (Heffernan, 2000, p. 177)

Explaining the elections of 1992 and 1997

If election results were simply determined by economic trends, the Conservatives would have lost in 1992 and won in 1997. The economy moved into recession around the time that John Major became Prime Minister in the autumn of 1990. The severest falls in output occurred in the first half of 1991 and this was followed by a year and a half of stagnation (Jay, 1994, p. 169). Putting the best possible gloss on it, Lamont maintains that 'The recession of 1990–93 was longer than that of the early 1980s but was less deep and the loss in output from peak to trough was smaller' (Lamont, 1999, p. 388). Unemployment remained high, peaking (in seasonally adjusted terms) at just under three million in December 1992. Inflation was brought down from its 1990 peak to 2.6 per cent by December 1992, but interest rates were still over 10 per cent at the time of the election. As John Major himself recalls (1999, p. 294), 'that period of early 1992 seemed like economic midwinter'. Recovery was imperceptible and there was considerable economic insecurity:

> Many home-owners who had bought in the inflated housing market of the boom years of the late eighties saw the value of their homes drop, and were trapped in negative equity. This became the first 'white collar' recession, and its worst effects were felt in the South and South-East, where Conservative support was traditionally strong. (Major, 1999, p. 294)

Despite all this bad news which suggested that the 'objective' economy was working against the Conservatives, the 'subjective' economy was working in their favour. Notwithstanding the fact that the economy was experiencing a long recession, 'voters' economic expectations – their sense of economic optimism – rose progressively in the 18 months prior to the 1992 election' (Sanders, 1999, p. 253). Moreover, the recession was not just a British one, although the British recession did start before that in the rest of the world, largely as a result of the bursting of the bubble of the Lawson boom which was characterized by unsustainable increases in house prices. Nevertheless, 'John Major's government in 1992 was simply not held responsible for the length and depth of the economic recession – which was blamed either on international factors outside the government's control or on the previous – Thatcher – Government' (*ibid.*, p. 252).

The Conservatives started, however, from a good base in so far as they were still perceived as the most competent party in terms of economic management. Although data on perceptions of economic competence was collected only intermittently between 1964 and 1989, the only time when Labour led the Conservatives on economic competence was when the first poll-tax bills were issued in March 1990. The Conservatives enjoyed a built-in advantage so that,

> even when Labour was well ahead of the Conservatives... in terms of voting intention, the Conservatives were almost invariably in the lead on the economy. In October 1989, for example, Labour enjoyed a 10-point lead over the Conservatives on voting intention, but the Tories enjoyed a 10-point lead over Labour on the economy. (King, 1998, p. 197)

The Conservatives, assisted by some errors made by Labour strategists, were able to successfully exploit this superior reputation for economic competence in the 1992 election campaign. They were able to suggest that the recession would soon be brought to an end, even if the green shoots of recovery were scarcely evident, while

Labour would only prolong it. Moreover, they will able to portray Labour as the party of high taxation. Labour produced a detailed shadow budget from which it was possible to deduce that, particularly as a result of abolishing the National Insurance contributions ceiling for those earning more than £22 000, there would be quite substantial increases in deductions from pay for moderately well-off voters. Although the overall impact of these proposed taxation increases was moderate, 'over half the electorate thought their own taxes would rise' (Wickham-Jones, 1997, p. 100).

The long-run electoral consequences of the ERM crisis

The centrepiece of Conservative economic policy was membership of the exchange rate mechanism that was seen particularly as a means of bringing inflation under control. In July 1992, the Chancellor, Norman Lamont emphasized, 'The ERM is not an optional extra, an add-on to be jettisoned at the first hint of trouble. It is and will remain at the very centre of our macroeconomic strategy' (Treasury press release, 10 July 1992).

Britain had entered the exchange rate mechanism at what many observers thought was a relatively high level against the deutschmark. It would have been possible to nudge the rate down before entry, but that would have contradicted the objective of using it as inflationary discipline. The inflationary pressures and high interest rates resulting from German unification imposed high interest rates elsewhere, and Britain's position in the ERM came under increasing strain. Even though the ERM had moved towards a quasi-fixed rate mechanism, it would have been possible to devalue within it. Lamont rejected this option in two short paragraphs in his July speech, claiming that it would not bring interest rates down. This might have been the main preoccupation of the Conservative Party's core supporters, but the real objective should have been to allow Britain to stay within the ERM, although it was not an objective which Lamont personally shared.

In any event, what is significant in terms of the concerns of this chapter is that Britain was obliged to withdraw from membership in humiliating circumstances, with Norman Lamont making the announcement from the pavement in front of the Treasury. Major regards it as 'a political and economic calamity' which 'changed the political landscape of Britain' (Major, 1999, p. 312). The Conservative lead over Labour in terms of perceptions of economic competence was quickly converted into a strong Labour lead: 'After autumn 1992 ... there was no month in which Labour did not lead the Conservatives on economic competence' (King, 1998, p. 187). This lead was still in place at the time of the 2001 election when 'a very substantial majority [of voters] believed that Labour would do a better job than the Conservatives in managing the economy in difficult times' (Clarke, Sanders, Stewart and Whiteley, 2001, p. 7).

Lamont (1999, p. 394) has argued that the ERM crisis 'became something of an excuse for the Conservative Party', pointing out that the Conservative lead continued to decline after the immediate crisis was over. It is the case that 'In the short term the exchange rate crisis gave Labour the most marginal of advantages on economic competence ... Moreover, the Government was able to pass some of the blame for the crisis on to others' (Wickham-Jones, 1997, p. 115). However, 'The Exchange Rate Mechanism crisis of September 1992 crystallised a number of important doubts that voters had already entertained about the Conservatives as competent economic managers' (Sanders, 1999, p. 252), and their reputation was not helped by the political storm over proposals to close the 31 remaining coal pits in October 1992. Major admits (1999, p. 669) that 'the timing of such a controversial announcement could scarcely have been worse' and regrets his failure to override the advice of the Treasury and the Department of Trade and Industry. The government was forced into 'a swift and undignified partial U-turn' (*ibid.*, p. 670).

Voters' doubts about government competence were reinforced when the 1993 budget substantially increased taxes, in particular introducing higher national insurance contributions and a two-stage introduction of VAT on fuel (the second stage was later voted down by Parliament). Opinion poll evidence 'indicated it was the most unpopular budget since records began in 1949' (Wickham-Jones, 1998, p. 105). Lamont was subsequently removed from office, but Ken Clarke's first budget in November 1993 also cut public spending and increased taxes. 'Together, the two budgets in 1993 had seen the largest peacetime increases in taxation ever introduced in the UK' (*ibid.*, p. 106).

Economists generally agreed that the tough fiscal policy was necessary to bring the public-sector deficit under control, although it was the Conservatives who had incurred it in the first case. However, it damaged beyond repair the one remaining economic card the Conservatives had in relation to Labour, that of being able to deliver lower taxation. The Labour Party was able to highlight the introduction of various 'stealth' taxes by the Conservatives in an effort to increase revenue, such as the airport departure tax and the insurance premium, although Labour continued to make use of these new taxes themselves.

The 1992 devaluation began an economic recovery, and by 1997 independent commentators agreed that the economy was in good shape. The 1996 annual report on the UK economy from the OECD gave a generally positive view of the economy, noting that 15 years of microeconomic reform had made it more flexible and competitive, less prone to inflation and with lower levels of unemployment (OECD, 1996). However, the Conservative government received little credit for this improvement from the electorate. In contrast to 1992, the objective economy was working in the government's favour, but the subjective economy was not. 'Between September 1992 and March 1997 the feel-good factor was negative for fifty months out of fifty-four' (Wickham- Jones, 1998, p. 113). Nearly half the electorate thought at the time of the 1997 election that the Major government had built strong foundations for Britain's economic recovery, but Labour had a seven-point lead in responses to the statement 'Labour would do a better job of running the economy than the Conservatives' (Worcester and Mortimore, 1999, pp. 63–4). The economic optimism index did move into positive territory by the time of the election but this in part seems to have been because Labour supporters 'anticipated victory at the polls and economic recovery brought about by their own, Blair government' (*ibid.*, p. 67).

The key to understanding the 1997 election is the way in which 'The Conservatives' loss of their longstanding reputation for competence in the immediate wake of the [ERM] crisis opened up an electoral space which allowed *politics* to affect voters' electoral preferences on a scale not encountered since 1979' (Sanders, 1999, p. 252). In realigning elections like those of 1979 and 1997, broader considerations than economic performance are likely to have an important impact on the outcome.

The importance of factors other than economic performance

There were many political factors other than an assessment of economic performance that affected the choices made by voters, although in a sense they were encapsulated by a widespread feeling that after 18 years of Conservative government it was 'time for change'. It has long been established that 'generalized beliefs about the desirability of periodic transfers of control do play a role in the behaviour of the mass electorate' (Butler and Stokes, 1969, p. 434). In the realigning election of 1964 that ended 13 years of Conservative rule, 'general beliefs in favour of alternation in power supplied the last margin needed to dismiss from office the aging Conservative Government' (*ibid.*, p. 435). In 1997 such a shift was made easier by the fact that 'voters who had remained at the centre of the political spectrum after 1992 found that Labour's rightward shift had, in classical Downsian fashion, moved the party closer to their own ideological position' (Sanders and Brynin, 1999, p. 226). Seventy-four per cent of those voters who converted directly from Conservative to Labour between 1992 and 1997 saw the perception that 'Labour had become "more moderate and responsible" under Blair as important in their decision' (Sanders, 1997, p. 52).

There were a number of political factors that affected voting decisions, but among the most important was concern about the state of public services on which most electors are reliant. By the first four months of 1997, health was ranked as the most urgent problem facing the country with education in third place (after unemployment) (King, 1998, p. 194). A survey in 1996 of 'lost Tories' who had voted Conservative in 1992 but no longer intended to support the Conservatives found that the most important reason given (mentioned by 66 per cent of respondents) was that the 'Conservatives were continuing to undermine the NHS'. The second most important reason (mentioned by 55 per cent) was that 'Public services – not just the NHS – continue to decline under the Conservatives' (*ibid.*, p. 195). In terms of the party best able to handle a particular issue, Labour had a massive 49 per cent lead over the Conservatives on health and a 39 per cent lead on education at the time of the 1997 election. Although the Conservatives led on only two issues out of ten, the leads on education and health were the biggest enjoyed by Labour with the figures displaying very little faith in the Conservatives' ability to handle these problems (Sanders, 1997, p. 50); 97 per cent of Labour voters 'cited the party's promises to improve the NHS and education as important reasons for voting Labour' (*ibid.*, p. 52).

Tony Blair's own personality and leadership style had a positive effect on the Labour vote. In terms of 11 qualities of party leaders,

Blair received better scores than Major on all of them in a 1996 poll, often by very substantial margins (Denver, 1998, p. 42). 'Blair's leadership obviously attracted votes from parts of the electorate that other Labour leaders could not possibly have reached' (Sanders, 1999, p. 265). Sanders suggests (*ibid.*, p. 268) that Blair's leadership and the consequent transformation of Labour into a moderate party 'cost the Conservatives in the region of eight percentage points in terms of the popular vote'.

The Conservatives' difficulties were increased by a reversal in the electorate's perceptions of which party was most divided. In May/June 1992, 65 per cent of those polled thought the Conservatives were united and 72 per cent thought Labour were divided, a striking contrast. By the first three months of 1997, 59 per cent thought Labour was united and 80 per cent thought that the Conservatives were divided, a remarkable transformation (Denver, 1998, p. 27). These negative perceptions were reinforced by a series of financial and sexual scandals referred to under the umbrella term of sleaze. The policy disaster represented by BSE also did nothing to help the government's reputation for competence (Grant, 1998). It is evident that 'models of competence which focus only on the economy are under-specified' (Evans, 1999, p. 147).

An assessment of economic voting models

There is no doubt that the 1997 election offered a particularly tough test of the economic voting model. The collapse of confidence in the competence of the Conservatives to manage the economy did have an effect on the normal relationship between economic indicators or perceptions of well-being and voting behaviour: 'Although the loss of the Conservatives' competence reputation failed to weaken the effects of expectations, it *does* seemed to have impaired the government's ability to buy electoral support by reducing taxation' (Sanders, 1999, p. 265).

Economic performance effects were far from completely absent from the 1997 election. First, there is evidence that those voters who were particularly adversely affected by the performance of the economy were more likely to change their vote. The available evidence suggests that 'Conservative defection was highest among those voters whose economic perceptions had deteriorated most' (Sanders and Brynin, 1999, p. 231). Sanders and Brynin note that:

respondents with financial difficulties at the beginning of the period and those who found themselves encountering financial difficulties between 1991 and 1995 were significantly more likely to switch to Labour than those who did not experience such difficulties. There is, in short, a limited amount of evidence to suggest that voters who experienced economic difficulties were indeed more likely to support the opposition party – as economic theories of voting would imply. (*Ibid.*, p. 235)

The evidence also suggests that the Conservatives might have performed even less well in the 1997 election if there had not been an economic recovery: 'Conservative support certainly increased as expectations rose in advance of the 1997 election' (Sanders, 1999, p. 266). However, they had to make their recovery from a very low baseline. Nevertheless, if there had been no expectations of recovery, Sanders estimates that their share of the popular vote might have been 26.2 per cent, more than 5 per cent below the historically low figure they actually achieved (*ibid.*).

Some journalistic commentators saw the outcome as a defeat for what they saw as a theory of economic determinism (Wickham-Jones, 1998, p. 101); although no such theory had ever been advanced by a serious academic analyst. Nevertheless, it was evident that economic models had some relevance even in the special circumstances of 1997. The way in which a government managed the economy continued to have a powerful effect on its standing with the electorate: 'The loss of the Conservatives' reputation for economic competence probably contributed more than any other single factor to their defeat in 1997' (King, 1998, p. 187). This effect was in many ways an indirect one as it allowed other political issues to gain a greater salience.

In 2001 the economic optimism index was actually negative, although this was offset by perceptions of Labour's economic competence while the MORI Financial Services index 'which measured how the public thought they themselves and their family would fare remained steady and positive' (Worcester and Mortimore, 2001, pp. 24–5). 'Managing the economy' was ranked sixth equal among a list of 17 issues which would be 'very important' in deciding how to vote. Only 31 per cent of respondents picked it, compared with 73 per cent mentioning healthcare and 62 per cent education.

There are a number of methodological issues that arise in any effort to assess voting behaviour. One arises from the need to analyse individual acts of choice that have an aggregate outcome. It is difficult to reconstruct all the different influences that enter the mind of the voter and their relative weight, hence the attractiveness of such shorthands as the 'feel good factor'. However, it is important to be cautious about the relationship between political preferences and economic perceptions. A positive assessment of the government's economic performance may be an adjustment to a partisan preference rather than the source of it. The evidence reviewed also suggests that we need to give some weight to perceptions of public-service delivery as well as to economic indicators.

The behaviour of the Labour Party after 1992 was consistent with Downsian notions of rationality, but in many ways the behaviour of the Conservative Party since 1997 seems inconsistent with the Downsian model. It may be, however, that defeated parties are particularly susceptible to the views of their activists. In the case of the Conservative Party, this tendency was accentuated by the anticipation of a likely second defeat and the need of the leader to retain popularity with the activists who are the final electoral college in the new system of leadership elections. The elderly and socially unrepresentative character of Conservative activists increases the risk, under such assumptions, of the party losing touch with the electorate.

In the 2001 campaign, the Conservatives concentrated on British membership of the euro, an issue that was not a priority for the electorate compared with education and health. Labour was to some extent vulnerable on these issues because of its failure to deliver on promises made in 1992, but the Conservatives failed to exploit this potential vulnerability. Labour thus had a relatively easy campaign and might well have won an even bigger majority if it had not been for the low turnout. The Labour victory in highly favourable economic circumstances, with the governing party dominating the centre-ground of politics, fits well with the standard economic models of voting behaviour. They do not provide a complete explanation of electoral outcomes, but the balance of evidence suggests that politicians who want to win re-election need to manage the economy competently, although forces such as globalization may undermine their ability to do so.

8

Economic Policy-Making

Introduction

Economic policy in Britain is made by a core group of decision-makers: the Prime Minister, the Chancellor and the Treasury, and the Bank of England. The extent of the influence they exert varies from time to time, but they are always involved to some extent in the making of key decisions. Cabinet and particularly Cabinet committees may also play a role, particularly in relation to public expenditure issues, but they do not usually shape overall economic strategy. The frequency of Cabinet meetings has declined from an average of two a week to a weekly meeting which under Tony Blair has rarely lasted more than an hour and has often finished in 30 minutes (Holliday, 2000, p. 89). Even before its current downgrading, it was not unknown for the Cabinet to be excluded altogether from important decisions. For example, between 1964 and 1966 it was a triumvirate of three ministers dominated by the prime minister 'and not the Cabinet that settled major issues of economic policy' (Cairncross, 1996, p. 99). The key issue of devaluation was kept away from the Cabinet altogether.

The Prime Minister

Table 8.1 attempts to categorize the involvement of postwar prime ministers in economic policy-making. Some of the categorizations may be open to challenge, but most analysts would probably accept the general picture of a variability of involvement. Five periods of prime ministerial office are characterized by high involvement; four by moderate involvement; and three by low involvement. The periods of low involvement are all before 1964, suggesting that a contemporary prime minister has to take some interest in economic

Table 8.1   Involvement of postwar prime ministers in the economy

Prime minister	Level of involvement
Attlee	Moderate
Churchill	Low
Eden	Low
Macmillan	High
Douglas-Home	Low
Wilson (1)	High
Heath	High
Wilson (2)	Moderate
Callaghan	High
Thatcher	High
Major	Moderate
Blair	Moderate

policy issues, if only for the reasons outlined in Chapter 5 about the electoral importance of economic policy management. As Callaghan put it, 'The economy is always there, like Banquo's ghost, to haunt you' (quoted in Hennessy, 2000, p. 382). The reasons for variability in involvement may include: the prime minister's personal interest and competence in the area; the extent to which he or she prioritizes other areas of activity; and the extent to which he or she has a strong chancellor to whom they are content to leave much of the general direction of economic policy. The question of the relationships between prime ministers and chancellors is discussed more fully later in the chapter.

The extent to which a range of factors influence the involvement of a prime minister in economic decision-making can be illustrated by considering the cases of the postwar prime ministers. Attlee generally occupies a high place in rankings of twentieth-century prime ministers (for example, third in a BBC poll of historians conducted in the year 2000), but Dell (2000, p. 205) challenges the conventional wisdom by dismissing him as 'obviously inadequate'. More specifically, he argues (*ibid.*, p. 204) that 'He played no part in economic policy before the summer of 1947, even though the country's economic plight was desperate.' Even his admirers admit the inadequacies of economic decision-making in the Attlee government, particularly in relation to the attempts to create a system of economic planning: 'Attlee's problem lay in his lack of a feel for economics' (Hennessy, 2000, p. 160). Attlee was quite frank about his lack of expertise. When asked about the economy when he was leader of the opposition, he replied, 'Why should I bother?

I have got Gaitskell and Wilson' (Brittan, 1995, p. 4). There were a number of aspects of Attlee's laconic style, particularly his attitude to the media, which could not be sustained in modern political conditions. In particular, what Wilson later called Attlee's 'tone deafness' on economic questions would disqualify a major aspirant to the office.

The aged and increasingly ill Churchill was preoccupied with other issues, notably his doomed attempt to bring about a reconciliation between the United States and the Soviet Union. Despite having served as Chancellor for five years, the economy was simply beyond his understanding (Hennessy, 2000, p. 205). His interventions on economic policy were largely confined to the quixotic, as when he objected to a proposal from the Chancellor, Butler, that a tax should be imposed on sweets to help reduce the Budget deficit (PRO: T 267/12, p. 5).

His successor, Anthony Eden, was also under the illusion that it was still possible for British prime ministers to make grand strategic interventions on the foreign policy stage, in his case leading to an increasing and eventually destructive preoccupation with Colonel Nasser and the Suez Canal. Eden simply lacked an understanding of domestic policy questions and allowed his Chancellor, Macmillan, to reconstitute the Economic Policy Committee of the Cabinet, with Macmillan in the chair (something Attlee had not permitted) (Hennessy, 2000, p. 210).

Harold Macmillan was one of the postwar prime ministers to display a strong interest in economic policy matters. In part, this was because the times required it, as economic growth assumed a greater importance as a policy objective. However, Macmillan was well-suited to being prime minister at a time when economic policy issues assumed greater importance. This arose from a recognition that the British economy was being out performed by its continental rivals and because post-Suez there was an awareness of the limits of what Britain could do on the international stage. In the 1930s Macmillan had written extensively on economic and industrial policy issues; although he allowed the Chancellor to chair the Economic Policy Committee, he was inclined to dominate his Chancellors.

Macmillan's short-term successor, Sir Alec Douglas-Home, confessed that he worked out economic problems with matchsticks, something out of which the opposition leader, Harold Wilson, made a great deal of political capital. Blackaby's (1978) standard account of economic policy in the period does not even find it necessary to make reference to Douglas-Home. It was probably the last time that a British prime minister would confess to a lack of understanding of, and interest in, economic problems.

Harold Wilson regarded himself as uniquely equipped to deal with questions of economic policy by virtue of his academic training and earlier ministerial experience. The Treasury's account was that 'from the first the Prime Minister himself took the leading part in the guidance of economic policy' (PRO: T267/22, p. 11). Wilson set up a 'creative tension' between the Chancellor, Callaghan, and the Secretary of State for Economic Affairs, George Brown, who was liable to be 'drunk and rather quarrelsome' (Cairncross, 1996, p. 101) by the evening when informal policy discussions often took place. It was not surprising that the result was not an entirely happy one with the organization of economic policy by government 'at its lowest point of efficiency in the early days of the Labour Government in 1964–6' (*ibid.*, p. 263).

The experiences of deflation and devaluation did not blunt Wilson's confidence in his ability in economic matters. Shortly before devaluation he took personal control of the government's economic policy, taking overall charge of the Department of Economic Affairs. He told Richard Crossman, 'If I can't run the economy well through the D.E.A., I'm no good. I was trained for this job and now I've taken the powers to run the economy' (Crossman, 1976, p. 463). Dell is ready with some jibes, dismissing Wilson as a 'statistician marketing himself as an economist' (2000, p. 303); Wilson 'thought he would be a great manager of capitalism but his ideas on the subject derived from the Attlee stone age' (*ibid.*, p. 306). Despite recent attempts to revive Wilson's reputation as a kind of modernizing precursor of Blair, the expectations that he aroused as a qualified manager of the economy were never fulfilled.

His Conservative successor, Edward Heath, may also be seen as a modernizer. The difficult economic circumstances of his period in office would have probably drawn any prime minister into a close involvement in economic policy. Despite his declared intention to reduce government intervention in the economy, Heath's own policy priorities combined with a continuing emphasis on the importance of the full employment objective led the Heath government into extensive forms of intervention. Heath 'was very much the economic and industrial overlord of his administration. He was the first Conservative Prime Minister to chair the Cabinet's Economic Strategy Committee' (Hennessy, 2000, p. 352).

When Harold Wilson returned to office in 1974, his approach to the task was very different from that he had pursued in 1964. Wilson was both more tired and less ambitious. Using a footballing analogy, Wilson told the Parliamentary Labour Party that he would no longer 'have to occupy almost every position on the field' but 'would be no more than what used to be called a deep lying centre-half' (Wilson, 1979, p. 17). For Wilson's second term, it is possible to categorize his involvement in economic policy as 'moderate' rather than 'high' (Table 8.1).

Wilson's successor, Callaghan, was one of only four prime ministers to have served a period of office as Chancellor, in his case hardly with conspicuous success. Dell suggests that he would have liked to follow Wilson's practice of leaving the day-to-day conduct of economic policy to the Chancellor, Dennis Healey, so that he could enhance his reputation through the exercise of statesmanship on the international stage; 'But such neglect of the country's main problem could not continue' (Dell, 2000, p. 451). Hence it fell to Callaghan to signal the end of the Keynesian consensus and to negotiate the 1976 agreement with the IMF that ushered in a new era in economic policy. The period from 1974 to 1979 was a transitional period in which the postwar economic consensus on objectives and policy instruments, and the broader postwar settlement, started to fragment and come to an end. Callaghan played an important role in that transition process; he was 'an agent of change himself ... rather than a mere victim of it' (Hennessy, 2000, p. 380). Dell is, as always, ready with a 'could have done better' rebuke from the headmaster's study: 'The loss of the 1979 election was perhaps James Callaghan's greatest service to the British people' (2000, p. 471).

Mrs Thatcher treated her title as First Lord of the Treasury with some literal seriousness. ' "There has never been a Prime Minister more interested in the *details* of the economy", said one of her colleagues. "Can you imagine Macmillan inviting two foreign economists to No.10 to explain the obscure details of monetary control?" ' (Keegan, 1984, p. 200). The revival and reorientation of the British economy so as to wipe out the years of corporatist decline was central to the Thatcherite project. This new interpretation of economic policy was not established overnight, nor was Mrs Thatcher initially unchallenged in her management of the economy. It is easy to forget that the initial assumption of Mrs Thatcher's accession to office was that after a couple of years there would be a U-turn, followed by a return of Labour to office. But as

Mrs Thatcher memorably told the Conservative Party conference in 1980, 'You turn if you want to. The lady's not for turning.' By 1981 most of the interventionist 'wets' had been purged from the Cabinet. Mrs Thatcher's critics saw her success as evidence that 'The power structure of economic policy in Britain is very much in favour of a determined Prime Minister and Chancellor' (Keegan, 1984, p. 184). Mrs Thatcher's later difficulties in her relationship with her second Chancellor, Nigel Lawson, suggest that a close interest by a prime minister in economic policy does not necessarily secure the desired policies.

The case of John Major is more difficult to assess. In part, this is because of the void that developed in economic policy after the forced exit from the ERM in 1992. Wilks (1997, p. 691) comments, 'Since 1992 macro-economic policy has been emptied of content. No targets, except the control of inflation; and no dominant theory of how the economy works; instead a rather welcome pragmatism'. Major was concerned with inflation, but it is perhaps significant that he devotes only one chapter of his autobiography (apart from the discussion of 'Black Wednesday') to economic policy during his period as prime minister.

The Blair premiership is also difficult to assess because so much depends on the special bilateral relationship between Blair and Brown (Naughtie, 2001). Thain (2000, p. 231) sees the distribution of roles between them as 'Blair the popularizer of the "Third Way" acceptable to middle-class "middle England", Brown as the engine of economic and social policy reforms giving substance to the claim to philosophical cohesion.' It is the Chancellor who chairs 'the key economic committees of Cabinet' (Thain, 2000, p. 231). Perhaps the electorate's perception of the Chancellor as the main driving force behind economic policy is not so far from the truth. Blair has taken a close interest in economic policy through frequent bilaterals with Brown, but it is the Chancellor who has been in the lead in economic policy matters. One consequence has been an enhancement of the authority of the Treasury which will be discussed more fully later in the chapter.

The Prime Minister–Chancellor relationship

In many ways this relationship is the key to understanding the making of economic policy, yet it has not been tackled very systematically in the literature. When it breaks down, as it did in 1988–89, the smoothness of the process of economic policy-making is considerably disrupted. Nigel Lawson's resignation can be seen as the start of a process that led to Mrs Thatcher's removal as Prime Minister. Two rather contrasting books covering different time periods written about the office of Chancellor of the Exchequer by two former Labour ministers (Dell, 1997; Jenkins, 1998) have as an underlying theme the importance of the relationship.

Chancellors are more expendable than prime ministers. Eleven individuals held the office of prime minister in the postwar period, but during this period there were almost twice as many chancellors (20). If the economy turns sour, it is the Chancellor rather than the Prime Minister who is likely to have to pay the price of loss of office. Even so, the average tenure of chancellors in office is lengthening, perhaps because of the increased emphasis on stability in economic policy and because the increased complexity of the job increases the need for accumulated expertise. A prime minister is unlikely to get through three chancellors again, as did Macmillan. Major considered that 'losing one chancellor was a desperate affair, and losing two would be above the normal ration' (Major, 1999, p. 681).

If one leaves aside the special case of Iain Macleod, who died after a few weeks in office, then five administrations have had the same chancellor for the whole of their period in office (Churchill/Butler; Home/Maudling; Heath/Barber; Wilson and then Callaghan/Healey; Blair/Brown). It is relatively rare for a chancellor to survive a change of prime minister of the same party, Healey being the most recent example. Although incumbents 'have tended to be political heavyweights... their reputations have usually not been enhanced in the office' (Deakin and Parry, 2000, p. 182). Jenkins is perhaps one exception. Only two Chancellors have moved directly to the office of Prime Minister (Macmillan, Major), fewer than have moved from the Foreign Office (Eden, Douglas-Home, Callaghan). Two other postwar Prime Ministers had been Chancellors in the past, but in neither case (Churchill, Callaghan) was there much relevance to their promotion to Prime Minister.

The various types of relationship between a prime minister and a chancellor may be conceptualized in terms of a simple two-by-two table (Table 8.2). One axis measures whether the relationship between the Prime Minister and the Chancellor is characterized by harmony or friction. A harmonious relationship does not mean that the Prime Minister and the Chancellor agree about all aspects of

Table 8.2   Prime minister–chancellor relationships

	Chancellor as political figure in his own right	Chancellor lacks independent political base
Harmonious relationship	Chancellor enjoys autonomy and support from prime minister	Chancellor faithfully executes prime minister's policies
Difficult relationship	Clashes over policy, ultimate breakdown of relationship	Prime minister lacks confidence in chancellor, dismissal likely

economic policy, or that they are warm personal friends. It does mean that they have an effective working relationship. As Major comments in relation to Clarke, '[I] knew that we could be at ease with one another even when we disagreed' (Major, 1999, p. 681). Such a relationship would be characterized by broad agreement about policy objectives and mechanisms to achieve them; a definition of their respective spheres of responsibility; and a willingness to support each other's authority when it is challenged in Cabinet or elsewhere. A relationship of friction where there is disagreement about policies, mutual mistrust and a lack of willingness to support each other is likely to end in the resignation or dismissal of the Chancellor. The other axis measures whether or not the Chancellor is a person of independent judgement with a political standing which is not solely dependent on the Prime Minister's support. If he has his own basis of support in the parliamentary party, it is more difficult for the Prime Minister to dismiss or remove him.

The top left-hand corner of Table 8.2 refers to those situations where the Chancellor enjoys an independent political standing, but there is an effective working relationship between him and the Prime Minister based on mutual respect. The Prime Minister recognizes the Chancellor's need for autonomy and support, while keeping himself or herself informed about economic policy and maintaining a dialogue with the Chancellor. A good example is the later period of Denis Healey's chancellorship when James Callaghan was Prime Minister. Callaghan believed that 'A Prime Minister must stand shoulder to shoulder with his Chancellor' (Hennessy, 2000, p. 386). Nevertheless, 'Although Healey had his support, the Chancellor had to understand that he must persuade' (Dell, 1991, p. 226). But when the chips were down, as in the International Monetary Fund crisis of 1976, the Prime Minister, admittedly after some delay, made clear both privately and publicly his support for the Chancellor. One mechanism that Callaghan used to keep in touch with policy developments was the so-called Economic Seminar involving himself, the Chancellor, the Governor of the Bank of England, and key officials. Callaghan did not wish to have a battle with Healey in the period after the 1976 IMF Settlement, and the Economic Seminar provided an 'alternative way of opening up economic policy' (Hennessy, 1990, p. 226). As a consequence of the existence of the Economic Seminar, Healey recalls that, 'We never had the sort of public argument between prime minister and chancellor that proved so damaging to market confidence during the Thatcher Government' (Healey, 1990, p. 450).

It is interesting to compare the Callaghan–Healey relationship and that between Blair and Brown; both relationships belong to the top left-hand corner of Table 8.2. It is worth noting that the economic circumstances in which the relationships were conducted were very different. Healey probably faced the most difficult economic and political circumstances of any postwar chancellor, whilst Brown inherited an economy in excellent shape and benefited from the substantial mandate enjoyed by New Labour. Blair's relationship with Brown in the Labour government's first term was certainly not free from tensions and conflicts. There were a number of sources of tension: Brown's greater sympathy to some of the 'Old Labour' agenda, particularly redistribution; Brown's ambitions to be leader himself one day; and perhaps a certain amount of envy on Blair's part in relation to Brown's success with the party and the electorate. Focus groups suggested that the Chancellor was the most popular member of the government, being regarded as more principled and intellectual and less careerist than the Prime Minister (*Financial Times*, 27 March 2001). Nevertheless, the relationship was managed effectively and was the fulcrum around which the whole government turned. Brown was perceived at the end of Labour's first term to be the most powerful Chancellor of modern times, with an ability to influence the whole range of government policy.

Moving across to the top right-hand corner of Table 8.2, there are chancellors who lack an independent political standing and have an acquiescent personality. The role of such a chancellor is to carry out the prime minister's wishes. The classic example in the postwar period is probably Derek Heathcoat Amory whom Harold Macmillan appointed as a malleable Chancellor after Peter Thorneycroft had resigned. Heathcoat Amory was well-equipped to calm the waters after a resignation. Middlemas describes him as 'compliant to the Prime Minister's wishes...a good administrator, a much-liked healer in the Treasury' (Middlemas, 1986, p. 249). Macmillan reciprocated at times by treating him with something like contempt; in a paper on Treasury control written by the Chancellor, he scribbled 'Rot' in the margins and concluded by giving the essay a low mark 'Chancellor of Exch. This is a *very bad paper*. It might have been written by Mr Neville Chamberlain's ghost' (Hennessy, 2000, pp. 265–6). Dell (1997, p. 257) delivers a predictable condemnation, 'he had been willing to follow his Prime Minister in an expansionary and politically convenient policy in which he himself did not believe. Chancellors should be made of sterner stuff.'

Heathcoat Amory belongs to a different age when provincial industrialists (in his case, Tiverton in Devon) became 'reluctant politicians' and entered politics out of a sense of public service. However, the acquiescent Chancellor has not disappeared. A more recent example of the loyal supporter of the Prime Minister is Margaret Thatcher's first Chancellor, Sir Geoffrey Howe. As Chancellor, 'he became Thatcherism's chief mechanic, the indispensable overseer of the machine, whatever direction it took' (Young, 1989, p. 142). 'Howe was at the Treasury as a reliable workmanlike figure who owed his advancement to the Prime Minister' (Dell, 1997, p. 451). Perhaps, as a consequence, he was prepared to tolerate public abuse by Mrs Thatcher in front of officials (Lawson, 1982, pp. 84–5). To a large extent he and Mrs Thatcher shared the same goals, although he was by no means an unquestioning Thatcherite and did not lack independence of mind. Eventually he came to be one of the main architects of Mrs Thatcher's downfall through his resignation speech.

A Chancellor who is located in the bottom right-hand corner of Table 8.2 is in an unhappy position indeed. Lacking an independent political following and not enjoying the confidence of the Prime Minister inevitably ends in dismissal. The clearest example in the postwar period is Selwyn Lloyd. A rather solitary figure, 'He had no power base, either in the House of Commons or in the country' (Thorpe, 1989, p. 444). He had moved up the ministerial ladder 'by performing competently and loyally in subordinate positions, the political staff officer *par excellence* (Thorpe, 1989, p. 207). Macmillan initially made him Chancellor because he hoped he 'would be a pliant master of the Treasury' (Horne, 1989, p. 340), but he came to be increasingly disappointed with Lloyd's performance and his lack of vigour and authority. Retrospective assessments of Lloyd make him one of the least successful Chancellors of the postwar period: 'good mechanics make bad drivers' (Harris, 1992). Dell (1997) is not sparing in his condemnation: 'a man with limited intellectual horizons... lacking the conviction or understanding to make an independent contribution to the discussion of economic policy (p. 258)... 'not up to the job' (p. 282). In Dell's judgement, probably only one person was up to the job, and he never held the position (Edmund Dell). In any event, Lloyd was dismissed along with a number of other members of Macmillan's Cabinet in 'the night of the long knives'.

The final phase of the relationship between Major and Lamont also falls into the bottom right-hand corner of Table 8.2. However, he started off in the top right-hand box, although he was not as acquiescent a personality as either Heathcoat Amory or Selwyn Lloyd. If Britain had experienced economic recovery instead of recession, he might have been able to develop a firmer base of support within the Cabinet and the parliamentary party and move across to the top left-hand box of Table 8.2. Continuing economic difficulties, culminating in the ERM exit, shifted the relationship to the bottom right-hand corner of the box. What this emphasizes is the way in which the relationship between a prime minister and a chancellor may shift over time, in part in response to external events, in part as a consequence of the dynamics of the relationship itself. The usual course of events is for the relationship to deteriorate; for example, Major hints that his relationship with Clarke began to be more difficult after 1996 (Major, 1999, p. 685).

Lamont was initially appointed to the post principally as a reward for his successful management of Major's campaign to be elected party leader. He lacked any substantial personal basis of support in the Parliamentary Party. Initially, matters went well enough; Lamont was content to apply the policies of the government, although his Euroscepticism was deepening and he had grave reservations about Britain's membership of the ERM. Major's confidence in him was not so strong that he would not have replaced him with Chris Patten after the 1992 election if he had not lost his seat at Bath (Hennessy, 2000, p. 466). After the ERM crisis, 'the crucial relationship between the Prime Minister and the Chancellor went into irreversible decline' (Hennessy, 2000, p. 463). Major urged Lamont not to resign on the grounds that he was a 'lightning conductor' for him (Lamont, 1999, p. 269). This is a role with which most politicians would have felt uncomfortable, but it is an illustration of how prime ministers can be shielded by their chancellors from sharing in the blame for a policy failure. It was evident 'from the autumn of 1992 to Lamont's eventual sacking in May 1993 that a never-commanding Chancellor was reduced to a weaker figure in the governing constellation than is good for any administration, let alone one in deep trouble as was Major's' (Hennessy, 2000, p. 467). Lamont's credibility was diminished, according to Major, by some of his economic pronouncements and some unfortunate and often false stories publicized by the media who pounced for the kill on a wounded minister. As a result 'in interviews ministers were questioned about Norman, while Norman himself was asked about trivia, and no one wanted to know about economic policy'. The final resignation scene 'illustrated the chill that had descended on our relationship' (Major, 1999, p. 679). Lamont was beyond the scope of Dell's reflections, but no doubt his verdict would have been a devastating one.

Moving to the bottom left-hand corner of Table 8.2, Nigel Lawson's relationship with Mrs Thatcher provides the clearest example of an independently-minded Chancellor with his own ideas about economic policy clashing with a Prime Minister with similar qualities. The main underlying cause of the tension was disagreement about whether Britain should join the ERM, which in turn was part of a wider and continuing dispute within the Conservative Party about Britain's role in Europe. Margaret Thatcher wanted Nigel Lawson as Chancellor, although in many ways she wanted to be her own Chancellor. 'Where the leader had hitherto tolerated a willing servant she now placed a man of dangerous zeal, but one whose congenial support for her own thinking she had no reason to doubt' (Young, 1989, p. 334). Their different views on the desirability of exchange-rate stability, with Mr Lawson seeking to shadow the mark, and Mrs Thatcher arguing that one could not buck the market, led to confusion at the centre of British economic policy. 'Other Chancellors have had their battles with No.10 but probably none worse than Lawson. In the end there was total breakdown in what had become an impossible partnership' (Dell, 1997, p. 493).

The experience of the postwar chancellors has not been a very happy one: 'Being chancellor cost Denis Healey certainly, and Roy Jenkins and Kenneth Clarke probably, the leaderships of their party and perhaps of their country' (Lipsey, 2000, p. 18). In many ways, it has been the prime ministers who have derived the most political benefit from the relationship with their chancellors. Six lost office because of general election results. Three were dismissed, although two of them later enjoyed a partial revival of their political careers. The relative rarity of dismissals suggests that prime ministers have to be careful about damaging themselves by removing a chancellor. Only Lloyd's dismissal was really an exercise of prime ministerial discretion and the 'night of the long knives' did little for Macmillan's reputation. Dalton had to go because of his own foolishness in tipping off a journalist about the contents of the budget before it was delivered. Lamont's reputation was damaged beyond repair, although he was offered, and not surprisingly rejected, the lesser job of environment secretary. Three chancellors were moved sideways and two died in office or resigned because of ill-health. Only two moved directly to the office of prime minister. There were just three resignations: Heathcoat Amory felt that the differences between him and Macmillan would widen and it was better to go while he was ahead; Thorneycroft resigned on the issue of public expenditure, but Macmillan was able to dismiss this as a 'little local difficulty'; Lawson's resignation considerably weakened Mrs Thatcher and was one of the events that contributed to her removal from office.

Because of the centrality of economic policy to modern government, an effective working relationship between the Prime Minister and Chancellor is crucial to a government's successful operation. It is possible 'that the concept of a strong axis only started with James Callaghan and Denis Healey in 1976 and has subsequenly been evident only intermittently' (Deakin and Parry, 2000, p. 20). In terms of short-term political management, the media will quickly pick up any hints of a rift in the relationship. The government's external image may be damaged, while its internal workings depend 'on the crucial alliance between Prime Ministers and Chancellors being stronger than the old but usually lesser *entente* between spending departments facing their common Treasury adversary' (Middlemas, 1991, p. 457). A recurrent Treasury concern is that prime ministers will be more susceptible to the pleas of the spending departments, hence the importance of the political strength of the Chancellor.

The Treasury

The Treasury has stood at the centre of the economic policy-making process in Britain throughout the twentieth century and particularly since 1945. Its reputation has fluctuated from time to time, but its considerable influence has remained one of the constants of British economic policy. Middlemas talks of Britain having a 'Treasury-based machinery of government regime' (Middlemas, 1991, p. 457). The functions of a ministry of economics and the preparation of the budget and the control of public expenditure that are separated elsewhere (for example, in Germany and the United States) are combined in one department. Among major economies, only France has a similar arrangement. Under the Blair government the role of the Treasury was strengthened further so that its remit appeared to extend into other areas of policy to an extent that concerned a House of Commons committee.

Because of the apparent extent of its influence, the Treasury has been a popular scapegoat for both politicians and commentators seeking to explain relatively poor British economic performance. This literature reached its peak in the 1980s and was characterized by charges that the Treasury was short-termist, cut off, arrogant and incapable of seeing the big picture (Ham, 1981; Pollard, 1982; Heseltine, 1987). As single-issue interest groups have grown in influence, the Treasury has attracted increased criticism as the department that has stopped them increasing government spending in a way they consider essential:

> Year in, year out, the reason most people hate the Treasury is because it is hard on public spending. To those in need – and still more to the pressure groups who claim to represent them – it is immoral. How can the Treasury deny more resources when the ill effects of the lack of them are so palpable? To other supplicants, it is irrational. How can the Treasury alone fail to see that putting more money into infrastructure would expand the economy and that the investment would pay for itself? (Lipsey, 2000, p. 134)

There is a close correlation between fluctuations in the reputation of the Treasury and its ability to control public expenditure. The Treasury emerged from the war with its traditional orthodoxies under challenge. The almost accidental way in which Stafford Cripps became Chancellor in 1947, bringing with him his responsibilities as Minister of Economic Affairs and the Central Economic Planning Staff from the Cabinet Office, helped to reassert the Treasury's authority. With the adoption of Keynesian techniques of macroeconomic management, the Treasury had acquired a new set of powers and responsibilities. But it was uncertain how to use them and found itself operating in 'uncharted waters' when it came to policy to control the level of demand:

> Although by 1953 the general principles of a counter-cyclical policy to stabilise the economy had been common ground among economists for a decade or more, there was no experience in Britain of putting such a policy into effect and hence little detailed knowledge of the rate at which the various components of demand were likely to change and the size and speed of the impact of the economy that measures of economic policy were likely to bring about. (PRO: T 267/12, p. 34)

The resignation of Thorneycroft as Chancellor in 1957 is recorded in the Treasury's internal history with a stark brevity: 'The Cabinet's refusal of a firm commitment that expenditure financed through Estimates should be held to the level proposed by Mr Thorneycroft led to his resignation in January 1958' (PRO: T 267/12, p. 5). The reference to the 'level proposed by Mr Thorneycroft' is an indirect reference to the fact that his stance, later praised by Thatcherites as an attempt to stem the inexorable increase of public expenditure, did not enjoy the backing of the official Treasury. The Treasury thought that the battle could not be won and it was sufficiently jealous of its reputation not to like losing battles (Dell, 1997, p. 238).

What the Treasury was able to achieve was a new multi-year public expenditure control system known as PESC (see Chapter 5). Before this system had bedded down, it faced a new institutional challenge through the formation of a Department of Economic Affairs by the incoming Labour government in 1964. This was partly a result of Wilson's desire to have as many 'crown princes' competing with each other as possible; partly a consequence of the need to find a suitable ministerial post for George Brown; and partly a product of Wilson's distrust of the Treasury. The new department was quickly and effectively outmanoeuvred by the Treasury which negotiated a 'Concordat' which gave the Treasury all the important tasks of economic management.

While the Treasury retained control of fiscal and monetary policy, the political pressures for higher spending tended to override any gains achieved by this new mechanism. The post-devaluation squeeze of 1967–69 represented a temporary victory for the Treasury. 'Once the economy was in better shape the dynamics of the PESC system...reverted to the pro-spending bias the Treasury had always feared' (Deakin and Parry, 2000, p. 36). This culminated in the scandal of the 'missing £5 billion' in 1974–75 that referred to an inability to relate actual spending to the plans made in 1971, an episode which severely dented the Treasury's reputation.

The 1976 IMF crisis placed the Treasury on a new footing:

> This episode marked the decisive break with the approach of Macmillan, Wilson and Heath who sought to balance the influence of the Treasury and the spending departments and more often than not came down on the side of the latter in the interests of political credibility. (Deakin and Parry, 2000, p. 38)

During the reforming and lengthy Chancellorship of Nigel Lawson, the Treasury's reputation was further enhanced: 'One of the most fruitful developments of the Thatcher years was the steady strengthening of the Treasury' (Lawson, 1992, p. 383).

These gains in status did not prove to be enduring, but remained susceptible to perceptions of the management of events:

> At the end of the 1980s, the Treasury went through a long down swing. Having ridden high, intellectually and politically, during the Lawson years, it was widely blamed for the bust that followed the irresponsible boom of those years. (Lipsey, 2000, p. 6)

The Treasury failed to keep control of public expenditure in the run up to the 1992 election, and the ERM withdrawal was perhaps the greatest economic policy disaster of the postwar period, further damaging the Treasury's reputation for competence. A slow process of rebuilding its authority occurred under Kenneth Clarke who exuded personal confidence.

It was the arrival of Gordon Brown, however, that really transformed the position of the Treasury. In part this was because 'Gordon Brown is the first Chancellor since Lawson to have a clear sense of a wider role for the Treasury in setting priorities for the government as a whole' (Deakin and Parry, 2000, p. 211). However, it was not just a question of Brown's personality, political priorities and growing authority, but of deeper structural needs of 'new Labour':

> the concept of a 'strong Treasury' can be seen as shorthand for approaches at ministerial and official level which go much wider than the Treasury itself and permeate government as a whole. A strong Treasury in this sense – not just a strong Chancellor – was a necessary condition if Labour wished to combine tight overall control of public expenditure with changed priorities and getting more out of available resources. (Deakin and Parry, 2000, p. 198)

The problem for the Treasury is that when it is weak it is criticized as incompetent, and when it is strong it is criticized for being too powerful. In a report on the Treasury published in 2001, the Treasury Select Committee commented, 'We are concerned that the Treasury as an institution has recently begun to exert too much influence over policy areas which are properly the business of other departments'. The Committee took the view that the Treasury's 'influence over the strategic direction of the Government has grown. The Treasury's role in leading the welfare reform programme and introducing stakeholder pensions and tax credits has led to the Treasury taking a greater role in social security policy.' Public Service Agreements had 'substantially increased the Treasury's influence over the affairs of spending departments' (Treasury Committee, 2001, para. 19)

The continuing sources of Treasury influence

Although there have been fluctuations in the Treasury's standing and influence, these variations in its prestige should not be allowed to obscure the substantial continuous influence it has exerted on the conduct of economic policy. One of its key assets has been the quality of its staff. It has always recruited the best candidates among the civil service's high-level intake; and Chancellors have testified to the high quality of the advice they received. Healey refers (1989, p. 376) to the Treasury commanding 'most of the best brains in a civil service that has no intellectual superior in the world'. The Treasury is 'a shaper and exporter of a civil service élite' (Deakin and Parry, 2000, p. 21). The 1994 Fundamental Expenditure Review led to a substantial reduction in staff in what was already a small department. However, it allowed the Treasury to develop new ways of working with other departments, as well to make its own internal structures less fluid and more hierarchical.

The Treasury has a reputation as an austere place in which to work. A stress audit of the Treasury's staff

> identifies excess workloads and hours as causing high stress levels, particularly for staff from ethnic minorities. Staff consistently identified the department as a 'cold, rather unfriendly and uncaring place to work' with a 'macho culture'. (Treasury Committee, 2001, para. 60)

The Treasury's view was 'that bullying and the other problems identified in the stress audit might be due to the type of people recruited by the Treasury, the work they did, and the pressure to produce high-quality work quickly' (*ibid.*, para. 62).

A number of the operating rules of government give important negotiating advantages to the Treasury. A standing order of the House of Commons which dates back to 1713 prevents an MP proposing a measure which would cost the Treasury money without government consent. A second rule, formalized in 1924, requires that no proposal for additional expenditure can be circulated to the Cabinet before it has been discussed in draft with the Treasury. A third rule, dating from 1884, is that any proposal involving an increase in expenditure or any new service requires Treasury sanction. Harold Wilson, in his second term as Prime Minister, promulgated 'a new ruling to the effect that Treasury ministers could not be overruled on financial matters in Cabinet committees' (Pliatzky, 1982, p. 140). Wilson spoke of it as 'giving the Treasury 51 per cent of the votes' (*ibid.*). Under Wilson's formulation, appeals could only be made to the full Cabinet if the chair of the committee concerned agreed, but Callaghan made this 'automatic', an arrangement written into the rules for ministers by Mrs Thatcher (Hennessy, 2000, p. 389).

Spending ministers gained the impression that the Treasury had a 'power of veto over everything that moved in Whitehall':

> For example, in the Cabinet Committee which dealt with plans for future legislation, the Treasury minister attending was always of junior rank, but always in a position to say 'The Treasury says no', quite often for arcane Treasury reasons, which were much more to do with the exercise of power within the confines of Whitehall than with the practicalities of what was being proposed. (Sheppard, 2000, p. 19)

As macroeconomic policy has declined in importance, the Treasury has sought out new roles. The Treasury has 'sought strategic control of a wide range of policy matters, using PSAs (Public Service Agreements) to set common values and objectives throughout Government' (Treasury Committee, 2001, para. 18). In part, the Treasury has filled a vacuum created by the lack of a central unit for strategic policy-making in government. This deficiency was offset by changes introduced after the second Labour victory in 2001. The Cabinet Office was recast as more of a prime-minister's department with a Delivery Unit to chase progress on manifesto pledges, an Office of Public Service Reform to help ensure delivery and a Forward Strategy Unit to provide greater strategic capacity.

Although the Treasury's influence may fluctuate again in the future, it is unlikely to experience a fundamental decline. Its role in the supervision of public expenditure places it at the heart of government, and any question of splitting the Treasury is generally agreed to be off the agenda. The Treasury is not necessarily just a neutral seeker after greater efficiency in the provision of public services; Deakin and Parry note (2000, p. 84) that a leaked paper of 1996 which stated that ' "Treasury officials have a high level of commitment to the efficiency of the market mechanism; to neo-classical welfare economics and to the utilitarian ethos on which they are based" lacks the usual civil service caution but is a fair formulation of the direction in which the Treasury was heading.' In a sense, all the Treasury was doing in such a formulation was to mirror the prevailing economic orthodoxy. However, a Treasury that was more representative of the society in which it operates might have a better understanding of the changing character of that society and be better placed to exert its undoubted influence.

The Bank of England

An in-joke at the Treasury used to refer to the Bank of England as 'the Treasury's East End branch'. It was certainly possible to portray the Bank as 'the executive arm of the Treasury in the financial markets' (Lawson, 1992, p. 383), but the relationship between the Treasury and the central bank has never been a simple one of the government issuing instructions to the Bank. Its nationalization in 1947 made relatively little difference to the way in which it operated; it continued to regard itself as the guardian of the City of London and its representative to government. As far as the Treasury was concerned, it had to treat the Bank of England as 'a centre of power in its own right' (PRO: T267/12, p. 4).

From the Treasury's perspective 'This was shown most clearly in August–September 1957, when there was disagreement between the Chancellor and the Governor over whether the commercial banks should be given a directive about the level of their advances' (PRO: T267/12, p. 4). The Bank of England was not disposed to comply and the Treasury lacked the powers to make them do so:

> The only alternatives would have been to pass new legislation to increase the Treasury's powers over the Bank and the banking system as a whole

or to call for the Governor's resignation...both would probably have exacerbated the foreign exchange crisis as well as causing a great political furore (PRO: T267/12, p. 4).

The Governor of the Bank appears as a shadowy but powerful figure in the accounts of prime ministers in office, usually urging cuts in public expenditure against the background of a looming sterling crisis (Horne, 1989, p. 50; Wilson, 1971, pp. 61–2). Interventions by the Governor were viewed with particular suspicion in the Labour Party. Crossman saw his colleagues as open to 'moral blackmail' by the Governor and the Bank, and whether they were on the right or left of the Labour Party, members of the Cabinet were 'weak and pliable in the hands of the City and the Bank of England when a crisis...blows up' (Crossman, 1979, p. 78). As the economic and political turmoil of the 1970s increased, the Bank seemed to be increasingly concerned about the extent to which it could exert such an influence. Dell, then Paymaster General, received a private message from the Bank asking to talk to him under the belief that he was 'some sort of socialist saviour of the City and industry to whom it could turn at all points' (Dell, 1991, p. 40).

The Bank's reputation was considerably damaged by the way it had handled the deregulation introduced by the Heath government's White Paper on Competition and Credit Control, and by the secondary banking crisis which followed. Relations between the Bank and the Treasury reached perhaps their lowest ebb in 1976 when the Bank was accused of having mismanaged the foreign exchange markets, leading to a substantial fall in sterling. Even the Prime Minister, James Callaghan, joined the chorus of criticism (Fay, 1988, p. 75). However, the outcome of the IMF crisis vindicated the stance taken by the Bank. 'It had been shown to be correct about the need to cut public spending and right in suggesting that an IMF loan would end speculation against sterling' (*ibid.*, p. 77).

As monetary concerns became a more central feature of economic policy from the late 1970s onwards, 'the activities of the Bank became central to the success of Government strategy' (Lawson, 1992, p. 83). Initial relations between Mrs Thatcher and the Bank were strained, in large part because the monetary indicators were not behaving as monetarist theory predicted. Mrs Thatcher came to the view that either the Bank was 'technically incompetent (it could not achieve the monetary target), or it was subversive (undermining monetarism)' (Fay, 1988, p. 117). The Prime Minister had a rather simplistic if clearly-defined view of the power relationships between herself and the Bank: 'It says on the plate on my front door that I'm the First Lord of the Treasury, so Richardson [the Governor] must do as I say' (Fay, 1988, p. 116). The idea of central-bank independence only won favour later in the government's term of office as Mrs Thatcher's power waned. Nigel Lawson presented a memorandum to Mrs Thatcher on the subject in November 1988 and made it a feature of his resignation speech.

Central bank independence

The idea of central-bank independence won increasing favour with commentators on economic policy. Politicians could not be trusted to run the economy because they would give undue weight to short- term electoral considerations. Central bankers were independent of such considerations, sympathetic to the market mechanism, either possessed or had ready access to relevant expertise and could be trusted to make prudent judgements. Credibility with the markets would thus be established and the chances of success in the fight against inflation increased. An independent central bank could take speedier action to anticipate and choke off the threat of higher inflation.

Politicians and officials were reluctant to surrender any key policy instruments to the Bank of England; Major's view (1999, p. 153) was that 'the person responsible for monetary policy should be answerable for it to the House of Commons'. The practical argument was that the Bank would be more cautious (even alarmist) about inflation than a politician would be. As a consequence, interest rates would go up relatively quickly and fall relatively slowly. Nevertheless, Major agreed that his Chancellor, Ken Clarke, should take two small steps towards greater Bank independence. The minutes of his monthly monetary meeting with the Governor of the Bank were to be published six weeks in arrears, so that the arguments made by both sides thus became public knowledge. It was also agreed that the Bank could publish its regular inflation report without prior approval by the Treasury.

Within a few days of coming into office, the Blair government took one of the most significant economic policy decisions of the postwar period by transferring responsibility for interest rate policy to the Bank. The letter from Gordon Brown announcing the decision is displayed in a glass case in the Bank's museum. The Blair government's decisiveness provides an interesting contrast with the unwillingness of the incoming Wilson government to contemplate devaluation. Not only did the transfer of responsibility enhance the credibility of the government with international financial markets, it also meant that political criticism of interest rate levels was deflected towards the Bank. Demonstrators started to appear outside the Bank of England.

It should be noted that this policy change gave the Bank instrumental or operational rather than goal or target independence. The arrangements made in Britain still fall far short of the degree of independence allowed to central banks in most other leading economies. Within G7, the central banks of the USA (and before the formation of the ECB) those of Italy, France and Germany enjoyed the freedom to set both interest rates and policy targets. The Bundesbank set its own interest rate policy, constrained only by an obligation to protect the value of the German currency. Even in terms of the deployment of the interest rate instrument, the dense network of relationships between the Bank and the Treasury means that it would be possible for the Treasury to give the Bank some indication of what a desirable change in the level of interest rates might be. A non-voting representative of the Treasury is present at meetings of the Monetary Policy Committee (MPC) whose principal task is to keep the MPC informed about government fiscal policy.

In Britain, the Bank of England works within an inflation target set by the government and has to account for a failure to keep within the target (which can include undershooting as well as overshooting as happened in 2001). The Bank therefore does not have to decide for itself what the objective of 'stable prices' means. It is also expected to support the government's economic policy and its growth and employment objectives. Government has also retained a so-called 'national interest power' enabling it in extreme economic circumstances to give instructions to the Bank on interest rates for a limited period. The government also continues to be responsible for exchange rate policy, another important economic lever. Moreover, the executive influences the appointment of the majority of the members of the Bank's nine-person MPC. Candidates for the governorship and deputy governorships are recommended by the Prime Minister, while the Chancellor is consulted on the appointment of the two other Bank representatives on the MPC and selects the four members appointed from outside the Bank. After Professor Charles Goodhart was not appointed by the Chancellor to a second term, he complained that the process of appointing members was 'opaque' (*Financial Times*, 10 June 2000).

The monthly meetings of the MPC are followed by the publication of extensive minutes two weeks later, including voting records. This has led to newspaper analyses categorizing individual members of the committee as hawks or doves. The hawkish contingent was seen as being led by the Deputy Governor of the Bank, Mervyn King. There was some ambiguity about the role of the four independent (perhaps better termed 'external') members of the MPC directly appointed by the Chancellor. All apart from Professor Goodhart effectively worked full-time on the role, spending a considerable amount of time as the public face of the MPC making speeches around the country. Martin Weale, director of the National Institute for Economic and Social Research, argued that the Chancellor's plan for part-time independent members had 'turned out not to be practical – they've been sucked into the Bank' (*Financial Times*, 30 October 1999). Nevertheless, independent members Sushil Wadhwani and DeAnne Julius were the most consistent 'doves' and 'continued to flex their intellectual muscles and challenge traditional Bank thinking' (*Financial Times*, 9 January 2001).

During the first year of the committee's work, the rate was cumulatively raised by one percentage point; it was then brought down gradually by two-and-a-half percentage points during the second year of the new system, before being adjusted upwards again. From February 2000 to February 2001 rates were kept unchanged at 6 per cent. Perhaps surprisingly, this period of stability attracted some criticism. John Edmonds, the general secretary of the GMB union, contrasted what he saw as the rapid 'racing-car' action of the US Federal Reserve with the 'supertanker' slowness of the MPC (*Financial Times*, 9 January 2001). There was broader concern among economists that the MPC had lost its ability to anticipate moves in the game. It was thought that the willingness of the MPC to play a deep-lying waiting game during this period had much to do with the pivotal influence on the committee of the Governor of the Bank of England, Sir Edward George.

The overall pattern from 1997 to 2001 was that while the official interest rate has been quite volatile, the changes made have generally been small and have been kept within a range of 5 per cent to 7.5 per cent. It was only after the events of September 2001 that the rate moved outside this range. The OECD (2000, p. 43) has commended the committee for showing 'that it is willing to hike rates when current inflation provided that the forecast suggests that it will ultimately rise above target, and *vice versa*'.

Inflation has been lower and more stable since the transfer of interest rate-setting powers to the Bank. However, this may not reflect the merits of the framework, but rather a generally benign global policy setting. In times of greater economic instability, the new framework may be called into greater question. If economic gains are no longer evident, questions about whether the loss of political control is worthwhile may be raised again. The arrangements could also be overtaken by British membership of the euro which would imply a diminished role for the Bank.

Domestic economic policy-making has been portrayed in this chapter in terms of what Hennessy (2000, p. 389) describes as the traditional and narrow triumvirate of No. 10 Downing Street, the Chancellor and the Treasury and the Bank. Although the balance of power between these three actors has shifted from time to time, they have continued to be preeminent. However, the fact that they make policy is not the same thing as saying that their decisions are effective; they may be held accountable for events, but they may not be able to control and influence them. The traditional levers of economic policy never worked all that well. Although there has been some adaptation of them to adjust to the imperatives of a globalizing world economy, most notably through the transfer of interest rate decisions to the Bank, would-be policy-makers may be even less able to influence the actions of economic agents than in the past.

9

Parliament, the Media and Organized Interests

Introduction

It was suggested in the last chapter that economic policy in Britain has been made by a limited number of key decision-makers. That does not mean, however, that there are no other actors that have an input into economic policy-making. Parliament would certainly like to make an impact on the policy-making process; the media, particularly the specialist broadsheet media, set the context within which policy-making takes place and have a particularly strong influence on the formation of policy agendas; and there are a number of pressure groups that are drawn into the policy-making process. If the policy-making process loses contact with public opinion, then exasperated members of the public may resort to direct action, as happened with the petrol protests in September 2000.

Parliament

Seen from the Treasury, Parliament is very much an outsider in the policy process. This is evident from the tone of documents in the Public Record Office over a long period of time. For example, during the Second World War, a minute on fire service provision noted with some condescension, 'But this question will eventually have to be argued with laymen, i.e., the local authorities and Parliament and a lay view may be of some value' (PRO: HO187/141). The Treasury's internal history of the management of demand from 1964 to 1970 contrasts the 'official' view with that of 'outsiders' whilst referring to 'a budget debate which was singularly barren of constructive content' (PRO: T267/22, p. 47). And it is doubtful whether attitudes have changed very much over the years; the British system of government is centred round the core executive and, if anything, the role of Parliament has been diminished by the emphasis on being 'on message' by the Blair government.

Lipsey's book often reads like an insider's account of the Treasury. He notes that 'Parliament and Treasury fail to work together' and refers to 'the traditional suspicion with which Whitehall views Westminster' (Lipsey, 2000, p. 240). There is also a perception of a difference in calibre:

> there is no hiding the fact that officials are on average cleverer than, and invariably better briefed than, MPs. Due official deference to MPs' democratic legitimacy is often tempered by understandable impatience with the quality of those whom the electorate has chosen. (Lipsey, 2000, p. 241)

It is perfectly possible for a former minister to write a cogent account of the making of economic policy over a number of years and make only a few references to the role of Parliament. Consider, for example, three books written by Treasury ministers in the 1974–79 Labour government – Barnett (1982); Dell (1991); Healey, (1990). This was a period when circumstances should have maximized the influence of Parliament: the government lost its majority in the House of Commons, and was eventually defeated by one vote on a 'no confidence' motion which led to an election. Yet in all three books there is far more discussion of, for example, the trade unions or international economic actors than there is of Parliament. When Parliament does appear, it is often as a set of wayward actors that upset the predictability of the decision-making process, but who are unable to exert any coherent or effective influence. Barnett writes:

> We in the Treasury would not want to go ahead with a tax we knew would really offend backbenchers, if we could help it. But the lack of an agreed policy ensured that the PLP [Parliamentary Labour Party] had less influence than might otherwise have been the case. (Barnett, 1982, pp. 63–4)

Dell has relatively little to say about Parliament, although noting that defeats in votes 'levied their own toll on the international credibility of the Government' (Dell, 1991, p. 214). Healey makes only the barest of mentions of the difficulties caused by an adequate, and then no, parliamentary majority, and of the subsequent pact with the Liberals.

A conclusion reached by the Study of Parliament Group over 20 years ago still seems to be valid. They commented that

> in many important aspects of economic affairs . . . the parliamentary dimension is of little importance and is characterised by more or less automatic procedures to approve government policies when required, while the real power and influence are exercised elsewhere. (Coombes and Walkland, 1980, p. 30)

This judgement is echoed by the Select Committee on the Treasury (Treasury Committee 2001, para. 53), 'In several respects, the opportunities for the House to debate and decide key aspects of economic and finance policy are limited'.

In part this situation arises from the limited formal powers of the House of Commons. As far as public expenditure is concerned, only the government can request Parliament to provide money. 'Parliament can only reduce, reject or accept the proposals for expenditure presented to it; it cannot increase the amounts proposed' (Likierman, 1988, p. 142). The voting through of the Estimates is more or less a formality and 'Parliamentary scrutiny of the Government's estimates of future expenditure has long been regarded as inadequate' (Treasury Committee, 2001, para. 53). The annual Finance Bill has to be passed by the House of Commons and its line-by-line scrutiny is an exhausting business for the MPs involved: 'The passage of Finance Bills through Parliament has been criticised for affording insufficient opportunities for scrutiny of the many complex measures such legislation contains' (Treasury Committee, 2001, para. 53).

The contribution of Parliamentary committees

If Parliament has an impact on economic policy, then it is through its committees. The Public Accounts Committee was established in 1861 and is chaired by a senior opposition figure. Since 1866 its work has been backed up by its own investigative staff in the Exchequer and Audit Department that became the National Audit Office in 1984. The Public Accounts Committee is generally regarded to be the House of Commons committee that has had the most consistent impact on the executive, particularly on civil servants. Bruce-Gardyne comments (1986, p. 142), 'This is the one Select Committee that the Whitehall villagers take seriously . . . Their reports can be damning, and they have, over the years, given generations of Per-

manent Under-Secretaries some most uncomfortable experiences.'
Nevertheless, many of the matters that the Public Accounts Committee deals with are a long way from the grand issues of economic
management. It is concerned with after the event, value for money
investigations. Even when it does find fault, it may be that its magisterial rebukes do not carry the weight they once did. Lipsey argues
(2000, p. 252) that it 'has failed to modernize its techniques' and
compares its methods unfavourably with those of the Audit Commission which is concerned with health trusts and local authorities.

The Treasury Select Committee is more directly concerned with
the core business of economic policy. It is the committee 'ambitious
MPs want to be on... Its membership has been well above the
Commons median in quality' (Lipsey, 2000, pp. 242–3). Nevertheless, the Committee admits that 'It is a challenge for us to scrutinise
adequately all of the areas within the Treasury orbit and in relation
to tax policy in particular, the case for more detailed scrutiny is
apparent' (Treasury Committee, 2001, para. 56). The Committee
can be an ally of a Chancellor and a useful sounding board for him.
Its limits are demonstrated by Lipsey's (2000, p. 248) comment that
'The chancellor needs to take the committee seriously, but not to get
in a stew about it.'

The Treasury Committee's role in relation to the MPC has opened
up a number of areas of uncertainty. Part of the arrangements for the
establishment of the MPC were supposed to be enhanced accountability of the Bank to the Treasury Committee. It should be noted
that the House of Lords has a committee concerned with monetary
policy and one of the MPC members claimed that he had 'been given
far too easy a ride by the [Commons] Committee', while he had been
given a 'harder time' by the Lords committee (Treasury Committee,
2001, para. 44) The Lords committee on monetary policy is to be
replaced by a permanent committee on economic affairs which it is
envisaged will hold a meeting with the Governor of the Bank once a
year.

The Treasury Committee sought a statutory right to conduct
confirmation hearings for MPC members, no doubt influenced by
American practice. The government refused to agree to such a check
on executive prerogatives so the committee decided to hold non-
statutory hearings to assess the personal independence and professional competence of the candidates. One candidate, Dr Wadhwani,
was confirmed on a majority decision, while Mr Allsopp was
rejected. Asked to reconsider his nomination, the Chancellor stated,

> Mr Christopher Allsopp fully satisfies the criteria for appointments to the Bank of England Monetary Policy Committee. He is one of a line of distinguished academics who serve on the MPC...His appointment has been widely welcomed, including personally by the Governor and Deputy Governor (Treasury Committee, 2000, para. 51)

The not surprising decision by the Chancellor to overrule the Treasury Committee's decision naturally led the committee to reflect on just what it was trying to achieve. (The Lords committee decided not to look at individual appointments, but to focus on the general process by which appointments were made.) It had to admit that if the Chancellor had not overruled their decision, it would have raised questions about his own judgement. Nevertheless, the committee took the view that its hearings acted 'as a stimulus to the Chancellor to choose candidates who are competent and independent' (*ibid.*, para. 52). It is difficult to believe that the Chancellor would choose candidates who were incompetent or beholden to outside interests, even without the presence of the committee.

The Treasury Committee does have a more convincing line of argument when it states that 'it is vitally important that MPC members are able to express themselves well in public and withstand robust questioning' (Treasury Committee, 2000, para. 54). The Governor of the Bank told the Lords committee that the Commons hearings might deter well-qualified candidates from applying. The Commons committee retorted with some justification, 'If the prospect of a confirmation hearing puts the candidate off from applying then he or she is probably not suitable for the post in the first place' (Treasury Committee, 2000, para. 55). 'Above all, the hearings underline the fact that MPC members are accountable to Parliament and to the public' (*ibid.*, para. 52). There is a tension here, however, as one reason for setting up the MPC was to insulate it from short-term political pressures that would undermine its credibility with the international financial markets. One senses that for all the talk of 'enhanced' accountability, what the Chancellor had in mind was something relatively limited in terms of answerability. In his letter of May 1997 he makes reference to the Bank making reports and giving evidence to the Treasury Select Committee. In other words, the committee will be told what the MPC is doing. The one success of the Treasury Select Committee in relation to the operating methods of the MPC has been to persuade them to publish their minutes more quickly.

The Treasury Committee has been engaging the Bank on its new territory, but with limited success. In terms of its more established territory, 'Parliament lacks the resources necessary to hold the Treasury fully to account' (*ibid.*, para. 57). Part of the long-standing conventional wisdom about Commons committees is that they require more staff in order to operate effectively, although some of the impact achieved by Lords committees often arises from their ability to draw on the varied experience of the members themselves. In its third report of 2001, the Treasury Committee follows this line of argument, calling for the employment of 'more permanent staff to help Parliament better hold the Treasury to account' (*ibid.*). Specific ideas discussed include the establishment of something along the lines of the Congressional Budget Office in the US Senate, more specialist staff with economics backgrounds in the House of Commons Library, along with a larger Treasury Committee with perhaps a sub-committee on tax policy. These are all worthy suggestions, but the executive is unlikely to entertain any of them if it led to a real transfer of power.

The underlying assumption of most discussions on these matters is that Parliament ought to be given more influence over economic policy. It could be argued, for example, that this would enhance the transparency of policy, making better known the assumptions behind policy decisions and exposing them to criticism and debate. In the modern world, however, effective transparency may be achieved more easily by making documents available on the internet for everyone to read if they wish, rather than having them unveiled before a Parliamentary committee.

It is also necessary to question the conventional wisdom that more influence for Parliament over economic policy would necessarily lead to more effective decisions. It might be argued that effectiveness is not the issue here, but rather inclusion. Economic policy decisions are made by a small circle of insiders whose preferences and methodologies are open to relatively little scrutiny. In Keynes' day, it might have been an acceptable for decisions to be made by a small metropolitan élite circulating between London, Cambridge and agreeable locations in the countryside, but that is not acceptable in a less deferential and more egalitarian society.

There is, however, one important difference between economic policy and other areas of policy, and that is the issue of 'credibility'. A credible policy is one which economic actors do not expect the government to renege on and is therefore much more likely to achieve its objectives. Institutional arrangements such as the MPC, and decision rules such as the 'golden rule' are designed to constrain decision-makers and reassure the markets that anti-inflationary commitments will be adhered to. A rules-based, depoliticized economic policy leaves less room for the intervention of democratic institutions such as Parliament. There is nothing inevitable about such a trend, however, and it could well produce a Polanyian 'double movement' in the opposite direction, particularly if the economic environment becomes more turbulent and central bankers are no longer able to deliver stable prices. Whether Parliament has the expertise, understanding and opportunism to seize such an opening, should it occur, remains open to question.

The media

Lipsey suggests (2000, p. 251) that 'There has been a general passing of power from Parliament to the media outside.' What does this power actually consist of? First, it may be suggested that the media performs an important role in setting the political agenda; Parsons argues that 'newspapers and magazines have been a major point of entry for economic theory and language into more generally currency and (mis)usage' (Parsons, 1989, p. 3). Second, the media is the means by which the views of politicians are transmitted to the electorate. It is no accident that Tony Blair's first-term press secretary, Alastair Campbell, has been regarded as one of the most significant members of his team. Third, the media can have a substantial impact on the reputations of politicians. It is here that broadsheet newspapers or magazines with a relatively small circulation can have a disproportionate influence. Members of the tabloid press have been known to point to their limited circulations, but this overlooks the fact that a high proportion of their readers are in decision-making positions which can have an influence on economic outcomes.

The agenda setting role of the media was most clearly demonstrated in the propagation of monetarist ideas in the 1970s. The 'two terrible monetarist twins', Samuel Brittan at the *Financial Times* and Peter Jay at *The Times*, advanced the new orthodoxy, leading to the charge that 'because of the coincidence of two people with such views having prominent positions in two heavyweight newspapers, half-baked journalism was undermining proper economics' (Brittan, 1995, p. 20). Brittan and Jay had 'slightly different starting points', but Brittan (1995, p. 20) acknowledges that 'Jay never flinched from the implications of the new (or rediscovered) ideas on the ultimate futility of traditional full employment policies'. Jay drafted, or according to some accounts largely wrote, Callaghan's famous 1976 speech to the Labour Party conference which marked the beginning of the end of the Keynesian consensus. He later became economics correspondent of the BBC, while Brittan became part of Lawson's group of unofficial economic advisers (the 'Gooies') in the last few years of his Chancellorship (Brittan, 1995, p. 21). What is evident from their experiences is the potential for crossover between the world of journalism and that of economic policy decision-making. 'The influence of Brittan and Jay derived from the way in which they acted as a channel between the world of economic ideas and political and economic events and public opinion' (Parsons, 1989, p. 175).

It is difficult to find such a striking example of agenda-setting by journalists since the 1970s, and there are a number of reasons why this may be the case. First, the agenda-setting role has been taken over to a considerable extent by think-tanks. These occupy a number of distinct niches in the market for ideas. The Centre for Policy Studies, established in 1974 by Sir Keith Joseph and Margaret Thatcher, played an important role in the development of neo-liberal ideas within the Conservative Party. The Adam Smith Institute, founded in 1977, sought to bring forward practicable policy ideas, placing a particular emphasis on privatization. It floated the idea of a poll tax, although in detail only after an informal meeting of ministers had launched the proposal (Butler, Adonis and Travers, 1994). The Social Market Foundation, established in 1989, started from 'the realisation that market economics is not enough' (Stone, 1996, pp. 249–50); it is interested in the performance of markets, but also the social framework in which they operate. The think-tanks of the 1970s and 1980s tended to be informally linked to the Conservative Party or at least to neo-liberal ideas. The Institute for Public Policy Research was established in 1988 to provide an alternative to the free market think-tanks. It provided a source of ideas for New Labour, for example through its Commission on Public Policy and British Business, which was chaired by Professor George Bain, a Labour supporter then head of the London Business School (Commission on Public Policy, 1997).

A rather different body is the politically neutral Institute of Fiscal Studies which works on taxation and public expenditure issues. Its work is more at the academic end of the spectrum, but it is regarded as highly authoritative and its views are much in demand at budget time. Its guess in its 'green' budget at what the Chancellor might do 'usually proved to be uncomfortably close to the real thing' (Lipsey, 2000, p. 120). It also originated the idea of a unified budget which was implemented in 1992, but abolished by Gordon Brown. Think-tanks offer a more systematic means of putting forward the ideas that might once have been developed by journalists, and can draw on a wider range of expertise.

Second, the policy vacuum that existed in the 1970s provided a particularly favourable context for the dissemination of new ideas. As Parsons observes:

> monetarist and supply-side economics and anti-big-government ideas as they were taken up by the media were manifestations of a search for a new legitimating discourse at a time when the economic system and political order were under severe pressure resulting from the prevailing international economic situation and the demise of the old economic nostrums and trade-offs. (1989, p. 193)

Third, Parsons argues (1989, p. 199) that 'the world is now driven along by structures of global communications and information which are more powerful than any government and more influential than any man of ideas'. National agenda are formulated in a more globalized context: 'In this brave new world ideas count for much less than is knowing what is going on at the moment.' Nevertheless, particular events may be underpinned by a structure of deeper premises and understandings. As Keynes observed (1936, p. 383), 'Practical men, who believe them to be quite exempt from any intellectual influences, are usually the slave of some defunct econo-mist.' The 24-hour news agenda is, however, characterized by con-siderable ephemerality and the constant switching of focus to an immediate presentation of the latest big story which can mean a reporter presenting something which is devoid of any meaningful content but authenticated by an appropriate background. This kind of journalism does not lend itself to an agenda-setting role.

The media remains the mechanism by which politicians commu-nicate with the electorate, and there has been an explosion in the number of outlets providing television news and the volume of programming. Over the 10 years to 2001 there was 'an eight-fold increase in the supply of TV news available to the average consumer with about 243 hours a week now available' (http://www.bbc.co.uk/ info/news/newsfuture/res_page4/shtml). Nevertheless, the BBC still dominates the market. 'Over two-thirds of all radio and television news consumption is produced by BBC News. Overall 93% of the population tune in each week to the radio or television news' (BBC, page3.shtml). These figures provide the BBC with a 70 per cent share of the total UK viewing and listening to networked news and current affairs. Viewers and listeners are particularly likely to turn to the BBC in times of crisis or emergency. However, 'the heaviest consumers of broadcast news are both older and more affluent. Broadly the split is between those under and over 44 years of age with a marked reduction in news consumption among those aged 16–34' (BBC, page7.shtml). Politicians are very sensitive to any reduction in news coverage at peak times, as was shown in the row over the temporary move at ITN's *News at Ten* to a different time slot.

An emphasis on television should not neglect the importance of radio as a medium, particularly as one that attracts individuals who are more interested in economic and political issues, and who hold positions of influence. Radio 4's *Today* programme may not enjoy the influence it had in the days when Mrs Thatcher used to ring up to put across her view. In part this is because of the news remit given to Radio 5. It is also important to remember that both television and radio are often reacting to an agenda set by stories in the print media. The day's newspapers are avidly read in television news-rooms for possible leads.

Governments have developed a variety of techniques for news management to try and influence the way in which information about their policies reaches the public. Effective government propaganda first developed, if in a rather crude way, under Lloyd George in the First World War. The lobby system was the main way in which the relationship between politicians and journalists was regulated; the journalists got their stories on an inside track and politicians' confidences were respected. There was always a tension between this rather cosy system and the notion of independent, objective and vigorous journalism. Lawson notes (1992, p. 867) that 'The Number 10 press secretary is such a regular source of information that no journalist is likely to risk biting the hand that feeds it.' This does not mean that critical or misleading stories about the government do not appear. The special character of the lobby system has been undermined by the fact that the briefings given to it by the Prime Minister's press secretary are now on record and available over the internet. There is also an increasing tendency for journalists to comment on the way in which government is trying to set the news agenda.

It is possible to exaggerate the influence that the media has on voters' perceptions of the government in office. Voters screen the information they receive in terms of an already established set of attitudes and preferences. Nevertheless, some recent research suggests that the bias in the print media can have an influence on voting behaviour in election campaigns (Worcester and Mortimore, 1999, pp. 144–51). When the news that the 2001 general election was to be delayed appeared first in the *Sun*, there were suggestions that this was an attempt to retain the paper's support for new Labour and prevent 'dithering Tony' stories. The likely stance of the *Sun* and of its proprietor, Rupert Murdoch, may also have reinforced New Labour's cautiousness about British adoption of the euro.

If nothing else, the media can have a substantial influence on the reputation of politicians. Norman Lamont was undoubtedly damaged as Chancellor by a 'relentless campaign to ridicule [him], with nothing too trivial to be peddled in the cause' (Major, 1999, p. 678). A reading of the memoirs of chancellors shows them to be sensitive to the reception given by the press to their budgets and other major policy announcements. The most heavily indexed newspaper in the memoirs of Lamont (23 times) and Lawson (19 times) is the *Financial Times*. Margaret Thatcher's press secretary, Bernard Ingham, 'once rebuked a newly appointed Press Secretary of mine for wasting time lunching with a senior *Financial Times* writer, instead of cultivating those who really mattered' (Lawson, 1992, p. 467). In fact, the *Financial Times* does matter, but in a different way from the *Sun*. It is read by decision-makers in the economy, including company executives and dealers in financial markets. Its website is an increasingly important source of information for those interested in the economy.

Any economic institution that does not lay itself open to media scrutiny is likely to be subject to criticism. The volume of demand is illustrated by the fact that the MPC granted 205 interviews to journalists over a 12-month period. Nevertheless, a number of journalists writing on financial matters for 'serious' newspapers complained 'that the MPC was not as open to the media as it could be' (House of Lords, 2001, para. 38). The House of Lords committee took the view that it was part of their duty to make themselves accessible through press conferences and other activities and they should have a bias in favour of responding to serious press inquiries. They should receive support and training to help them fulfil this role. It is difficult to imagine the House of Lords making such a request of the Bank of England even 20 years ago. In an increasingly fragmented society, the media has an important role in explaining what is happening, and this applies as much to the arcane mysteries of economics as it does to any other area of policy.

Pressure groups

Ideas are not simply justifications produced to serve a particular set of interests. Perceptions of interest can be shaped by new ways of thinking, although these may interact in an interesting way with market forces. For example, a farmer may convert to organic farming because she becomes convinced by the ecological arguments of the organic movement, but also because it offers an opportunity to secure higher returns.

Nevertheless, the operations of the economy in particular do give rise to particular sets of interests that coalesce around particular positions. Most farmers consider that the continuation of agricultural subsidies is desirable, even essential if they are to remain in business. Concentrated groups of rent-seekers like farmers tend to win out over more diffuse interests such as those of consumers and taxpayers. This can be partly explained in terms of an Olsonian logic of collective action, and partly in terms of the ways in which particular constructions of reality are perpetuated. For example, it was a common assumption during debates about food safety issues in Britain in 2000/01 that the country had a 'cheap-food' policy, whereas in fact the Common Agricultural Policy kept British prices well above world market levels.

Neo-Keynesianism and the emergence of tripartism

The interpretation of Keynes's ideas by politicians and civil servants tended to increase the importance of some kinds of vested interest: by vested interest is meant an interest that is related to a definable location in the economy in terms of control of a particular factor of production. These developments were both a cause and an effect of the spread of Keynesianism. It was a cause in the sense that 'the political viability of Keynesianism in the post-war period turned on the advantages it offered for constructing a new coalition between business and labor in many nations' (Hall, 1989, p. 17). It was an effect in the sense that neo-Keynesianism, particularly through its ultimate reliance on incomes policies, led government into a bargaining relationship with unions and employers.

This process was variously referred to as corporatism, neo-corporatism or tripartism. It spawned a large literature concerned both with whether the category was analytically useful (for example, how distinct was it from pluralism?), and whether neo-corporatism offered a more effective means of running the economy. A large literature may be summarized in the following terms:

1 Corporatism seemed to work best as a form of elite accommodation in smaller European countries such as Austria and Sweden, although its proponents claimed that it was also present in Germany (particularly during the period before unification when the German economy appeared to be more successful).

2 Britain experimented with relatively weak forms of corporatism, perhaps more appropriately referred to as 'tripartism' through devices such as the National Economic Development Council (NEDC) set up by Macmillan and abolished under the Major government. The Thatcher belief that corporatism was actually a cause of relatively poor British performance overlooks the fact that it was only tried in Britain in what Lawson (1992, p. 714) appropriately terms a 'half-hearted' way.

3 This does not mean that it could have worked in Britain if properly developed or applied. The constituent organizations of the new constitutional trinity, particularly the decentralized trade union movement, but also the incoherent system of employer representation, lacked sufficient authority over their members. They could not effectively share in any delegation or sharing of authority by government because they could not deliver their side of the bargain.

Nevertheless, the tripartite temptation was a persistent one, reaching its height from the Heath government's U-turn in 1972 to the defeat of Labour in 1979 when James Callaghan so accurately foresaw before the election that a 'sea change' was occurring in British politics. Under the Labour government of 1974–79, but to some extent under Heath as well, the trade unions exerted a level of influence on government policy which they have not enjoyed since or before. Dell's interpretation was that the Social Contract meant that the government 'would concede to the trade union leadership influence over every aspect of government policy' (Dell, 1991, p. 14). Similarly, another Treasury minister at the time, Joel Barnett, recalls, 'We frequently paid a high price to obtain the cooperation of our trade union friends' (Barnett, 1982, p. 33). It was even suggested that 'the TUC/Labour Party Liaison Committee was sometimes a more important body to lobby than was the Cabinet' (Field, 1982, p. 44).

A distancing of relationships with producer groups

All this changed after 1979. The appearance of a trade union delegation in No. 10 Downing Street or even at the Department of Employment, the normal channel of communication with government, was so infrequent that it attracted media attention. Mitchell (1987) has traced the way in which the success rate of the TUC in terms of government agreeing to take the action it advocated fell from between 40.5 per cent and 47.0 per cent in the last three years of the Labour government to between 4.5 per cent and 22.5 per cent in 1979 to 1984. Even so, the unions seemed to retain some veto power. Lawson had suggested getting rid of the NEDC after the 1987 election, but Mrs Thatcher was 'wholly opposed; she was terrified of what the unions might do' (Lawson, 1992, p. 717).

The somewhat more conciliatory style of the Major government did produce 'a slight thawing of relations between the trade unions and the Conservative government' (Baggott and McGregor-Riley, 1999, p. 77). However, there were also considerable continuities with the Thatcher period, particularly in terms of the general policy stance of the government. The trade unions 'continued to find themselves frozen out of the decision-making process' (Baggott and McGregor-Riley, 1999, p. 79) in spite of a few meetings with the Prime Minister and a 1993 meeting with the Chancellor which was the first in five years. However, tripartism was further undermined, not just by the abolition of the NEDC, but perhaps more significantly through the final dismantling of tripartite arrangements in training policy which were a standard feature of policy-making in this area in countries such as Germany.

Membership of the trade union movement fell throughout this period so that by the time Labour returned to office it was only just over half the level it had been in 1979. 'New Labour' had little enthusiasm for a return to the traditional relationship between the Labour Party and the trade unions, and the Trades Union Congress (TUC) did not want to return to the social contract corporatism of the 1970s (Grant, 2000, p. 177). The unions have made some gains under the Labour government that they would not have got under the Conservatives, for example the minimum wage. Even here they owed a debt to Professor George Bain for the careful way in which he managed its introduction: minimum wage, minimum fuss. Nevertheless, in uprating the minimum wage in 2001 the government did pay some attention to union concerns, so that even if they did not get as big an increase as they wanted, they were reasonably happy with the outcome.

The creation of the Monetary Policy Committee (MPC) did, however, give the trade unions some cause for concern. They saw it as having an implicit bias against, or at least disregard for, the interests of manufacturing industry which they did not see as being taken into account in the composition of its membership. They were concerned that the problems of an overheating economy in the south-east were being solved at the expense of the rest of the country. It cannot be denied that the establishment of the MPC represents a significant change in the rules of the game in the economic policy arena that does not favour the interests represented by the trade unions.

In some ways, the end of tripartism was as much a blow for the Confederation of British Industry (CBI) as it was for the TUC. Mrs Thatcher regarded the CBI with some suspicion, seeing it as tainted with corporatism and often seemed to prefer the more ideologically compatible Institute of Directors. Nevertheless, high-level contacts continued. Lawson recalls (1992, p. 716):

> I made a practice of telling each incoming CBI President that my door was always open whenever there was any aspect of Government policy that was troubling them and which they wished to discuss with me, frankly and in private. They invariably took me up on this.

Labour as 'the natural party of business'

Nevertheless, there were undoubtedly strains in the relationship between the Conservative Party and business. From a business perspective, the Conservatives often appeared to be too influenced by the views of their core voters and activists, particularly on European issues. By contrast, Tony Blair's ambition was to make Labour 'the natural party of business' (10 Downing Street Newsroom, speech in New York, 14 April 1998) just as Harold Wilson had sought to make it the 'natural party of government'. Before he was elected he made it clear that he wanted to have a close relationship with big business: 'People don't even question for a moment that the Democrats are a pro-business party. They should not be asking that question about New Labour. New Labour is pro-business, pro-enterprise' (*Financial Times*, 16 January 1997). This stance seems in part to be a reflection of Blair's personal reverence for big companies and his empathy with professional managers and partly a strategic calculation about what was necessary to establish New Labour's credibility with the international financial markets.

This rhetoric was transformed into a close, consultative relationship with business and with the CBI in particular which was careful not to trumpet all the concessions that it was given. The general business reaction was positive. As one chief executive put it, 'Businesses support centre-right policies. This [Labour government] is a centre-right government' (*Financial Times*, 8 November 1997). However, there have been tensions over particular issues, and it did seem as if the issue of what was seen by business as the increased regulatory burden, particularly on smaller businesses, might lead to a more serious rift in Labour's second term.

One consequence of this reinvigorated relationship between government and business was an enhanced relationship between the CBI and the Treasury. The CBI has always enjoyed good access to the Treasury (Grant and Marsh, 1977, pp. 120–1), although when governments were more interventionist, the relationship with the Department of Trade and Industry (DTI) was probably more significant than it is now. Under New Labour the DTI has been effectively subordinated to the Treasury and the CBI has enough political sophistication to focus its efforts where the power is concentrated. Indeed, as the CBI is now a greatly slimmed-down organization in terms of staff resources, it has to be careful about how it deploys its lobbying resources.

Before the CBI was formed, the relationship was perhaps not handled with as much sophistication on the industry side as it was later. The Treasury's reconstruction of a meeting between Selwyn Lloyd and industrialists notes:

The Chancellor did not get much light from his talk with leading industrialists... All agreed that the confidence of industry needed to be restored but were divided about how this should be done; and, as the note-
taker said afterwards, 'the noise of grinding axes filled the room. (PRO:
T267/20, p. 24)

The modern relationship is perhaps exemplified by the decision to
set up a Treasury inquiry into planning policy, since a long-standing
concern of the CBI has been related to the slowness of planning
procedures and a lack of transparency and certainty. The inquiry
'was initiated quietly... at the instigation of the [CBI]' (*Financial
Times*, 3 February 2001). This was in spite of complaints about the
Treasury meddling too much in questions that are the concern of
other departments. Tripartism has not been restored, nor will it be,
but the bilateral relationship between government and business was
strong in the Labour government's first term.

The limits of insider decision-making

As was noted in the last chapter, the economic policy-making process
is dominated by a small group of insiders, but there are a number of
external influences on those insiders. Probably the least important
of them is Parliament. Parliamentary committees, those in the Lords
as much as those in the Commons, make an important contribution
to the scrutiny of economic policy. Nevertheless, there is widespread
agreement about 'the marginal importance of the legislature in the
detailed processes of policy formation and implementation' (Judge,
1990, p. 77) and this applies to economic policy more than to many
other areas of public policy. Pressure groups, particularly business
interests, can have a significant input to the decision-making process,
but it is the Treasury and other departments that determine at what
level and to what extent access is given: 'The most important lobbyists may get to see a minister. Less important lobbyists will see
officials, or be confined to written representations' (Lipsey, 2000,
p. 126). Of the three main sets of external influences identified in
this chapter, the most important is the media, because of the way in
which it sets the political agenda and its impact on the reputation of
the government and individual ministers. During the first term
of the Labour government, ministers were occasionally rebuked by
the Speaker for releasing information to the media about policies and
decisions before they informed Parliament.

This insider-oriented system of decision-making received a rude shock in September 2000. Relatively small groups of hauliers and farmers, communicating by E-mail and mobile phone, blockaded petrol refineries and distribution depots. Fuel supplies at petrol stations quickly ran out and food supplies were placed at risk, demonstrating the vulnerability of a 'just-in-time' modern economy to this form of action. It is evident that the protests had widespread public support, although they were brought to an end before that support started to erode. As a consequence, the government was obliged to permanently abandon the 'escalator' which increased fuel prices above the rate of inflation, and to make further concessions on the rate of duty leading to a substantial negative impact on its revenues. Economic policy may appear to be largely the business of expert insiders, but it can be affected by populist surges in public opinion.

10
Conclusions

The last quarter century has seen substantial changes in both the focus and the conduct of economic policy in Britain. The form of the state itself has changed, and the physical controls of the economy have been gradually dismantled. First to go were the controls introduced in wartime over the allocation of raw materials and of finished goods for consumers (rationing). A whole series of financial controls was dismantled in 1971 and controls over the import and export of currency disappeared in 1979. The disappearance of the old command state was no accident: 'Where it attempted to direct the economy it simply could not deliver the efficiency and adaptability needed in a world of increasingly global competition' (Moran, 2000, p. 11). The other part of the Keynesian welfare state, the service delivery state, also came under challenge because of the perceived 'failure of government to deliver public services efficiently and effectively' (Loughlin and Scott, 1997, p. 207). The emphasis shifted from government directly providing services, to making arrangements for their provision, a shift accelerated under the second Blair government.

Nevertheless, up until 1979 the state retained a series of major roles in the area of economic policy: as a macroeconomic manager; as an owner of key industries; and as a provider of substantial subsidies. Privatization substantially reduced the decision-making load of ministers in the area of economic policy, a point that is sometimes overlooked. Subsidies have not been eliminated completely, but there is no group of supplicant 'national champion' firms reliant on government largesse for their continued existence. Government does still have macroeconomic management roles, but its actions in this area are much more rules-based than they used to be. The conduct of monetary policy has been transferred to the Bank of England.

225

The regulatory state

Government has substantially developed its role as a regulator, to the extent that many analysts now talk of a 'regulatory state'. This tendency has been reinforced by the fact that the EU, largely lacking fiscal policy instruments, has been substantially dependent on regulation for the expansion of its sphere of competence. Much regulation – for example of the professions – is not directly relevant to economic policy. Other forms of regulation have non-economic policy objectives, but have a substantial impact on economic actors – for example environmental and health and safety regulation. Some forms of regulation, such as utilities regulation and the reregulation of the financial services sector, are directly economic in character: 'Three decades ago it was impossible to find a market which was not governed by the traditional British version of self-regulation; now it is impossible to find a significant City market which is not subjected to elaborate state regulation' (Moran, 2000, p. 8).

What is clear is that there is a strong regulatory imperative at work. Traditional models of a core bureaucracy operating on the basis of lifelong careers and a peer-driven public-service ethic have been eroded. There has been 'broader change in the social habitat of public services, with more litigious and less compliant consumers and less deference to public-service professionals' (Hood, James and Scott, 2000, p. 295). A consequence is that the state starts to expand again, but in a more chameleon-like form. There is a 'tendency for statism and bureaucracy to creep back "pragmatically" in response to particular "shocks" liable to provoke the hysteria of the media and as a consequence a public demand that "something should be done" '. (Skidelsky, 1999, p. 280). For example, the enquiry into the deaths of babies at Bristol Royal Infirmary between 1991 and 1995 led Alan Milburn, the Health Secretary, to promise to establish two new regulatory bodies: an Office for Information on Healthcare Performance will coordinate data collection about medical outcomes, with an overarching Council for the Regulation of Healthcare Professions to ensure that individual professional regulatory bodies act in a consistent manner (*Financial Times*, 19 July 2001).

The emergence of a regulatory state does not mean that state power necessarily diminishes, but that its form changes. It becomes more diffuse, but remains susceptible to central direction and command. It becomes less direct, but also more penetrating. A regulatory state is in many ways a more fragmented state with responsibility divided among a host of different regulators or auditors. Wolfe, J. suggests that 'withdrawing from direct control makes state power more efficient'. Markets function as 'self-organizing media of indirect control...complementing direct power concentrated in core state institutions' (Wolfe, J. 1999, p. 905). Moran suggests (2000, p. 2) that in the shift from what he calls a command state to a regulatory state, 'this new order of rule actually marks a different kind of command – in many ways more pervasive than the old, defunct order of command.'

The disappearance of economic orthodoxies

Whatever form the state takes, it does not operate in an intellectual void. British government policy towards the economy for much of the postwar period was informed by one of two prevailing orthodoxies: neo-Keynesianism and monetarism, although the former had a much longer life than the latter. These orthodoxies influenced the relative priorities given to different objectives of economic policy, and the instruments used to achieve those objectives. From the early 1990s onwards there has been no dominant orthodoxy; policy has become a more eclectic and pragmatic mix. In part this is because a dominant orthodoxy is no longer needed in an era of depoliticization, and also because the orthodoxies promised more than they proved able to deliver.

The content of economic policy has changed considerably reflecting a change in the ranking of objectives, with a greater emphasis on inflation than unemployment. The shift in emphasis from the demand side to the supply side has also had far-reaching consequences. Some of the policy instruments that were the subject of considerable discussion in the 1960s and 1970s have virtually disappeared off the policy map: incomes policy; indicative planning; industrial policy. There has been a new emphasis on issues of skill formation and social exclusion. The cottage industry that concerned itself with the management of the nationalized industries has been replaced by a new debate about regulation and deregulation. In the 1970s there was an active debate about the national distribution of income and wealth and the possibility of introducing a wealth tax, which has given way to a debate about distributive injustice between north and south and the extent to which this can be attributed to globalization.

One of the reasons that the politics of economic policy has changed is that economic policy has appeared to become much more successful. Reading through the Treasury's internal histories of the 1950s through to the 1970s, one senses a restrained note of quiet despair. There is a sense that everything has been tried at least once and nothing seems to work. In contrast in 2001 the International Monetary Fund was able to report (2001, p. 1):

> The United Kingdom is experiencing the longest period of sustained noninflationary output growth in more than 30 years. Output growth has averaged 2.9 per cent in 1993–2000, the rate of unemployment is at its lowest level in a quarter century, and inflation has remained at or below 3 per cent.

There was no assurance, however, of continued and uninterrupted success. During 2001 the high-technology boom in the United States and elsewhere came to a shuddering halt. A full-scale recession was only avoided by continuing consumer confidence and, in the United States at least, this appeared to be undermined by the terrorist attacks of 11 September. The US stockmarket subsequently fell substantially. Britain's high level of engagement in the international economy and its continued weak productivity performance made it vulnerable to any sustained international economic downturn. The British economy was increasingly characterized as a two-tier one; rapid increases in house prices and a continuing retail boom occurred alongside weakening performance in manufacturing.

Although this book has generally accepted Burnham's depoliticization thesis, it has its limits. A prolonged economic downturn in the economy might lead to increasing questioning of the wisdom of a policy of 'all power to the central bankers', and the head of the Federal Reserve, Alan Greenspan, was starting to lose his status as an unchallenged guru and sage as the American economy weakened. The response to the events of September 2001 showed that the instinct to turn to government for solutions in conditions of crisis remained strong. Airlines are commercial entities which were already facing commercial difficulties before the terrorist attacks, but it appeared to be accepted as reasonable in both America and Europe that they should apply for government financial aid. In addition, globalization has increasingly been the subject of violent challenge whenever world leaders attempted to meet. A repoliticization of economic policy is possible, and indeed the question of whether Britain should adopt the euro is one of the most highly-politicized issues facing the country in the early twenty-first century.

A Polanyian movement 'to resist the pernicious effects of a market-controlled economy' (Polanyi, 1944, p. 76) is a real possibility, and this might offer a new opportunity for Keynesian approaches. As Baker notes (2001, p. 19):

> The Keynesians bring with them notions such as the possibility of market failure, the efficacy of fiscal policy as a tool of demand management, the inherent capacity of financial markets to produce crisis, and the economic worth of public investment. They also refuse to bow down before the God of central banking as the fount of all economic power and wisdom.

Following the events of September 2001, there was a reversal of policy orthodoxy in the United States. President Bush indicated his support for lower taxes and higher public spending. A temporary deficiency in aggregate demand was to be met in Keynesian manner by a shift from surplus to deficit in the conduct of government finances. In Europe, however, the eurozone's stability and growth pact sets limits on budget deficits, although there are 'automatic stabilizers' that come into operation when there is an economic slowdown. Nevertheless, there is still a concern in Europe about the trade-off between fiscal and monetary policy and the risks of driving up long-term interest rates. It should also be remembered that Keynesian theory evolved in very different international economic circumstances when there was much more scope for action by national governments.

The limits of the Third Way

Blair's Third Way is an attempt to construct a framework of ideas for an era of globalization. It starts from the premise that globalization is both inevitable and desirable, even for poorer people in the third world. At a basic level it seeks to offer what most of the public evidently want: 'an economically competent government that shared their sense of social justice' (Blair, 2001, p. 3). A modest element of redistribution in favour of the 'deserving' poor made up of working families is therefore back on offer.

More generally, it seeks to offer a renewal of social democracy that is nevertheless very much based on a market philosophy. Blair's view (2001, p. 1) is that in the past 'Markets were poorly understood, their obvious limits leading the left to neglect their great potential for enhancing choice, quality and innovation' Blair has no doubt that 'Effective markets are a pre-condition for a successful modern economy. The question is not whether to have them, but how to empower individuals to succeed within them' (*ibid.*, p. 2).

This rhetoric appears to offer a superficially attractive combination of social justice and supply-side competitiveness, but the difficulty for Blair's approach is that market values are not deeply held by the population. Although Thatcher imposed a new postwar economic settlement that involved a reordering of policy priorities and substantial changes in the deployment of policy instruments, there was not a fundamental change in popular attitudes towards the market or to the public provision of health and education services.

This is evident when one considers public attitudes towards profits. In a market economy, provided there is no exploitation of a monopoly position, making substantial profits is seen as an indicator of a firm's efficiency. Such a firm is seen as meeting a demand present in the market in a way that is attractive to consumers and uses available resources and technology in a cost-effective way. However, large profits are commonly described as 'excessive' or 'obscene', the companies that make them as 'greedy' and there are calls for the application of 'windfall' taxes. Mr Blair's enthusiasm for the market and for globalization is not widely shared by the electorate. Market values are not deeply embedded. Despite the experience of Thatcherism, the instinct and habit of government intervention in the economy has not disappeared, and there is a constant search for new ideological justifications of intervention.

Engagement or disengagement with Europe?

The market-oriented approach is combined in the Third Way with a philosophy of engagement with Europe, with one principal objective being to seek to make European structures more market-oriented. Until a referendum on the euro is called, however, ambiguities will remain about New Labour's attitude towards the EU. Blair is personally enthusiastic about the EU, but also realizes that it is politically unpopular. Because he is himself someone who evidently believes in the benevolence of an élite with a clear vision of the future, it is perhaps difficult for him to see why technocratic élitism is not necessarily popular.

The more thoughtful opponents of EMU accept that the UK would have to develop a different kind of political relationship with Europe if it continued to remain outside euroland. Redwood (2001) sets out three alternatives to what he terms a 'United States of Europe'. One option 'would be to go it alone' (Redwood, 2001, p. 27); Britain would leave the EU altogether and attempt to be an independent force in the world. Given the growth of regional arrangements in most parts of the world, this is not a viable option and Redwood does not pursue it in any depth.

An alternative would be a closer relationship with the United States. This might involve joining NAFTA or, in its most radical form, becoming 'the 51st state of the American Union' (*ibid.*, p. 28). The EU is unlikely to allow Britain to negotiate a separate deal with the United States, and although an Atlantic Free Trade Area has been discussed the chances of it being achieved under the Bush administration are slim. There is no serious or substantial political support in the USA for a closer relationship with a UK outside the EU. Apart from anything else, it is quite useful for the USA to have the UK as its political stalking-horse within the EU. Even if these objections could be overcome, a closer UK relationship with the USA would be more asymmetric than its relationship with the EU.

Redwood's preference is to renegotiate the relationship with the EU, creating 'a new kind of relationship that makes sense for us and them' (Redwood, 2001, p. 178). Britain would renationalize the common fisheries policy and pull out of most of the CAP, but continue to cooperate in areas such as trade policy, competition policy, transport policy and environmental policy. What Redwood fails to address is why other member states, already exasperated by British behaviour, should offer the UK such a special and favourable deal. Faced with a threat of the UK leaving, they might simply respond that if Britain is not prepared to abide by the commonly agreed rules, it should leave the club, an outcome that would have serious and adverse effects on the UK economy.

The underlying concern of the Eurosceptics is that most European countries favour a more interventionist, organized market economy than the neo-liberal American model, including in particular a high degree of social protection for workers. Joining the euro would be a further step down the road of unravelling all that was won through the new postwar settlement achieved by Mrs Thatcher.

Concepts such as 'social partnership' that involve close consultation with the trade unions are anathema to Mrs Thatcher's heirs. The reintroduction of a Thatcherite model in the UK would therefore be permanently constrained.

Economic policy needs to strike a balance between the principles of efficiency, equity and harmony. Resources are scarce and they need to be used in the most efficient possible combination to provide desired goods and services. We have moved a long way since the prevalence of the version of social democracy 'for which market capitalism was simply a superior means of producing taxable wealth for redistribution' (Skidelsky, 1999, p. 281). It may be, however, that efficiency has come to predominate to too great an extent over other values, threatening the society on which a successful market economy depends. Society may need once again to protect itself 'against the perils inherent in a self-regulating market system' (Polanyi, 1944, p. 76).

Part of that protection would be a greater emphasis on issues of equity, perhaps going beyond the Blairite idea agenda of equal opportunity and combating social exclusion. There is also, however, an important place for harmony which is interpreted here as harmony with nature, but also that inner harmony that comes from allowing individuals sufficient space and time for the development of a personal 'hinterland'. Both these objectives are in conflict with the pressures generated by a modern competitive economy: hence the need for government intervention to protect the environment and to give individuals enough social protection to be able to lead balanced lives. We are economic men and women, but we are much more besides.

One of Polanyi's insights was that a fruitless effort to shape a universal capitalism would culminate 'in the end of universalism and an emerging pattern of regionalism' (Lindberg, 2001, p. 13). The EU is the most highly developed form of regionalism available in the world today; its supporters often despair of its inability to develop a bond with the individuals it calls European citizens, its lack of democracy, its embedded preference for technocratic élitism and its inability to reform policies such as the CAP. Its critics see it as leading Britain away from its traditional alignment with the United States into a more regulated, statist entity dominated by France and Germany.

At some point the question of whether Britain is to join the euro will have to be resolved one way or another; there are few benefits in continuing uncertainty. If Britain joins, the nature of economic policy-making will be fundamentally changed; Britain will become part of a complex system of multi-level economic governance. If Britain does not join, the future is less certain, although the country could muddle through, half in and half out of Europe, half influenced by American and half by continental European values. Scotland might see its future increasingly linked with Europe rather than England and even one day join the euro as an independent nation.

There are too many uncertainties to enable us to predict the future with any hope of success. Globalization may slow down, or even experience periods of reverse, but it is unlikely to disappear as a phenomenon. Harder times may make it more difficult to depoliticize economic policy. Whatever else happens, in the long run economic policy is likely to remain close to the centre of the political agenda, whatever new and surprising institutional configurations are created by future generations to seek to manage the economy.

Further Reading and Web Site Guide

Introduction

Burnham's (1999, 2001) work introduces the theme of the depoliticization of economic policy which is pursued throughout this book.

1   From the Postwar Settlement to Thatcherism

Middleton (2000) provides a text on British economic policy and performance since 1945, and Marquand (1988) provides a broad contextual understanding of the development of British economic policy. Dell (2000) provides a somewhat jaundiced and provocative overview in terms of the fall of traditional democratic socialism in Britain. Heffernan (2000) offers an excellent analysis of the intellectual links between the Thatcherite settlement and New Labour.

2   Globalization and Europeanization

Scholte (2000) provides an excellent overview of the globalization debate, while Giddens (1998a, 1998b, 2000) offers an understanding of the Blair government's stance on globalization. The work of the global governance agencies can be tracked through their web sites:

IMF: http://www.imf.org/
OECD: http://www.oecd.org/
WTO: http://www.wto.org/
G8 Information Centre: http://www.g7.utoronto.ca/

3   Economic Theory and Economic Policy

The importance of Polanyi's (1944) work in providing a perspective on these issues has increasingly been recognized, and Hirsch's book (1977) on the social context of the market mechanism has stood the test of time well. English and Kenny (2000a) reviews and challenges the relative economic

234

decline debate. Students seeking to understand Keynesianism should read, pending the arrival of an abridged complete volume, the second volume of Skidelsky's (1992) biography.

4 Monetary Policy

Dimsdale (1991) provides a useful account of how the role of monetary policy evolved and changed; Britton (1991) gives an understanding of how Keynesianism was displaced by monetarism, and the problems of using monetary targets in practice; and Lawson (1992) offers an understanding of the development of policy from the perspective of a participant. The many-sided debate about British participation in the single currency is effectively reviewed in Baimbridge, Burkitt and Whyman (2000).

5 Public Expenditure and Taxation

Two web sites are of crucial importance in this area. The Treasury's own web site offers key speeches, press releases and background documents (http://www.hm-treasury.gov.uk/) and an invaluable site in terms of objective data and analysis is that of the Institute of Fiscal Studies (http://www.ifs.org.uk/). Lipsey (2000) offers a readable account of the Treasury's role in this area, and a good overview of the policy debates surrounding taxation and public spending is provided in Commission on Taxation and Citizenship (2000).

6 The Supply Side and Competitiveness

Wilks (1999) is a key and carefully-nuanced study of the development of competition policy, whilst an overview of the European dimension is to be found in Cini and McGowan (1998). On transport, a useful web site is that of the Commission on Integrated Transport (http://www.cfit.gov.uk/). Ainley (1999) and Kendall and Holloway (2001) offer a context for understanding New Labour's learning policy, and Wolfe, J. D. (1999) is a key article on the implications of regulation for state power. Young (2001) provides an authoritative and succinct account of the development of utility regulation.

7 The Electorate and the Economy

The work of Sanders (1999) has been of crucial importance in this area, and Downs (1957) is still worth reading. Chapter 7 of Alt and Chrystal (1983) is still a helpful introduction to the theoretical issues. King (1998) can be used for an overview of the 1997 election, and Worcester and Mortimore (2001) provides useful data on the 2001 election.

8 Economic Policy-Making

Dell (1997) is a readable exercise in acerbity from which none of the postwar chancellors emerges very well. Hennessy (2000) often appears to think that the country would be better if it was run by civil servants, but there are few writers better at making good use of Public Record Office material to understand changing patterns of decision-making. Lawson (1992) has written the most comprehensive account offered by a former chancellor. There is quite a substantial literature on the Treasury, but Deakin and Parry (2000) is one of the most valuable recent contributions, particularly in terms of understanding its relationship with other departments. There is a less good literature on the Bank of England, but the web site is worth visiting (http://www.bankofengland.co.uk/).

9 Parliament, the Media and Organized Interests

Reports from the Treasury Select Committee are usually worth reading and can be downloaded from <http://www.parliament.uk/commons/selcom/treahome.htm>. Parsons (1989) remains a classic in terms of understanding how the media affects the agenda of economic policy, and Bruce-Gardyne (1986) is a readable account of the various pressures that come to bear on Treasury ministers and how they are dealt with.

10 Conclusion

Moran's (2000) analysis of the regulatory state is brief, but full of insights. Skidelsky (1999) offers a good analysis of the pressures that operate on contemporary policy-makers, and Redwood (2001) offers an alternative approach to that of the prevalent conventional wisdom.

Bibliography

Addison, P. (1987) 'The Road from 1945', in P. Hennessy and A. Seldon (eds), *Ruling Performance: British Governments from Attlee to Thatcher* (Oxford: Basil Blackwell).

Ainley, P. (1999) 'New Labour and the End of the Welfare State? The Case of Lifelong Learning', in G. R. Taylor (ed.), *The Impact of New Labour* (Basingstoke: Macmillan – now Palgrave).

Alt, J. E. and Chrystal, K. A. (1983) *Political Economics* (Brighton: Wheatsheaf).

Anderson, M., Meaton, J., Potter, C. and Rogers, A. (1998) 'Greener Transport Towns: Publicly Acceptable, Privately Resisted?', in D. Banister (ed.), *Transport Policy and the Environment* (London: E. and F. Spon).

Annaert, J. (1999) 'Globalisation of Financial Markets', in F. Buelens (ed.), *Globalisation and the Nation-State* (Cheltenham: Edward Elgar).

Apel, E. (1998) *European Monetary Integration 1958–2002* (London: Routledge).

Artis, M. (1999) 'The UK and EMU', in D. Cobham and G. Zis (eds), *From EMS to EMU: 1979 to 1999 and Beyond* (Basingstoke: Macmillan – now Palgrave).

Baggott, R. and McGregor-Riley, V. (1999) 'Renewed Consultation or Continued Exclusion? Organised Interests and the Major Governments', in P. Dorey (ed.), *The Major Premiership* (Basingstoke: Macmillan – now Palgrave).

Baimbridge, M., Burkitt, B. and Whyman, P. (2000) 'Introduction: An Overview of European Monetary Integration', in M. Baimbridge, B. Burkitt and P. Whyman (2000) *The Impact of the Euro: Debating Britain's Future* (Basingstoke: Macmillan – now Palgrave).

Baker, D. and Seawright, D. (2000) 'Nation for Market: Modern British Conservatism and Hyperglobalism as Hypernationalism', paper presented at the IPSA World Congress, Quebec City.

Baker, G. (2001) 'The Keynesian Genie is Recalled from the Bottle', *Financial Times*, 3 May 2001, p. 19.

Barnett, J. (1982) *Inside the Treasury* (London: Andre Deutsch).

Baumol, W. J. (1967) 'The Macroeconomics of Unbalanced Growth: The Anatomy of the Urban Crisis', *American Economic Review*, vol. 57, pp. 415–26.

Bean, C. and Crafts, N. (1999) 'British Economic Growth since 1945: Relative Economic Decline ... and Renaissance', in N. Crafts and G. Toniolo (eds), *Economic Growth in Europe since 1945* (Cambridge: Cambridge University Press).

Benn, A. (1979) *Arguments for Socialism* (London: Cape)

Bennett, R. J. and Payne, D. (2000) *Local and Regional Economic Development: Renegotiating Power Under Labour* (Aldershot: Ashgate).

Blackaby, F. T. (1978) 'Narrative, 1960–74', in F. T. Blackaby (ed.), *British Economic Policy 1960–74* (Cambridge: Cambridge University Press).

Blackhurst, R. (1998) 'The Capacity of the WTO to Fulfill Its Mandate', in A. O. Krueger (ed.), *The WTO as an International Organization* (Chicago: University of Chicago Press).

Blair, T. (2001) 'Third Way, Phase Two', *Prospect*, March 2001.

Blake, D. S. and Walters, R. S, (1983) *The Politics of Global Economic Relations* (Englewood Cliffs: Prentice–Hall).

Blank, S. (1973) *Industry and Government in Britain: the Federation of British Industries in Politics* (Farnborough: Saxon House).

Blank, S. and Taillander, A. (1998) 'Atlantic Interdependencies and Free Trade', in G. Boyd (ed.), *The Struggle for World Markets* (Cheltenham: Edward Elgar).

Boyer, R. (1997) 'The Variety and Unequal Performance of Really Existing Markets: Farewell to Doctor Pangloss?', in J. R. Hollingsworth and R. Boyer (eds), *Contemporary Capitalism: the Embeddedness of Institutions* (Cambridge: Cambridge University Press).

Bretherton, R. F. (1999) *Demand Management 1958–64* (London: Institute of Contemporary British History).

Brittan, S. (1964) *The Treasury under the Tories 1951–64* (Harmondsworth: Penguin Books).

Brittan, S. (1971) *Steering the Economy* (Harmondsworth: Penguin Books).

Brittan, S. (1995) *Capitalism with a Human Face* (Aldershot: Edward Elgar).

Britton, A. J. C. (1991) *Macroeconomic Policy in Britain 1974–1987* (Cambridge: Cambridge University Press).

Browning, P. (1986) *The Treasury and Economic Policy, 1964–1985* (Harlow: Longman)

Bruce-Gardyne, J. (1986) *Ministers and Mandarins* (London: Sidgwick & Jackson).

Bruce-Gardyne, J. and Lawson, N. (1976) *The Power Game* (London: Macmillan – now Palgrave).

Bulpitt, J. and Burnham, P. (1999) 'Operation Robot and the British Political Economy in the Early-1950s: The Politics of Market Strategies', *Contemporary British History*, vol. 13, pp. 1–31.

Burnham, P. (1999) 'The Politics of Economic Management in the 1990s', *New Political Economy*, vol. 4, pp. 37–54

Burnham, P. (2001) 'New Labour and the Politics of Depoliticisation', *British Journal of Politics and International Relations*, vol. 3, pp. 127–49.

Butler, D., Adonis, A. and Travers, T. (1994) *Failure in British Government: the Politics of the Poll Tax* (Oxford: Oxford University Press).

Butler, D. and Stokes, D. (1969) *Political Change in Britain* (London: Macmillan – now Palgrave).

Cairncross, A. (1985) *Years of Recovery: British Economic Policy 1945–51* (London: Methuen).

Cairncross, A. (1996) *Managing the British Economy in the 1960s: A Treasury Perspective* (London: Macmillan – now Palgrave).

Cairncross, A. (1999) *Diaries: the Radcliffe Committee and the Treasury 1961–64* (London: Instittute of Contemporary British History).

Cairncross, A. and Eichengreen B. (1983) *Sterling in Decline* (Oxford: Basil Blackwell).

Cairncross, A. and Watts, N. G. M. (1989) *The Economic Section 1939–1961: a Study in Economic Advising* (London: Routledge).

Chennels, L., Dilnot, A. and Roback, N. (2000) *A Survey of the UK Tax System*, IFS Briefing Note no. 9 (London: Institute for Fiscal Studies).

Chester, Sir N. (1975) *The Nationalisation of British Industry 1945–51* (London: Her Majesty's Stationery Office).

Cini, M. (1997) 'Administrative Culture in the European Commission: The Cases of Competition and the Environment', in N. Nugent (ed.), *At the Heart of the Union* (Basingstoke: Macmillan – now Palgrave).

Cini, M. and McGowan, L. (1998) *Competition Policy in the European Union* (Basingstoke: Macmillan – now Palgrave).

Clarke, H., Sanders, D., Stewart, M. and Whiteley, P. 'The 2001 British Election Study: An Interim Report', *British Politics Group Newsletter*, Summer 2001, 5–8.

Coates, D. (1994) *The Question of UK Decline* (Hemel Hempstead: Harvester Wheatsheaf).

Coen, D. and Grant, W. (2001) 'Corporate Political Strategy and Global Policy: A Case Study of the Transatlantic Business Dialogue', *European Business Journal*, vol. 13, pp. 37–44.

Coen, D. and Willman, J. (1998) 'The Evolution of the Firm's Regulatory Affairs Office', *Business Strategy Review*, vol. 9, pp. 31–8.

Commission on Public Policy (1997) *Promoting Prosperity: A Business Agenda for Britain* (London: Vintage).

Commission on Taxation and Citizenship (2000) *Paying for Progress* (London: Fabian Society).

Coombes, D. and Walkland, S. A. (1980) (eds) *Parliament and Economic Affairs* (London: Heinemann).

Crafts, N. (1985) *British Economic Growth during the Industrial Revolution* (Oxford: Clarendon Press).

Crafts, N. (1988) 'British Economic Growth Before and After 1979: A Review of the Evidence', Centre for Economic Policy Research Discussion Paper Series no. 292.

Crafts, N. (1997) *Britain's Relative Decline 1870–1995* (London: Social Market Foundation).

Crafts, N. (2000) 'Globalization and Growth in the Twentieth Century', International Monetary Fund Working Paper, Washington D.C.

Crafts, N. (2001) 'Britain's Relative Economic Decline, 1879–1999', unpublished paper.

Crafts, N. and Toniolo, G. (1996) 'Postwar Growth: An Overview', in N. Crafts and G. Toniolo, *Economic Growth in Europe since 1945* (Cambridge: Cambridge University Press).

Crewe, I. and Särlvik, B. (1980) 'Popular Attitudes and Electoral Strategy', in Z. Layton-Henry (ed.), *Conservative Party Politics* (London: Macmillan – now Palgrave).

Crooks, E. (2001) 'Taxing time with the calculations', *Financial Times* 29 March, p. 8.

Crossman, R. (1976) *The Diaries of a Cabinet Minister: Volume Two* (London: Hamish Hamilton and Jonathan Cape).

Crossman, R. (1979) *The Crossman Diaries* (London: Hamish Hamilton and Jonathan Cape).

Crouch, C. (2000) 'Introduction: The Political and Institutional Deficits of European Monetary Union', in C. Crouch (ed.), *After the Euro* (Oxford: Oxford University Press).

Crouch, C. and Streeck, W. (1997) 'Introduction: the Future of Capitalist Diversity', in C. Crouch and W. Streeck (eds), *Political Economy of Modern Capitalism* (London: Sage).

Currie, D. (1997) *The Pros and Cons of EMU* (London: HM Treasury).

Curtice, J. (1999) 'Can Britain Join the Euro? Political Opportunities and Impediments', in D. Cobham and G. Zis (eds), *From EMS to EMU: 1979 to 1999 and Beyond* (Basingstoke: Macmillan – now Palgrave).

De Haan, J. and Eijffinger, S. C. W. (2000) 'The Democratic Accountability of the European Central Bank', *Journal of Common Market Studies*, vol. 38, pp. 393–407.

Deacon, A. (2000) 'Learning from the USA. The Influence of American Ideas upon New Labour Thinking on Welfare Reform', *Policy and Politics*, vol. 28, pp. 5–18.

Deakin, N. and Parry, R. (2000) *The Treasury and Social Policy* (Basingstoke: Macmillan – now Palgrave).

Dell, E. (1991) *A Hard Pounding: Politics and Economic Crisis 1974–1976* (Oxford: Oxford University Press).

Dell, E. (1997) *The Chancellors* (London: HarperCollins).

Dell, E. (2000) *A Strange Eventful History: Democratic Socialism in Britain* (London: HarperCollins).

Denver, D. (1998) 'The Government That Could Do No Right', in A. King (ed.), *New Labour Triumphs: Britain at the Polls* (Chatham, N.J.: Chatham House).

Department of Environment, Transport and Regions (2000) *Transport 2010: The 10 Year Plan* (London: Department of Environment, Transport and Regions).

Dimsdale, N. (1991) 'British Monetary Policy since 1945', in N. Crafts and N. Woodward (eds), *The British Economy since 1945* (Oxford: Oxford University Press).

Dinan, D. (1999) *Ever Closer Union* (Basingstone: Macmillan – now Palgrave)

Dorey, P. (1999) 'Despair and Disillusion Abound: The Major Premiership in Perspective', in P. Dorey (ed.), *The Major Premiership* (Basingstoke: Macmillan – now Palgrave).

Dornbusch, R. and Fischer, S. (1990), *Macroeconomics*, 5th edn (London: McGraw-Hill).

Downs, A. (1957) *An Economic Theory of Democracy* (London: Harper-Collins).

Dunleavy, P. (1991) *Democracy, Bureaucracy and Public Choice* (London: Harvester Wheatsheaf).

Emmerson, C. and Frayne, C. (2001) *The Government's Fiscal Rules*, IFS Briefing Note no. 16 (London: Institute for Fiscal Studies).

English, R. and Kenny, M. (1999) 'British Decline or the Politics of Declinism?', *The British Journal of Politics and International Relations*, vol. 1, pp. 252–66.

English, R. and Kenny, M. (2000a) 'Conclusion: Decline or Declinism?', in R. English and M. Kenny (eds), *Rethinking British Decline* (Basingstoke: Macmillan – now Palgrave).

English, R. and Kenny, M. (2000b) 'Martin Wiener', in R. English and M. Kenny (eds), *Rethinking British Decline* (Basingstoke: Macmillan – now Palgrave).

English, R. and Kenny, M. (2001) 'Public Intellectuals and the Question of British Decline', *British Journal of Politics and International Relations*, vol. 3, pp. 259–83.

Evans, G. (1999) 'Economics and Politics Revisited: Exploring the Decline in Conservative Support, 1992–5', *Political Studies*, vol. 47, pp. 139–51.

Fay, S. (1988) *Portrait of an Old Lady: Turmoil at the Bank of England* (London: Penguin).

Field, F. (1982) *Poverty and Politics* (London: Heinemann).

Gamble, A. (1984) *Britain in Decline* (London: Macmillan – now Palgrave).

Gamble, A. (1988) *The Free Economy and the Strong State* (London: Macmillan – now Palgrave).

Gamble, A. (1994) *Britain in Decline*, 4th edn (Basingstoke: Macmillan – now Palgrave).

Gamble, A. (2000) 'Theories and Explanations of British Decline', in R. English and M. Kenny (eds), *Rethinking British Decline* (Basingstoke: Macmillan – now Palgrave).

Garavoglia, G. (1984) 'From Rambouillet to Williamsburg: A Historical Assessment', in C. Merlini (ed.), *Economic Summits and Western Decision-Making* (London: Croom Helm).

Giddens, A. (1998a) *The Third Way: The Renewal of Social Democracy* (Cambridge: Polity Press).

Giddens, A. (1998b) 'After the Left's Paralysis', *New Statesman*, 1 May, pp. 18–21.

Giddens, A. (2000) *The Third Way and its Critics* (Cambridge: Polity Press).

Goldstein, J. (1998) 'International Institutions and Domestic Politics: GATT, WTO and the Liberalization of International Trade', in A. O. Krueger (ed.), *The WTO as an International Organization* (Chicago: Chicago University Press).

Grant, W. (1982) *The Political Economy of Industrial Policy* (London: Butterworth).

Grant, W. (2000) *Pressure Groups and British Politics* (Basingstoke: Macmillan – now Palgrave).

Grant, W. and Marsh, D. (1977) *The CBI* (London: Hodder & Stoughton).

Griffiths, A. and Wall, S. (1993) *Applied Economics*, 5th edn (Harlow: Longman).

Hajnal, P. I. (1999) *The G7/G8 System* (Aldershot: Ashgate).

Hall, P. (1989) 'Introduction', in P. Hall (ed.), *The Political Power of Economic Ideas* (Princeton: Princeton University Press).

Hall, P. and Taylor, R. C. R. (1996) 'Political Science and the Three New Institutionalisms', *Political Studies*, vol. 44, pp. 936–57.

Hall, P. and Taylor, R. C. R. (1998) 'The Potential of Historical Institutionalism: a Response to Hay and Wincott', *Political Studies*, vol. 46, pp. 958–62.

Ham, A. (1981) *Treasury Rules* (London: Quartet).

Harris, A. (1992) 'What it takes to be Chancellor', *Financial Times*, 27 January 1992.

Hay, C. (1999) *The Political Economy of New Labour* (Manchester: Manchester University Press).

Hay, C. and Marsh, D. (2000) 'Introduction: Demystifying Globalization', in C. Hay and D. Marsh (eds), *Demystifying Globalization* (Basingstoke: Macmillan – now Palgrave).

Hay, C. and Watson, M. (1999) 'Labour's Economic Policy: Studiously Courting Competence', in G. R. Taylor (ed.), *The Impact of New Labour* (Basingstoke: Macmillan – now Palgrave).

Headicar, P. and Curtis, C. (1998) 'The Location of New Residential Development: Its Influence on Car-Based Travel', in D. Banister (ed.), *Transport Policy and the Environment* (London: E. & F. N. Spon).

Heald, D. (1983) *Public Expenditure* (Oxford: Martin Robertson).

Healey, D. (1990) *The Time of My Life* (Harmondsworth: Penguin).

Healey, N. M. (2000) 'The Case for European Monetary Union' in M. Baimbridge, B. Burkitt and P. Whyman (eds.) *The Impact of the Euro* (Basingstone Macmillan – now Palgrave).

Hedges, A. and Bromley, C. (2001) *Public Attitudes towards Taxation* (London: Fabian Society).

Heffernan, R. (2000) *New Labour and Thatcherism* (Basingstoke: Macmillan – now Palgrave).

Helm, D. (1986) 'The Assessment: The Economic Borders of the State', *Oxford Review of Economic Policy*, vol. 2, pp. i–xxiv.

Henderson, D. (1986) *Innocence and Design: The Influence of Economic Ideas on Policy* (Oxford: Basil Blackwell).

Henderson, D. (1998) 'International Agencies and Cross-Border Liberalization: The WTO in Context', in A. O. Krueger (ed.), *The WTO as an International Organization* (Chicago: University of Chicago Press).

Hennessy, P. (1990) *Whitehall* (London: Fontana).

Hennessy, P. (1993) *Never Again: Britain 1945–1951* (London: Vintage).

Hennessy, P. (2000) *The Prime Minister* (London: Allen Lane).

Heseltine, M. (1987) *Where There's a Will* (London: Hutchinson).

Hirsch, F. (1977) *Social Limits to Growth* (London: Routledge & Kegan Paul).

Hirst, P. and Thompson, G. (1996) *Globalization in Question: the International Economy and the Possibilities of Governance* (Cambridge: Polity Press).

HM Treasury (1997) *UK Membership of the Single Currency: an Assessment of the Five Economic Tests* (London: HM Treasury).

HM Treasury (2001) *Productivity in the UK: Enterprise and the Productivity Challenge* (London: HM Treasury and Department of Trade and Industry).

Holliday, I. (2000) 'Executives and Administrations', in P. Dunleavy, A. Gamble, I. Holliday and G. Peele (eds), *Developments in British Politics 6* (Basingstoke: Macmillan – now Palgrave).

Hollingsworth, J. R. and Boyer, R. (1997) 'Coordination of Economic Actors and Social Systems of Production', in J. R. Hollingsworth and R. Boyer (eds), *Contemporary Capitalism: the Embeddedness of Institutions* (Cambridge: Cambridge University Press).

Hood, C., James, O. and Scott, C. (2000) 'Regulation of Government: Has it Increased, Is it Increasing, Should it be Diminished?', *Public Administration*, vol. 78, pp. 283–304.

Horne, A. (1989) *Macmillan 1957–1986* (London: Macmillan – now Palgrave).

IMF (2001) 'IMF Concludes Article IV Consultation with the United Kingdom', Public Information Notice no. 01/15.

Institute of Fiscal Studies (2000) *Fiscal Reforms since May 1997* (London: Institute for Fiscal Studies).

Institute of Fiscal Studies (2001) *The IFS Green Budget* (London: Institute for Fiscal Studies).

Jay, P. (1994) 'The Economy 1990–94', in D. Kavanagh and A. Seldon (eds), *The Major Effect* (London: Macmillan – now Palgrave).

Jenkins, R. (1998) *The Chancellors* (London: Macmillan – now Palgrave).

Johnson, C. (1991) *The Economy under Mrs Thatcher* (London: Penguin).

Jones, A. (1977) 'Inflation as an Industrial Problem', in R. Skidelsky (ed.), *The End of the Keynesian Era* (London: Macmillan – now Palgrave).

Jones, D. T. (1981) 'Catching up with Our Competitors: the Role of Industrial Policy', in C. Carter (ed.), *Industrial Policy and Innovation* (London: Heinemann).

Judge, D. (1990) *Parliament and Industry* (Aldershot: Dartmouth).

Kay, J. (2000) 'The Social Route to Economic Success', *Financial Times*, 15 March 2000.

Keegan, W. (1984) *Mrs Thatcher's Economic Experiment* (Harmondsworth: Penguin).

Kendall, I. and Holloway, D. (2001) 'Education Policy', in S. P. Savage and R. Atkinson (eds), *Public Policy under Blair* (Basingstoke: Palgrave).

Keynes, J. M. (1936) *The General Theory of Employment, Interest and Money* (London: Macmillan – now Palgrave).

King, A. (1975) 'Overload: Problems of Governing in the 1970s', *Political Studies*, vol. 23, pp. 284–96.

King, A. (1998) 'Why Labour Won – at Last', in A. King (ed.), *New Labour Triumphs: Britain at the Polls* (Chatham, N.J.: Chatham House).

Krueger, A. O. (1998) 'Introduction', in A. O. Krueger (ed.), *The WTO as an International Organization* (Chicago: Chicago University Press).

Lamont, N. (1999) *In Office* (London: Little Brown).

Lawrence, P. (1980) *Managers and Management in West Germany* (London: Croom Helm).

Lawson, N. (1992) *The View from No.11* (London: Bantam).

Layard, R. (1982) *More Jobs, Less Inflation* (London: Grant McIntyre).

Layard, R. (2000) 'Joining Europe's Currency', in M. Baimbridge, B. Burkitt and P. Whyman (eds), *The Impact of the Euro: Debating Britain's Future* (Basingstoke: Macmillan – now Palgrave).

LeGrand, J. (1991) 'The Theory of Government Failure', *British Journal of Political Science*, vol. 21, pp. 423–42.

Lembke, J. (2001) *Competition for Technological Leadership: EU Policy for High Technology* (Aldershot: Edward Elgar).

Leruez, J. (1975) *Economic Planning and Politics in Britain* (Oxford: Martin Robertson).

Levitt, M. and Lord, C. (2000) *The Political Economy of Monetary Union* (Basingtoke: Macmillan – now Palgrave).

Lewchuk, W. (1989) 'Fordist Technology and Britain: The Diffusion of Labor Speed-Up', University of Warwick Economic Research Paper no. 340.

Leys, C. (1990) 'Still a Question of Hegemony?', *New Left Review*, vol. 181, pp. 119–28.

Likerman, A. (1988) *Public Expenditure* (London: Penguin).

Lindberg, L. N. (2001) 'Acceptance Remarks by Leon N.Lindberg', *EUSA Review*, vol. 14 (3), pp. 12–14.

Lipsey, D. (2000) *The Secret Treasury* (London: Viking).

Loughlin, M. and Scott, C. (1997) 'The Regulatory State', in P. Dunleavy, A. Gamble, I. Holliday and G. Peele (eds), *Developments in British Politics 5* (Basingstoke: Macmillan – now Palgrave).

Lowndes, V. and Wilson, D. (2001) 'Social Capital and Local Governance: Exploring the Institutional Design Variable', *Political Studies*, vol. 49, pp. 629–47.

MacDougall, D. (1987) *Don and Mandarin: Memoirs of an Economist* (London: John Murray).

McGowan, F. (2000) 'Competition Policy', in H. Wallace and W. Wallace (eds) *Policy-Making in the European Union*, 4th edn (Oxford: Oxford University Press).

Major, J. (1999) *The Autobiography* (London: HarperCollins).

Maloney, W., Smith, G. and Stoker, G. (2000) 'Social Capital and Urban Governance: Adding a More Contextualised "Top-down" Perspective', *Political Studies*, vol. 48, pp. 802–20.

Marquand, D. (1988) *The Unprincipled Society* (London: Jonathan Cape).

Marwell, G. and Ames, R. E. (1981) 'Economists Free Ride, Does Anyone Else?', *Journal of Public Economics*, vol. 15, pp. 295–310.

Middlemas, K. (1986) *Power, Competition and the State. Volume 1: Britain In Search of Balance, 1940–61* (London: Macmillan – now Palgrave).

Middlemas, K. (1991) *Power, Competition and the State. Volume 3: The End of the Postwar Era: Britain since 1974* (London: Macmillan – now Palgrave).

Middleton, R. (2000) *The British Economy since 1945* (Basingstoke: Palgrave).

Minford, P. (2000) 'The Single Currency – Will it Work and Should We Join', in M. Baimbridge, B. Burkitt and P. Whyman (eds), *The Impact of the Euro: Debating Britain's Future* (Basingstoke: Macmillan – now Palgrave).

Mitchell, N. J. (1987) 'Changing Pressure Group Politics: The Case of the Trades Union Congress, 1976–84', *British Journal of Political Science*, vol. 17, pp. 509–17.

Moran, M. (2000) 'From Command State to Regulatory State?', *Public Policy and Administration*, vol. 15, pp. 1–13.

Moran, M. and Alexander, E. (2000) 'The Economic Policy of New Labour', in D. Coates and P. Lawler (eds), *New Labour in Power* (Manchester: Manchester University Press).

Naughtie, J. (2001) *The Rivals* (London: Fourth Estate).

Newbery, D. M. (1999) *Privatization, Restructuring and Regulation of Network Utilities* (Cambridge, Mass.: MIT Press).

Nordhaus, W. (1975) 'The Political Business Cycle', *Review of Economic Studies*, vol. 42, pp. 169–90.

Nugent, N. (2001) *The European Commission* (Basingstoke: Palgrave).

OECD (1996) *OECD Economic Surveys: United Kingdom* (Paris: Organisation for Economic Cooperation and Development).

OECD (2000) *OECD Economic Surveys: United Kingdom* (Paris: Organisation for Economic Cooperation and Development).

Office of Fair Trading (2000) *Annual Report of the Director General of Fair Trading* (London: Office of Fair Trading).

Ohame, K. (1990) *The Borderless World* (London: Collins).

Olson, M. (1965) *The Logic of Collective Action* (Cambridge, Mass.: Harvard University Press).

Owen, G. (2000) *From Empire to Europe* (London: HarperCollins).

Parsons, W. (1989) *The Political Power of the Financial Press* (Aldershot: Edward Elgar).

Peake, L. (1997) 'Women in the Campaign and in the Commons', in A. Geddes and J. Tonge (eds), *Labour's Landslide* (Manchester: Manchester University Press).

Peters, G. (1999) *Institutional Theory in Political Science* (London: Pinter).

Pliatzky, L. (1989) *The Treasury Under Mrs Thatcher* (Oxford: Basil Blackwell).

Polanyi, K. (1944) *The Great Transformation* (Boston: Beacon Hill)

Pollard, S. (1982) *The Wasting of the British Economy* (London: Croom Helm).

Pretty, J. (1998) *The Living Land* (London: Earthscan).

Price, S. and Sanders, D. (1991) 'Government Popularity in Postwar Britain', Essex Papers in Politics and Government no. 78.

Price, S. and Sanders, D. (1995) 'Economic Expectations and Voting Intentions in the UK, 1979–87', *Political Studies*, vol. 43, pp. 451–71.

Pringle, R. and Turner, M. (1999) 'The Relationship between the European Central Bank and the National Central Banks' in D-Cobham and G-Zis (eds) *From EMS to EMU* (Basingstoke: Macmillan – now Palgrave).

PRO (Public Record Office): BT 258/2498 'Future investment plans: approaches to individual firms in the chemical industry'.

PRO: HO 187/141 'Commissions, Committees and Conferences: Select Committee on Expenditure: emergency fire brigade appliances and equipment'.

PRO: T 267/12 'Policy to Control the Level of Demand, 1953–58'.

PRO: T 267/20 'The Control of Demand, 1958–64'.

PRO: T 267/22 'The Control of Demand, October 1964 to June 1970'.

Prosser, T. and Moran, M. (1994) 'Privatization and Regulatory Change: The Case of Great Britain', in M. Moran and T. Prosser (eds), *Privatization and Regulatory Change in Europe* (Buckingham: Open University Press).

Pryke, R. (1971) *Public Enterprise in Practice* (London: MacGibbon & Kee).

Pryke, R. (1981) *The Nationalized Industries: Policies and Performance since 1968* (Oxford: Martin Robertson).

Pulzer, P. G. (1972) *Political Representation and Elections in Britain* (London: George Allen & Unwin).

Putnam, R. (1984) 'The Western Economic Summits: A Political Interpretation', in C. Merlini (ed.), *Economic Summits and Western Decision-Making* (London: Croom Helm).

Putnam, R. D. (2000) *Bowling Alone* (New York: Simon & Schuster).

Rainbird, H. (1990) *Training Matters* (Oxford: Basil Blackwell).

Redwood, J. (2001) *Stars and Strife: The Coming Conflicts between the USA and the European Union* (Basingstoke: Palgrave).

Roach, S. (2001) 'Back to Borders', *Financial Times*, 28 September 2001.

Robertson, D. (1976) *A Theory of Party Competition* (London: John Wiley).

Rosamond, B. (1999) 'Discourses of Globalization and the Social Construction of European Identities', *Journal of European Public Policy*, vol. 6, pp. 652–68.

Rose, R. (1979) 'Ungovernability: Is There Fire Behind the Smoke?', *Political Studies*, vol. 27, pp. 351–70.

Sanders, D. (1997) 'Voting and the Electorate', in P. Dunleavy, A. Gamble, I. Holliday and G. Peele (eds), *Developments in British Politics 5* (Basingstoke: Macmillan – now Palgrave).

Sanders, D. (1999) 'Conservative Incompetence, Labour Responsibility and the Feelgood Factor: Why the Economy Failed to Save the Conservatives in 1997', *Electoral Studies*, vol. 18, pp. 251–70.

Sanders, D. and Brynin, M. (1999) 'The Dynamics of Party Preference Change in Britain, 1991–1996', *Political Studies*, vol. 47, pp. 219–39.

Scholte, J. A. (2000) *Globalization: A Critical Introduction* (Basingstoke: Macmillan – now Palgrave).

Senior British Official (1998) 'Background Briefing by American and British Senior Administration Officials and Spokesmen', Office of the Press Secretary, The White House, 6 February 1998.

Shephard, G. (2000) *Shephard's Watch* (London: Politico's Publishing).

Skidelsky, R. (1992) *John Maynard Keynes: Vol.2, the Economist as Saviour, 1920–1937* (London: Macmillan – now Palgrave).

Skidelsky, R. (1999) 'Unfinished Business', in A. Kilmarnock (ed.), *The Social Market and the State* (London: Social Market Foundation).

Skidelsky, R. (2000) *John Maynard Keynes: Vol. 3, Fighting for Britain, 1937–1946* (London: Macmillan – now Palgrave).

Smaghi, L. B. and Casini, C. (2000) 'Monetary and Fiscal Policy Co-operation in EMU', *Journal of Common Market Studies*, vol. 38, pp. 375–91.

Smith, A. (1986) *The Wealth of Nations Books I–III* (London: Penguin).

Smith, M. (1998) 'Competitive Co-operation and EU–US Relations: Can the EU be a Strategic Partner for the US in a World Political Economy?', *Journal of European Public Policy*, pp. 561–77.

Stedward, G. (2000) 'New Labour's Education Policy', in D. Coates and P. Lawler (eds), *New Labour in Power* (Manchester: Manchester University Press).

Stone, D. (1996) *Capturing the Political Imagination: Think Tanks and the Policy Process* (London: Frank Cass).

Strange, S. (1986) *Casino Capitalism* (Oxford: Basil Blackwell).

Strange, S. (1996) *The Retreat of the State* (Cambridge: Cambridge University Press).

Streeck, W. (1997) 'Beneficial Constraints: On the Economic Limits of Rational Voluntarism', in J. R. Hollingsworth and R. Boyer (eds), *Contemporary Capitalism: the Embeddedness of Institutions* (Cambridge: Cambridge University Press).

Talani, L. (2000) 'Who Wins and Who Loses in the City of London from the Establishment of European Monetary Union', in C. Crouch (ed.), *After the Euro* (Oxford: Oxford University Press).

Tanzi, V. and Schuknecht, L. (2000) *Public Spending in the 20th Century: A Global Perspective* (Cambridge: Cambridge University Press).

Taylor, C. (1995) *EMU 2000? Prospects for European Monetary Union* (London: Pinter).

Taylor, C. (2000) 'The Role and Status of the European Central Bank: Some Proposals for Accountability and Cooperation', in C. Crouch (ed.), *After the Euro* (Oxford: Oxford University Press).

Tew, J. B. H. (1978) 'Monetary Policy – Part 1', in F. T. Blackaby (ed.), *British Economic Policy 1960–74* (London: Cambridge University Press).

Thain, C. (2000) 'Economic Policy', in P. Dunleavy, A. Gamble, I. Holliday and G. Peele (eds), *Developments in British Politics 6* (London: Macmillan – now Palgrave).

Thain, C. and Wright, M. (1995) *The Treasury and Whitehall* (Oxford: Clarendon Press).

Thatcher, M. (1993) *The Downing Street Years* (London: HarperCollins).

Thomas, R. (2001) 'UK Economic Policy: The Conservative Legacy and New Labour's Third Way', in S. P. Savage and R. Atkinson (eds), *Public Policy under Blair* (Basingstoke: Macmillan – now Palgrave).

Thorpe, D. R. (1989) *Selwyn Lloyd* (London: Jonathan Cape).

Tomlinson, J. (1985) *British Macroeconomic Policy since 1940* (Beckenham: Croom Helm).

Treasury Committee (1997) *Second Report: The Barnett Formula* (London: the Stationery Office).

Treasury Committee (2000) Select Committee on Treasury, *Ninth Report 2000–1* (London: the Stationery Office).

Treasury Committee (2001) Select Committee on Treasury, *Third Report 2000–1: The Treasury* (London: Stationery Office).

Trichet, J.-C. (2001) 'The Euro after Two Years', *Journal of Common Market Studies*, vol. 39, pp. 1–13.

Tsoukalis, L. (1993) *The New European Economy*, 2nd edn (Oxford: Oxford University Press).

Vines, D. (1998) 'The WTO in Relation to the Fund and the Bank: Compe-
tencies, Agendas and Linkages', in A. O. Kruger (ed.), *The WTO as an
International Organization* (Chicago: Univeristy of Chicago Press).

Wallace, H. (2000) 'The Policy Process', in H. and W. Wallace (eds), *Policy-
Making in the European Union*, 4th edn (Oxford: Oxford University Press).

Wickham-Jones, M. (1997) 'How the Conservatives Lost the Economic
Argument', in A. Geddes and J. Tonge (eds), *Labour's Landslide* (Manchester: Manchester University Press).

Wiener, M. J. (1981) *English Culture and the Decline of the Industrial Spirit,
1850–1980* (Harmondsworth: Penguin).

Wilkinson, R. (2000) 'New Labour and the Global Economy', in D. Coates
and P. Lawler (eds), *New Labour in Power* (Manchester: Manchester
University Press).

Wilks, S. (1997) 'Conservative Governments and the Economy, 1979–97',
Political Studies, vol. 45, pp. 689–703.

Wilks, S. (1999) *In the Public Interest: Competition Policy and the Monopolies
and Mergers Commission* (Manchester: Manchester University Press).

Williams, E. E. (1896) *Made in Germany* (London: William Heinemann).

Wilson, H. (1971) *The Labour Government 1964–70* (Harmondsworth: Penguin).

Wilson, H. (1979) *Final Term* (London: Weidenfeld & Nicolson and
Michael Joseph).

Winch, D. (1989) 'Keynes, Keynesianism and State Intervention', in P. Hall
(ed.), *The Political Power of Economic Ideas* (Princeton: Princeton University Press).

Wincott, D., Buller, J. and Hay, C. (1999) 'Strategic Errors and / or
Structural Binds? John Major and Europe' in P. Dorey (ed.) *The Major
Premiership* (Basingstoke: Macmillan – now Palgrave).

Wincott, D. (2000) 'Globalization and European Integration', in C. Hay
and D. Marsh (eds), *Demystifying Globalization* (Basingstoke: Macmillan
– now Palgrave).

Wolf, C. (1993) *Markets and Governments: Choosing Between Imperfect
Alternatives*, 2nd edn (Cambridge, Mass.: MIT Press).

Wolf, M. (2001) 'Why Mr Brown should not Stick to the Rules', *Financial
Times*, 5 March 2001, p. 23.

Wolfe, J. D. (1999) 'Power and Regulation in Britain', *Political Studies*, vol.
47, pp. 890–905.

Wolfe, R. (1999) 'The World Trade Organization', in B. Hocking and S.
McGuire (eds), *Trade Politics* (London: Routledge).

Worcester, R. and Mortimore, R. (1999) *Explaining Labour's Landslide*
(London: Politico's Publishing).

Worcester, R. and Mortimore, R. (2001) *Explaining Labour's Second Landslide* (London: Politico's Publishing).

Young, A. (2001) *The Politics of Regulation: Privatized Utilities in Britain*
(Basingstoke: Palgrave).

Young, H. (1999) *One of Us* (London: Macmillan – now Palgrave).

Zis, G. (1999) 'The European Monetary System: in Unexpected Sucess'
in D. Cobham and G. Zis (eds) *From EMS to EMU* (Basingstoke:
Macmillan – now Palgrave).

Index